MARTIN LUTHER KING

Godfrey Hodgson has worked as a journalist for newspapers, magazines, radio and television in Britain and the United States. Born in 1934, he trained as an historian at Oxford and the University of Pennsylvania, and holds a doctorate *honoris causa* from the University of the South at Sewanee, Tennessee. He is the author of a number of books, most of them about twentieth-century American history. Godfrey Hodgson met Martin Luther King on a number of occasions between 1956 and 1967.

MARTIN LUTHER KING

GODFREY HODGSON

Quercus

First published in Great Britain in 2009 by Quercus

This paperback edition published in 2010 by
Quercus
21 Bloomsbury Square
London
WC1A 2NS

A CIP catalogue record for this book is available
from the British Library

ISBN 978 1 84916 262 3

10 9 8 7 6 5 4 3 2

Typeset by Ellipsis Books Ltd, Glasgow

Printed and bound by Clays Ltd, St Ives plc

Contents

1

A Dream Deferred

What happens to a dream deferred?

Does it dry up
like a raisin in the sun?
Or fester like a sore –
and then run?
. . .
Maybe it just sags
like a heavy load.

Or does it explode?
Langston Hughes

On the morning of the great day, Washington was tense, like a capital braced for revolution. Many stayed indoors. At the intersections of the broad avenues that diagonally score the trim residential streets of the white suburbs in Northwest, detachments of heavily armed soldiers were on guard. The fear, in what was still a southern city under its glaze of Camelot sophistication, was the deep-seated slave owners' dread of servile rebellion. Thousands of demonstrators were converging on the city. Black demonstrators. What would be their mood? How would they behave?

Down by the Lincoln Memorial, it was plain from the start that such fears were unfounded, unworthy of the spirit of the day. The crowds were far bigger than expected, and far more peaceful. In the end at least a quarter of a million people turned up, perhaps 300,000. But they were white as well as black. They had their children with them. They were in their best clothes, and the mood was benign, even uplifted. As the summer day warmed up, some swung their bare legs in the reflecting pool in front of the memorial. The atmosphere was not riot, but holiday.

Behind the scenes, though – and the headquarters of the march were directly behind the great seated sculpture of Abraham Lincoln in his marble monument near the broad Potomac River – the atmosphere was indeed tense, but not with insurrectionary fervour. A political struggle was being played out over the fire-eating speech written by one of Dr King's allies, John Lewis, then the chairman of the Student Nonviolent Coordinating Committee (SNCC, pronounced 'Snick'), and now a respected veteran member of Congress for Georgia. Lewis, like all the speakers, had handed in overnight a copy of what he planned to say. He was attacking the Kennedy administration's draft civil rights bill as too little, too late. Blacks, he said, 'would take matters into their own hands and create a source of power outside of any national structure'. They would 'march through the South, through the heart of Dixie, the way Sherman did, leaving a scorched earth with our nonviolence'.

It was just what the organizers, the veteran labour union leaders A. Philip Randolph and his subtle ideologist, Bayard Rustin, did not want to hear. The purpose of the march was not to scare white folks, but to reassure them, to convince a still hesitant white majority, North and South, that black people were only asking for their constitutional rights, and demanding them not in a hostile, hectoring tone, but with the voice of quiet moral authority. The aim was to put pressure on Congress to implement the emancipation already promised, nine summers earlier, by the Supreme Court in its judgement that legal segregation was contrary to the United States Constitution as amended after the Civil War a century before.

There was a practical problem. The march's organizers were anxious to display the broadest possible coalition behind their demands, including labour unions and religious leaders. Now word came that Patrick O'Boyle, Cardinal Archbishop of Washington, was displeased. He was threatening to pull out of the march, with all the authority of a Church that the President and a rough quarter of the American people belonged to, unless John Lewis washed his mouth out.

John Lewis would be listened to with respect. But it was not him the vast crowd had come to hear. The man of the hour was Dr Martin Luther King Jr. Son of a tough preacher of the old school from Atlanta's Ebenezer Baptist Church, King had won a reputation at Dexter Avenue Church in Montgomery, the capital of Alabama, as a preacher who combined the Old Testament grandeur and populist fervour of traditional black

Christianity with a sophisticated understanding of modern theology and social thought.

He was then thirty-four years old, short – under five foot seven inches – elegantly dressed in Ivy League style, with a broad mouth under a neatly trimmed moustache. He had a deep, thrilling voice, which started low and could build up until he communicated an irresistible shared passion to his congregation in church or to his followers in the streets. When he graduated from Boston University, he had toyed with the idea of becoming a theological scholar, and there had been offers of jobs in safe northern universities. He became a minister, he said, more because of his father's example and the tradition of a family of preachers than because of any intense 'call', though his Christian commitment was unshakeable. Behind a smooth face and the incomparable ability to move an audience was hidden a complex personality, passionate and sensuous as well as subtle and staunch.

He became a political leader, almost in spite of himself, in the boycott by the African-American population of Montgomery of its bus system after Rosa Parks famously refused to get up and move to the back of the bus to make room for a white passenger, as custom, backed by municipal regulation, dictated. The bus boycott, King's courage and his charismatic gifts as an orator threw him into the front rank of leadership of a divided 'Negro' movement, and of an aroused people. In Montgomery, then else-where, King had put himself at the head of mass protests. He had been repeatedly imprisoned and in other ways 'despitefully used'.

In Birmingham, the tough steel town that was the hardest bastion of segregation in all the South, he had experienced moments of despair, but he had emerged, if not triumphant – the white civic leaders of Birmingham were too stubborn to allow Negroes to triumph – at least successful. At long last he had finessed President Kennedy and national Democratic politicians to commit themselves to action. And from Birmingham jail he had written his famous letter to white clergy, magisterially rebuking them for asking the Negro to wait. Now, in Washington, he had his opportunity to shame the northern half of the national Democratic Party into overriding the prejudice and the pride of their southern colleagues, entrenched in Congress as the chieftains of their one-party states.

Rustin and Dr King did their best to change Lewis's mind. Both failed. Lewis was small, dark, and psychologically adamant. Only Randolph himself, the patriarchal leader of the black sleeping-car porters' union, was able to persuade him that his flight of rhetoric was endangering the whole enterprise. There was, in truth, danger on two sides. It would be bad to alienate the white liberals, the churchmen and the rabbis whose support would be needed for the fight ahead in Congress for the civil rights bill. It would be worse to drive a wedge between Dr King and his moderate allies on the one side and the young firebrands of SNCC on the other; their trust could be destroyed if their chairman's passionate speech was to be censored with too heavy a hand.

With desperate urgency, as the minutes ticked by to the opening of the ceremony, Lewis's SNCC colleagues redrafted his speech on a portable typewriter propped up behind the Lincoln statue. They did not take all of its sting away. Lewis still promised to 'splinter the segregated South into a thousand pieces and put them back together in the image of God and democracy'.

By the time he had agreed to the toned-down draft, the crowd had heard protest songs from some of the stars of the then fashion for political folk music. There was Josh White, famous for his powerful anti-lynching ballad, 'Strange Fruit'; Joan Baez, coolly beautiful in a cotton dress and sandals; and the young, acoustic Bob Dylan. Randolph had opened the programme, welcoming the crowd to what he called 'the largest demonstration in the history of this nation'. 'We are the advance guard,' he proclaimed, 'of a massive moral revolution for jobs and freedom.'

When Lewis had finished, it was time for the speaker the thousands had come to hear. From his first words, he touched deep chords of association with the great traditions of the American past. 'Five score years ago,' he began, and not a man or woman in that huge crowd could have been unaware that by quoting the opening words of Lincoln's Gettysburg address he was clothing himself in the mantle of the man seated in majesty behind him. King spoke with the slow rhythms of the Baptist pulpit, and with a rhetorical trick of his own. As he ended each period, he would hurry on to the opening phrase of the next paragraph, then pause, leaving his audience in suspense for a moment before the torrent of his words tipped over the edge and swept on down the great rapids of his peroration.

The speech was at once sermon and political argument. He was talking to several audiences at once. He was directly addressing the thousands who were there in front him in Washington's Mall. Over their heads he was reaching out to southern blacks and northern whites, to the tens of millions of undecided white Americans, willing to be persuaded that the time was ripe to end the embarrassing southern folkways of segregation, yet reluctant to be carried away on radical paths. He was reaching out to the powerless in southern plantations and the angry in northern ghettos, and most of all to the powerful, only just beyond the reach of his voice a mile or so up the Mall on Capitol Hill. So he wove together different languages for different listeners. He borrowed the emotional power of the Old Testament with an echo of the stately music of Handel's *Messiah*. He also appealed to the sacred texts of the American secular religion, echoing the grand simplicities of Jefferson's Declaration of Independence and Lincoln's Gettysburg address.

The march, and the movement he had led to this culmination, were not an end, he said, but a beginning. 'The whirlwinds of revolt will continue to shake the foundations of our nation until the bright day of justice emerges.' Some asked, he said, when the devotees of civil rights would be satisfied. 'We can never be satisfied,' he replied, until the evils of segregation, of police brutality and discrimination have been abolished, as long as 'the Negro in Mississippi cannot vote and the Negro in New York believes he has nothing for which to vote'. 'No! No!' he cried in the first climax of the speech. 'We are not satisfied, and we will not be satisfied until' – in a resonant verse from the Book of Amos that had been a favourite passage since his days in theological seminary – '. . . let justice roll down as water, and righteousness as a mighty stream'.

The first passages of the speech, he read. He had been writing them until four that morning in his Washington hotel. Then the idea came into his head of adapting a trope he had tried out in a speech in Detroit a year earlier. In words the whole world remembers, he told the great company in front of him, reaching back for half a mile along the Mall, that he had a dream. And the dream was that 'one day on the red hills of Georgia, the sons of former slaves and the sons of former slave owners will be able to sit down together at the table of brotherhood'; and that his own four small children would 'not be judged by the color of their skin but by the content of their character'.

Then again he reached for the language of the Old Testament, for the remembered words of Isaiah, to ratchet up the emotional power of his rhetoric. 'Every valley shall be exalted,' he cried, 'and every hill and mountain shall be made low. The rough places will be made plain and the crooked places will be made straight, and the glory of the Lord shall be revealed, and all flesh shall see it together.' So he moved from dream to hope, from his own vision to the shared pride of the national anthem, and at the end he reached into the deepest recesses of his vision, that of drawing a final line under traumas that haunted slaves and slave owners alike. Let freedom ring, he said on the day when 'all God's children, black men and white men, Jews and Gentiles, Protestants and Catholics, will be able to join hands all over the nation and sing in the words of the old Negro spiritual: "Free at last! Free at last! Thank God Almighty, we are free at last!"'

It has become the best-known political speech of the twentieth century, in America and around the world. When in 2007 *The Guardian* distributed the texts of the greatest speeches of the century, there was young Dr King, the martyred outsider, alongside Winston Churchill. 'I Have a Dream', as it has come to be known, has been sold in millions, in book form, tapes, discs and recordings of every kind. The manuscript from which part of it was read has been sold at Sotheby's for an undisclosed but very large sum. Dr King's papers have been auctioned for $32 million. Copyright of his words has been disputed in the courts. Two corporations, Apple Computers and the giant French telecommunications-equipment manufacturer, Alcatel, have used it in commercials. Martin Luther King is commemorated by hundreds of streets, avenues and boulevards in American cities, and by a public holiday that puts him in the quasi-apostolic company of George Washington, Thomas Jefferson, Andrew Jackson and Abraham Lincoln. The speech, its author and the Dream have passed into the postmodern world where cultural icons become international brands.

In the process, not only the context of the speech and its purpose and effect, but its author and the real nature of his Dream have been forgotten, misunderstood and even deliberately misinterpreted. He is often misremembered, as an unthreatening, relatively conservative leader, when in reality his vision was profoundly and unrelentingly radical; and as a Christian preacher, when – though he was indeed a Christian – his message was always consciously political. He is widely seen as a leader whose relevance was chiefly to the black people of the South, when in truth he sought to transform American life in the North as well, for whites as well as for blacks. He is seen as the champion for African-Americans; of equality before the law; he came to believe that his mission was to fight for economic equality for all.

His great speech was the hinge between the demanding and dangerous task of giving the southern blacks, de jure, full citizenship, and the less glorious, more frustrating task of giving to both black and white people, in the North and West as well as in the South, de facto economic opportunity and equal human status. King saw himself, from early on, as committed to human rights everywhere, not just in the South or even just in America. He was fiercely hostile to colonialism, and to racism wherever he saw it.

The first task, that of overthrowing legally sanctioned segregation in the South, he knew better than anyone, had been hard enough. But even he did not guess, on that day of triumph, just how difficult the next task would be.

King's speech at the march on Washington was a truly cardinal moment in the modern history of the United States. Barack Obama could not, arguably, have been elected president without it. But its meaning has been subtly distorted by what came after it. Immediately, and in part as a result of King's actions, President Kennedy laid before Congress a civil rights bill that did not become law until Kennedy had been assassinated. His successor Lyndon Johnson was both a master parliamentary tactician and, as a southerner, more deeply aware of what was at stake in the racial upheaval than ever Kennedy was. By the summer of 1964, the civil rights legislation had passed Congress. The following year Johnson succeeded in cajoling and pressuring Congress to pass the Voting Rights Act. It was, as Johnson knew, a political catastrophe for the Democratic Party he had served all his life. It touched off a political cataclysm. Conservative white southerners, who would once have voted, as they said, for a 'yellow dog' if the animal had the Democratic nomination, turned into Republicans.

Johnson invested his political capital in the bill because he believed that only access to the vote would enable southern blacks to free themselves. On Independence Day 1965 in a speech at Howard University, the historically black college in Washington, he went further than any national leader had ever gone to commit America to full racial equality. Freedom, the President said, in what many consider his own noblest speech, was not enough. It was not enough just to open the gates of opportunity. Black Americans must be helped to walk through those gates. 'This is the next and more profound stage of the battle for civil rights. We seek not just freedom but opportunity – not just legal equity but human ability – not just equality as a right and as a theory but equality as a fact and as a result.' That year, the Johnson administration made the equality of black citizens, and their economic advancement, its priority. The President poured money into visionary schemes to bring African-Americans into the mainstream of American life. There was Head Start for black children in the Mississippi Delta and the northern ghettos. The slums were to be abolished and turned into Model Cities. A War on Poverty, inherited from the Kennedy agenda, was to be fought in the name of Equal Opportunity.

But by April 1968 Martin Luther King was dead, his throat shattered by a bullet from a Remington rifle fired by a man who – whatever his other motives may have been – did not like black people. By then his dream was dead too, of many wounds.

In that same spring of 1965, when Lyndon Johnson was making the intellectual leap from freedom to equality, he also found himself drawn into war in Vietnam. The war on Vietnamese Communism ultimately siphoned off the resources that would have been needed to win a war on poverty. The will to win at home was dissipated. The poverty warriors of the Office of Economic Opportunity, many of them young African American activists, came up against the stubborn resistance of the Democratic regulars. King himself, when he campaigned for equal housing in Chicago, came up against the city's orthodox Democratic mayor, Richard Daley – a man, as even his press secretary said, who thought that equal opportunities meant 'nine Irishmen and a Swede'.

The black civil rights movement itself was fractured too. In the summer of 1965 the young firebrands of SNCC, men and women who had shown unimaginable courage in their campaigns in the most benighted backwoods of Mississippi and Alabama, began to talk about black power. This was largely 'consciousness raising', a rhetoric to persuade black people that they could and must dare to stand up for their freedom. But to white ears it sounded ungrateful, frightening and profoundly un-American. George Wallace, the cocky little ex-boxer who had been elected Governor of Alabama on a promise to defend segregation today, tomorrow and for ever, marched north. As a candidate for the Democratic nomination for president, he won an alarming share of the vote in working-class neighbourhoods in Maryland, Indiana and Wisconsin, the supposedly liberal North, among lifelong Democrats.

It was not only working-class people, and certainly not only racists and segregationists, who felt that the movement of which Martin Luther King was still seen as the symbol and the commander had gone altogether too far. On the one hand, even before his death, King came to be seen by young black activists and also by many in the white media, as somehow outmoded, with his pathetic – as too many saw it – attachment to the misunderstood concept of non-violence and his naive talk of Christian forgiveness. On the other, he was seen by many white people as the prophet of a black movement that was going beyond the goal of equal citizenship, which most Americans more or less grudgingly accepted, to what many saw as a profoundly un-American project for discriminating in favour of black people.

By the presidential election in November 1968, all of these perceptions and misperceptions had come together, aggravated by the heightened emotions of frustration and threatened humiliation in Vietnam as well as rioting and civil disturbance, from the campuses of elite universities to the black slums of several hundred American cities. Together, they ended the ascendancy of the Democratic Party that had lasted since the election of President Franklin Roosevelt in the nadir of the Great Depression, nearly forty years earlier. Richard Nixon was elected President. The liberal consensus, represented in masterly fashion by Lyndon Johnson, was shattered. Martin Luther King, his speech and his crusade, were remembered with nostalgia and even with pride. But their hour, it seemed, had passed.

Almost exactly one hundred years earlier, in the elation of victory over the Confederacy, the Radical Republicans had tried to destroy the system that kept the newly emancipated slaves in subjection. Their attempt at the Reconstruction* of the South collapsed, and was remembered and taught in American history books as a misguided, even wicked aberration, a 'fool's errand'.† By 1968, the second Reconstruction was over too. Martin Luther King was widely revered, but his message was neither understood nor seen as relevant to a new age of conservative ascendancy. Yet it was not a fool's errand. It has lasted – even, to an extent, triumphed. His life remains both a model and a hinge on which American history has turned.

---

* When, at the end of the Civil War, the Radical Republicans among the leaders of the victorious Union set out to 'reconstruct' the South without slavery, they passed three constitutional amendments: put simply, the Thirteenth abolished slavery, the Fourteenth guaranteed the civil rights of the freed slaves, and the Fifteenth granted them the right to vote.

† The title of a nineteenth-century best-seller by 'one of the fools', a northern white liberal 'carpetbagger', Albion W. Tourgée, who became a judge in Reconstruction North Carolina and a pioneer civil rights activist.

2

Sweet Auburn

... a citizen of no mean city ...
give me leave to speak unto the people.
Acts 21: 39

In 1878, a twenty-year-old black boy set off from the ironically named plantation village of Social Circle, forty miles from the raw young railroad town of Atlanta. He was one of many who set out to make their fortunes there, and one of the few who succeeded. The boy, Alonzo Herndon, had had only one year of schooling, but he had managed to accumulate eleven dollars in savings, earned by selling molasses, peanuts and axle grease. He had been born a slave. In fact, his mother was a slave, and his father was her white master, Frank Herndon.

After Emancipation in 1863 Herndon had turned his slaves loose, and they worked the land for him as best they could as sharecroppers. The system was that the master provided the land, the seed, the tools and a 'furnish' of cash to tide them over for a year while they, by means of back-breaking labour, 'made a crop' – in Georgia, normally of cotton. Usually they worked 'on the halves', meaning that half of the crop went to the landlord, sometimes more. Materially these freedmen were little better off than they had been in slavery. There were plenty of white sharecroppers as well, and they too were often miserably poor.

On his way to Atlanta, Alonzo Herndon stopped off to work on a farm and then learned the trade of barbering.[1] In 1878 he set up a barber's shop in a small town, Jonesborough. In 1883 he finally reached Atlanta, where he worked for a Negro barber, one Hutchins, on Marietta Street. Within six months he had bought a half-interest in the business, and before long he owned three barber-shops. In those days, it was the custom for white men to be shaved and have their hair cut by black barbers, and Herndon, expert, discreet and almost white in appearance, was soon the barber favoured by the tight circle of Atlanta's business elite. He saved money, and invested his savings in domestic property.

Before long he owned more than a hundred houses, not to mention an estate in Florida. In 1905 he rescued a small, failing mutual insurance society and turned it into what became, as the Atlanta Life Insurance Company, one of the biggest black-owned businesses in the United States.

John Wesley Dobbs, too, grew up on a farm.[2] He was born in Marietta, sixteen miles north-west of Atlanta. Dobbs's grandfather, too, had been a slave, owned by Josiah Dobbs of Cobb County; and his father was probably Dr John McAfee, a wealthy white slave owner. In 1851, aged thirty-two, grandfather Dobbs was valued at $800.

In 1897 John Wesley went into town and got a job in an Atlanta drugstore. He was hoping to pay his way through the secondary school run by the Atlanta Baptist College, which later became Morehouse College, sometimes called 'the black Harvard'. A few years later he had to drop out of school and get a job. Shrewdly, in hard times, he got a job with the federal government as a mail clerk working on the railway post office run by the Nashville & Atlanta Railway, one of ten railroads that converged on Atlanta and made the town's fortune. While sorting mail on the trains, John Wesley Dobbs also sold insurance. This provoked some jealousy from his white co-workers, but Dobbs successfully defended his behaviour, and ended up being put in charge of them. He must have been good at his job.

Certainly, he was soon doing well enough to marry an educated African-American woman and to buy, for $3,767, a fine house from a German woman in a neighbourhood where German Jews were just being replaced by middle-class black families. John Wesley Dobbs, like Alonzo Herndon, prospered. He became the grand master of a Negro Masonic order, and was known to everyone along Auburn Avenue, the commercial heart of black Atlanta until the 1950s, as 'the Grand'. He never made money on the scale of Alonzo Herndon, but he did cut quite a figure on the street he called 'Sweet Auburn', after Oliver Goldsmith's line in *The Deserted Village* – 'Sweet Auburn, loveliest village of the plain'. He liked to stand outside the Yates & Milton drugstore, preaching about the need for blacks to get involved and improve their condition via the political system.[3]

He knew everyone in black Atlanta and in black America beyond.

The black Congressman from Harlem, Adam Clayton Powell, would stay at the Grand's home when he came to town, and at least once Duke Ellington played the piano there. The Grand went to cover the Joe Louis–Max Baer fight at Yankee Stadium for the local Negro newspaper. His daughter, Mattiwilda Dobbs, went to Paris to study classical singing, won an international prize in Geneva, and was the first African-American to sing at La Scala in Milan. That was only the start of a glittering career as an internationally acclaimed operatic diva. Later she sang at Covent Garden, Glyndebourne, the Vienna Staatsoper, the Paris Opéra and the New York Met. Grand Master Dobbs was one of the leaders of the campaign to register black Atlantans to vote in the 1930s, and his grandson Maynard Jackson was the first black mayor of the city in the 1960s.

Herndon and Dobbs made money. Another path to respect in black Atlanta was religion. In 1893, ten years after Alonzo Herndon went to work at Hutchins's barber-shop, yet another poor black country boy with more ambition than money came to Atlanta to seek his fortune. His name was Adam Daniel Williams, and his goal was to succeed as a minister. He had been an itinerant preacher, and had worked at a textile mill that went bust. Then, working in a saw mill, he lost his thumb in an accident. He arrived in Atlanta with only one dime and a gold five-dollar piece, which he used to pay a doctor to treat a sore throat. He worked in a machine shop, and was invited to preach in a couple of local black churches. Finally, in 1894, he took over Ebenezer Baptist Church in the city. The pastor had just died, and there were then just thirteen church members and no church house.

Within a year his luck had turned, and so had Ebenezer's. Williams prospered mightily. Together with a radical black clergyman, Bishop Henry McNeal Turner, he promoted a dodgy scheme for investment in the Silver Queen mine in Mexico. The local black paper didn't like it. 'Thousands of poor Negroes ... are being defrauded,' it said. Williams denied this, and the scheme seems to have done his reputation no lasting harm. By 1914 Ebenezer had 750 members and was building a new church for over a thousand more on the corner of Auburn Avenue and Jackson Street. He went on to be one of the founders of the National Association for the Advancement of Colored People (NAACP, or often simply the N-Double-A) in Atlanta, and he helped to found the Booker T. Washington High School. He also helped to register thousands of Atlanta Negroes to vote. His motto was: 'Bucks, ballots and books are the answer.' In 1899 he had married Jennie Celeste Parks, and in 1903 she gave birth to Alberta Christine Williams, the mother of Martin Luther King Jr.

So there were opportunities for young black men as well as for the whites brought up on the code of self-improvement promoted by the works of Horatio Alger in late-nineteenth-century America, and nowhere more than in Atlanta. The city was the transport hub and commercial capital of the cotton kingdom. It had been founded, as plain Terminus, only in 1837, and was not incorporated as Atlanta, short for Atlantica-Pacifica, until 1847. From the beginning, the inhabitants had grandiose ambitions for the town. But in 1864 it was besieged for a month by General Sherman and his Union army. It was burned to the ground, probably not by the Yankees (as suggested in *Gone with the Wind*), but as a result of the defeated Confederates blowing up munitions, before Sherman's 'dashing Yankee boys' set off, ripping up the tracks as they went, on their historic March to the Sea. By the turn of the century, with the agricultural depression of 1893 driving black families off the land, tens of thousands of blacks had poured into the city, where they made up 40 per cent of the population.

It was in Atlanta that Henry W. Grady, editor and part-owner of the *Atlanta Constitution*, began to preach the cause of what he called the New South. He exhorted his fellow citizens to forget the romantic mythology of the *ante bellum* years and the Confederacy, and bring in northern capital and expertise to promote industry and business. In 1895, when Herndon, Dobbs and A. D. Williams were all starting out on the road to segregated fortune, Booker T. Washington gave his famous speech at the Cotton States and International Exposition in Atlanta.

Booker T. Washington was the arch-accommodationist, respected by the white southern elite because he called on his fellow African-Americans to lift themselves by their own efforts. He believed that education was the key to the advancement of the American Negro, and he founded the Tuskegee Institute to promote his vision. He later developed his philosophy, and told the story of his own journey, in a best-selling autobiography, *Up from Slavery*. In his speech in Atlanta he began by quoting from Herman Melville's classic, *Moby-Dick*. Lost in the wastes of the Atlantic, a ship's company is desperate for water when the captain spies another ship and signals his plight. The master of the other ship signals back, 'Cast down your bucket where you are!' Irritated, the captain repeats the message a second and a third time. Each time he gets the same answering signal. Finally, he does lower a bucket, and it comes up full of sweet fresh water. The explanation is that they are close to the mouth of the Amazon, and the great river's water has diluted the ocean's salt.

Washington's point was that white southerners, anxious to develop their businesses, ought not to try to recruit the European immigrants who were then flooding into the North, but should educate and train the black workforce they already had living among them. He ended the speech with a plea for racial cooperation without social integration: 'In all things that are purely social we can be as separate as the fingers, yet one as the hand in all things essential to mutual progress.'

Booker T. Washington had great prestige with the dominant white business elite as well as with black Atlantans. He was even invited to the White House to meet Theodore Roosevelt, to the horror of many whites, North and South. But by no means every black leader in Atlanta shared his vision. The great radical black intellectual W. E. B. Du Bois was then teaching at Atlanta University; he was later for a time a member of the Communist Party, editor of the National Association for the Advancement of Colored People's magazine *The Crisis*, and author of an impassioned plea for black pride and progress, *The Souls of Black Folk*, published in 1903. 'My real life work,' he wrote, however, 'was done at Atlanta for thirteen years, from my twenty-ninth to my forty-second birthday' while he was teaching black students there. When he died at ninety-five, there was a great deal more work to be done. Among many other achievements, he organized a Pan-African Congress in Paris in 1919 for black leaders from what was still then an almost wholly colonized continent.

Du Bois had no time for Booker T. Washington's respectful attitude to white men. So far as he 'preaches Thrift, Patience, and Industrial

Training for the masses,' Du Bois wrote, 'we must hold up his hands and strive with him … But so far as Mr Washington apologizes for injustice, North or South, does not rightly value the privilege and duty of voting, belittles the emasculating effects of caste distinctions, and opposes the higher training and ambition of our brighter minds … we must unceasingly and firmly oppose him.[4] Du Bois insisted that Negroes must stand up for themselves, and he shocked almost everyone by declaring as early as 1914 that they must have 'social rights'. Those rights, he explained – and it took real courage to say it in those days – included 'the right to be treated as a gentleman when he behaves like one, to marry any sane, grown person who wants to marry him, and to meet with and eat with his friends without being accused of undue assumption'. Social equality? he wrote elsewhere. 'Of course we want social equality. Social equality is the right to demand the treatment of men from your fellow men. To ask less is to acknowledge your own lack of manhood.'

One particular event ended the mood of cautious confidence that Booker T. Washington personified, and considerably dented his reputation by making it painfully clear to any thoughtful black man or woman that they could not count on living and working next to white people in Atlanta, or anywhere else in the Deep South like two fingers of the same hand as Booker T. Washington wrote. That event was a sudden violent outbreak of racial violence. Even in the first decade of the twentieth century Atlantans thought their city was relatively tolerant. But it was strictly segregated, and there was tension in the air, especially after the publication in 1905 of Thomas Dixon's best-selling novel, *The Clansman*, which portrayed the Ku Klux Klan romantically as the heroic defenders of white women.

The courageous activist Walter White, who was to lead the National Association for the Advancement of Colored People (NAACP) in its campaign against lynching, grew up in Atlanta. Of a younger generation than Du Bois, as a boy of thirteen, he and his father, both of them light-skinned enough to pass as white, witnessed the wild rioting that broke out in the city one hot night in the summer of 1906. The violence was triggered by newspaper reports that three white women had been assaulted or insulted by black men. Officially, twenty-five blacks were recorded as killed, plus one white person. But official casualty counts always seemed to minimize the death toll of African-Americans in these violent outbreaks. Some reports say that after mobs ranged the streets of Atlanta shouting 'Kill the niggers!', as many as a hundred black people were killed. Walter White saw a lame black bootblack chased by a white mob and beaten to death. He remembered all his life his father handing him a gun and telling him not to use it unless someone set foot on the family's lawn. 'But if anyone does, don't miss!' (Sixty years later, an old African-American minister told me that his parishioners would invite him to go out rabbit-shooting with them; when they hit their target, it would be blown apart. They were hunting with the high-powered rifles they or their fathers had bought after the riot of 1906.)

Ever since the end of slavery, whenever there was sudden social change in the South, and sometimes in the North too, race riots were likely to break out. There was a racial dimension to the draft riots during the Civil War in New York; and the terrible riot in New Orleans of 1866 is well documented.

The end of the nineteenth and the beginning of the twentieth century were a time of special racial tension. All over the nation, and especially in the South, white people were attempting to increase 'control' of blacks, who were seen as threatening both white jobs and, in a vaguer sense, the social order. The cry was for white supremacy, and many whites did not care who knew how much they disliked and despised blacks. They wanted their labour, but not their presence.

The year 1898, for example, saw a serious riot in Wilmington, North Carolina. A future Congressman, Alfred Moore Waddell, led the white rioters. They burned down the offices of a black-owned newspaper on the grounds that its editor had insulted the virtue of white women. Josephus Daniels, a future Cabinet minister in the supposedly progressive Cabinet of Woodrow Wilson, who was devoted to the principle of self-determination everywhere but in the South, egged the rioters on with violently racist editorials. Again, official reports said that at least twenty-two black people were killed. Others speak of a massacre in which hundreds of blacks perished, their bodies thrown into the river. What is not in doubt is that Waddell's mob, hundreds strong, overthrew the duly elected Republican government of the city and by naked force installed a segregationist Democratic regime there instead. Then came a few years of relative calm. But in 1906 there was a famous riot in Brownsville, Texas. African-American soldiers were accused of insulting and shooting white people. President Theodore Roosevelt disbanded an entire black battalion, unjustly blaming them for what has happened.

There were riots in many places in the North and along the border of the old confederacy during and after the First World War, when blacks were moving out of the South – for example, in East St Louis in 1917 and in Chicago in 1919. In Tulsa, Oklahoma, in 1921, black soldiers, back from the war in Europe, fought pitched battles in the streets against their former white comrades, and perhaps as many as three hundred people were killed.

It is always hard to assign precise causes for these sudden murderous outbreaks. Economic conditions are relevant, and so are local circumstances, such as newspaper coverage of alleged crimes or insults by blacks. There were often political motives, or tensions arising from political campaigns or disputes. Even the weather often played a part. The general background to the violence of 1898 to 1906, however, is not in doubt. It was 'Jim Crow'. This was the term, taken from a popular song about a black character of that name, applied to the attempt on the part of whites to set a limit to black advancement and reimpose new, harsh legal codes of segregation and racial domination. A symbol of this reactionary process was the Supreme Court's decision in the case of *Plessy v. Ferguson*, upholding a local ordinance imposing segregation on travel. All over the South a new generation of populist demagogues were calling for the legal repression of black people, and state legislatures were passing Jim Crow laws. In Georgia, white politicians like Tom Watson, previously a radical populist, and Hoke Smith, appealed to the economic fears and visceral prejudices of white working people. African-Americans, many of whom had been able to vote in the South during the Reconstruction years after Emancipation, were disenfranchised after the mid-1870s.

One consequence might seem paradoxical or counterintuitive. Between Emancipation and the coming of the Jim Crow era, which was fully established by the 1890s, it had been possible for some fortunate black people to prosper by catering to the needs of white customers. Black barbers, chefs, livery stable owners and less reputable entrepreneurs could and sometimes did prosper with white protection. After the Jim Crow era, that all ended. But in turn some avenues of opportunity were opened up for black businessmen operating segregated enterprises within a Negro world that was even more segregated than before. Now money could be made by taking on functions that white people would not perform for blacks, such as those of druggist or funeral director. In this new world, money could be made, saved and invested. At its apex a new black bourgeoisie began to appear, led by the likes of Alonzo Herndon. This was the world of Sweet Auburn, a mile and a half of stores, bars and Negro enterprises of all descriptions, including the *beaux arts* offices of Herndon's Atlanta Life Insurance Company, several black newspaper offices, and venues where entertainers such as Duke Ellington and B. B. King would perform.

There were also big churches along Auburn Avenue, for every denominational taste. There was Big Bethel, belonging to the African Methodist Episcopal Church. There was First Congregational. There was Wheat Street Baptist. Smaller, but beginning to grow, was A. D. Williams's Ebenezer Baptist. For alongside the new black bourgeoisie, like the lords spiritual alongside the lords temporal of the feudal age, there prospered modestly a new, respected and influential class of black teachers and above all black ministers. This was the world into which Martin Luther King Jr was born. 'In the quiet recesses of my heart,' he said later in life, by which time he had become many things to many people, 'I am fundamentally a clergyman, a Baptist preacher. This is my being and my heritage, for I am also the son of a Baptist preacher, the grandson of a Baptist preacher, and the great-grandson of a Baptist preacher.'

The great-grandfather, Willis Williams, was an 'old slavery time preacher' who joined Shiloh Baptist Church in Greene County, Georgia, in 1846. He was a slave, but in those days in country places slaves sometimes worshipped alongside their masters.[5] 'Willis, servant boy of William N. Williams', was received by the pastor. Almost all we know about Williams is that he was one of the wealthiest slave owners in the county – white, of course – and that he served as 'patrol commissioner', in charge of the county's 'slave catchers', who pursued runaways. After Emancipation, Willis married Lucretia, or 'Creecy', recorded as 'servant to Mrs N. E. Daniel', who was half his age. She was the mother of Adam Daniel Williams, the grandfather of Martin Luther King Jr.

Martin Luther King Sr was not baptized with that name, nor was Martin Luther King Jr. The father was originally Michael King, and so was the son. Daddy King, as he came to be known, was the son of James King and his wife Delia, born Linsey. (James King's own grandfather was used by his owner to breed slaves on several slave women, for sale.) The older Michael King was born to a family of sharecroppers who lived in grim rural poverty in Stockbridge, Georgia. He experienced racism in its rawest form. Once, after his mother knocked down a white man who hit her son, his father took a rifle and threatened the man. In danger of being lynched, his father had to hide in the woods for months. He never forgot the insults of his childhood. Once, later, he was called 'boy' by a traffic cop. 'No,' he said, pointing to his son. 'That's a boy! I'm a man.'

In 1918, like Alonzo Herndon, A. D. Williams and so many unknown others before him, Michael King went to Atlanta to seek his fortune. Later he said that he arrived in Atlanta 'smelling like a mule'.[6] He found work in a tyre plant, loading bales of cotton and driving a truck. But what he had always wanted to be was a preacher. His schooling was limited. At fifteen, he could read but not write. His religious training came from his pastor in the black Baptist church in Stockbridge.

In the city, he lodged at first with his older sister. When she went as a lodger at A. D. Williams's house, young Mike King started paying court to Alberta Williams. Eventually he was accepted by the family. His father wanted him to go back to Stockbridge and help on the farm, but Mike was determined to study to be a minister. He was turned down several times, but he persevered, and in 1926 entered the Morehouse School of Religion. That same year he and Alberta were married at Ebenezer. It was assumed that he would succeed his father-in-law. But he did not want to feel that he had inherited his church, and it was only after A.D. Williams's death in 1931 that King took over as pastor. At first, the church was burdened with debts, and it took hard work to build up the membership and repair the finances.

It was not until later, and in curious circumstances, that he acquired the name that was to become so celebrated in his son.[7] By 1934 Ebenezer's finances, and Mike King's, had prospered to the point where he could attend the World Baptist Alliance meeting in Berlin. With a group of other ministers he sailed for France, and went on by way of Paris to Rome, then on to Egypt and the Holy Land before returning to Germany. Perhaps he visited Wittenberg, where Luther had nailed his Reformation theses to the church door. Certainly it was in Germany that he decided to change his name from Michael King to Martin Luther King. On his son's birth certificate his name was first given as Michael, then Michael was later crossed out and 'Martin Luther' written in. Biographers and historians have argued about exactly when and why the five-year-old's name was changed. The simplest explanation is that Martin Luther King Sr, proud of his new name, had his son's changed to echo it. It was a name, after all, fitting for a leader who would give his life to bringing reformation to his people.

Young Martin Luther King was born into a happy and increasingly prosperous household. He went in due course to the high school that his grandfather had helped to found, and to the college, Morehouse, which his father, now the best-paid minister in black Atlanta, had attended. He grew up in the very centre of the world of the people who would soon insist that they were not Negroes, but black men and women, then African-Americans. The boy's life was not cloudless, however. He was not especially bright at school. His father could be hard and demanding, and he used the switch to enforce his idea of discipline. Young Michael was deeply fond of his grandmother, who died of a heart attack when he was six. When he was told of her death, he jumped out of a first-floor window and was fortunate not to sustain any serious injury. Neither King nor his father ever referred to this suicide attempt, but King Jr later said that his grandmother's death was the first occasion when he discussed with his parents death and immortality.

In the 1960s a white mayor of Atlanta, William B. Hartsfield, coined the clever slogan that Atlanta was 'too busy to hate'. It was not true then, and it was certainly not true in 1906 or indeed in 1915, when a Jew, Leo Frank, was accused of assaulting and then murdering a white girl.

The Governor of Georgia, unconvinced (correctly, as it turned out) that Frank was guilty, commuted the death sentence, whereupon a white mob broke into the jail and hanged Frank. It may not, even today, be a city wholly free from racial hatred, in either direction. But it is true that over the past hundred years it has been on the whole the most tolerant city in the Deep South, and the one where opportunities of every kind for African-Americans have probably been greatest.

When Martin Luther King Jr was growing up there it was a city that offered possibilities, financial but also educational, cultural and spiritual, to black men and women as well as to whites. In 1929 when he was born, it was already the real capital of the South, a centre of political and financial power and a magnet for talented and ambitious people of both races. Its complex of black colleges, funded with generous help from benefactors including the founder of Standard Oil, John D. Rockefeller, was the intellectual dynamo of the black South. Its African-American churches, with their rich tradition of mesmeric preaching and sonorous communal music, possessed a religious culture that was vital, ambitious and committed to their congregations' worldly as well as religious well-being. In a word, it was the best possible place to grow up for a young man who was to lead black people on their troubled and dangerous pilgrimage through the Red Sea to the Promised Land.

It was by no means, though, a haven from the dark experience of African-Americans. Young Mike King was in direct touch, through his father, his mother's father, his mother and his grandmother, with the African-American folk memory of the savagery and sheer meanness of which southern whites were capable. He did not have to be told that slaves were bred to work and to be sold as a commodity; that had happened in his own family. He knew that after Emancipation the freedmen were left to survive as best they could. He could see with his own eyes that white society not only did little to help black people, but passed and enforced countless petty and hateful regulations to enforce segregation and subordination.

In spite of this knowledge, Martin Luther King Jr grew up in the neighbourhood of Auburn Avenue in a society that remained convinced of the promise of America, and he was determined to share in that promise. His people were a people of faith. They had faith in their God, and also in themselves – faith in their own determination to endure, and to overcome. Like Paul of Tarsus, young Mike King of Auburn Avenue and Ebenezer Church was a citizen of no mean city.

3

A Higher Education

My call to the ministry was not a miraculous or supernat-
ural something; on the contrary it was an inner urge
calling me to serve humanity.

Martin Luther King Jr, aged twenty-one

On 22 November 1950 Martin Luther King Jr, then twenty-one years
old and a graduate student at Crozer Theological Seminary near Chester,
Pennsylvania, wrote an 'autobiography' of his religious development.[1] It
was an essay written for Professor George W. Davis's course on 'The
Religious Development of Personality'. In it, young King put the main
emphasis on the happy childhood he had been lucky to have and the
warmth and closeness of his family. He wrote of the 'intimate relationship' he had with his older sister Christina and his younger brother
Alfred Daniel, always known as A.D. His parents, he said, were very
close to one another, and maintained a most affectionate relationship
with their children.

It was in this essay that he mentioned the effect on him of his 'saintly'
grandmother's death (though without alluding to his suicide attempt).
He described early memories of the Depression, when he saw people
standing in bread queues. Although he was only five at the time, he
believed as a student it had caused his 'present anti-capitalistic feelings'.
The emphasis of the essay was on what William James might have called
'the religion of healthy-mindedness'. He had been, King said, 'an extraordinarily healthy child' and, to the day he wrote the paper, 'I hardly know
how an ill moment feels.' Nature, he believed, had been kind to him,
and his childhood environment had been 'very congenial'. No one in
the community in which he grew up 'attained any great wealth', but nor
was it a slum district. There was little crime, and most of the neighbours
were deeply religious. His playmates all went to Sunday School – not
that he chose them for that reason, but it would have been hard to find
children in his community who did not.

The religion taught at that Sunday School was fundamentalist, and until he was about twelve years old he accepted the infallibility of the Scriptures uncritically. This was, however, as his sophisticated twenty-one-year-old self reflected, 'contrary to the very nature of his being'. At thirteen, he remembered, he shocked the Sunday School class by denying the bodily resurrection of Jesus, and at fifteen, when he went to college, he became more and more aware of the gap between what he had learned at Sunday School and what he was being taught at college.

This continued, he recalled, until he took a class in Bible studies at college and came to see that behind 'the legends and myths of the Book were many profound truths'. The phrase reflects the 'modernist' atmosphere of the seminary where he was writing his essay, which prided itself on a 'liberal' theology that he was himself partially to reject. Religion, he saw clearly, was 'just something that I grew up in'. There was no abrupt conversion, no 'crisis moment'. Later, as we shall see, in a sleepless night at a time of fear and stress he went down to the kitchen to make a cup of coffee and experienced what has been called his 'kitchen conversion'.

He also mentioned in that early essay a number of experiences that brought him face to face, from a very young age, with the inescapable facts of race, of segregation and of the subordinate situation of his people. From the age of three until he was six, he wrote, he had a white playmate whose father owned a store across the street from the King home. They were inseparable until they went to school – 'separate schools, of course,' King wrote, to which his white, northern, liberal professor replied 'How tragic!' in the margin of his paper. From that point the friendship faded, until his friend told him outright that his father had ordered that he must no longer see his Negro playmate. It was, and remained, a great shock. At dinner that night King asked his parents why this had happened. His mother took him on her lap, he explained in a later, fuller account and told him about slavery and how it had ended with the Civil War. She explained the segregated schools, restaurants and housing of the South, the 'white' and 'colored' signs on drinking fountains and lavatories, 'as a social condition, not a natural order'. 'Then,' he wrote in a later autobiography, 'she said the words that almost every Negro hears before he can yet understand the injustice that makes them necessary: 'You are as good as anyone.'[2]

It was the frequent practice in the South to let little children play together, but by the age of puberty at the latest they must be taught that 'never the twain shall meet'. Many years later President Jimmy Carter movingly described the emotional impact of the same separation from the other side of the racial divide in a memoir of the rural Georgia of his childhood. In Carter's case, he was about fourteen when the boy who had been his closest friend stepped aside to let him, as the white man, go through a gate first.[3]

King's religious experience in the ten years of his formal education, as an undergraduate at Morehouse in Atlanta, as a theological student at Crozer and later as a doctoral student at Boston University, was a gradual and, at least superficially, a gentle progression from the accepting world of a Baptist minister's home and Sunday School, through adolescent rebellion to faith, to scholarship. It was not, however, the spotless path of which hagiography is made. His might have been the youth of a modern saint, but he was not an altogether saintly youth. He was a great deal more interesting than that.

King had absorbed from his happy Christian childhood a deep religious faith. He had also inherited from his tough and in many ways worldly father an irrepressible ambition. Although he thought seriously about becoming a teacher and a scholar, he was always drawn to his father's and his grandfather's calling, to preach the Word. In the context of the realities of Negro life in the South, that implied social and political, as well as spiritual, leadership. Tempted as he was by the comfortable and dignified world of the academic – not to mention the prospect of escaping from the segregated South – everything in his family tradition and his own instinct drew him into the conflicts of a world in which racial struggle was inevitable. Learning was good; but it was instrumental. As a scholar, King trod close to and sometimes crossed over the line that separates learning from plagiarism. As Dr Clayborne Carson, the admiring editor of his papers, put it, 'he increasingly saw himself as a preacher appropriating theological scholarship rather than as an academic producing such scholarship'.[4]

He was also less than saintly in a more obvious way. He was personally proud of his appearance to the point of vanity, very concerned with his appearance. At Crozer, too, he developed his interest in women, and acquired a habit of sexual adventure that continued after his generally happy marriage. These less admirable traits were, though, marginal to his religious, intellectual and political education. Much that was important in his mature life and political career cannot easily be understood in isolation from the experiences of his student years. At Morehouse, at Crozer and at Boston, King strengthened and shaped his faith. In those ten years he confronted the arguments that were deeply dividing Protestantism in the mid-twentieth century, and found his own way through the theological labyrinth. He developed a political orientation that was influenced by and sympathetic to democratic socialism, but he flatly rejected communism. And he came into contact, but did not fully explore, the ideas and the political achievement of Mahatma Gandhi, the pioneer of non-violent political action.

At Morehouse he came under the influence of Benjamin Mays, the president of the college. He was a significant figure in black Atlanta, a Chicago-trained theologian of national import in the Baptist communion, and the author of the pioneering book about African-American Christianity, *The Negro's God as Reflected in his Literature*, published in 1938.[5] Later King called Mays 'one of the great influences' in his life. In truth, as one of the youngest in his class, his classmate and friend Walter McCall remembered, King was at first more interested in meeting girls and organizing dances when his father was in church. Once the uncritical faith of childhood was gone, both religious commitment and an interest in racial injustice came slowly. In his second year at Morehouse, King was taught the first of several sociology courses by Walter R. Chivers, an outspoken opponent of segregation. In his third year, still only seventeen, he took a Bible class with George D. Kelsey, which he cited in his Crozer essay as igniting his growing interest in religion. (Kelsey gave him the only A of his undergraduate years.) Gradually he began to take more interest in his academic work and also in public speaking on campus. By his junior (penultimate) year he told his father, to the latter's intense joy, that he wanted to be a minister. 'It came,' he told a Baptist educator later, 'neither by some miraculous vision nor by some blinding light experience on the road of life . . . it was a response to an inner urge [which] expressed itself in a desire to serve God and humanity.'[6]

27

It was arranged for him to study at Crozer, the then struggling northern Baptist seminary, historically white, but where there were at the time about a dozen black students out of a total of ninety. While still in high school, King had done holiday work on a farm in the North and was amazed, as he wrote to his father, that 'we go to any place we want to and sit anywhere we like'. When he first arrived at Crozer, he was similarly impressed at first by the racial tolerance he found on campus, then depressed to find that some 'southern' attitudes and behaviour were to be found even in Pennsylvania the moment he and his African-American friends stepped out of the campus haven. On two occasions, he had a gun pulled on him.

King's grades at Crozer show a young man slowly developing real intellectual curiosity and confidence. In the first year he took fourteen courses and was given As in only three of them. Two of these were awarded in courses teaching the technique of preaching, an art in which he was to become one of the great masters. Preaching was taught at Crozer, by Robert E. Keighton, in a manner at once imaginative and practical. Keighton was a man of some culture, devoted to Shakespeare and fond of modern poets such as Auden and Eliot. But he taught sermons as a master craftsman might pass on the secrets of the trade to an apprentice. 'There was the Ladder Sermon, the Jewel Sermon, the Twin Sermon, the Surprise Package Sermon, and many others. The Ladder Sermon climbed through arguments of increasing power towards the conclusion the preacher hoped to make convincing. The Jewel Sermon held up a single idea from many different angles, as a jeweller might examine a precious stone.'[7] And so on.

In his second year King took ten classes and received only two As, both in theology, taught by Professor George W. Davis. But in his third and last year, out of eight grades he got no fewer than seven As and one A minus. King was now refining his own personal theology. It involved a compromise between the conservative, even fundamentalist, traditions of his African-American Baptist roots and the 'liberal' theology for which Crozer was known and which was dominant in the mainstream white Protestant denominations in the middle decades of the twentieth century.

American liberal theology flowered in many forms. Its common foundation was the Enlightenment instinct that the truth of religious belief must not be imposed by any external authority. In the nineteenth century American Protestantism, like American intellectual life generally, was much influenced by German thought, especially by that of Adolf von Harnack and Albrecht Ritschl. The dominant Protestant tradition in the progressive years of the early twentieth century, when many of King's Crozer teachers were studying at the Union Theological Seminary in New York, in Boston or Chicago, was the 'Social Gospel'. This was most powerfully preached by Walter Rauschenbusch, who had studied in Germany. It evaluated the Church primarily in terms of its progress towards a just society on this earth.

In the hands of some scholars, liberal theology, battered by nineteenth-century biblical criticism and evolutionary science, had evolved in the direction of an ethic that attenuated specific Christian tradition and biblical authority almost to vanishing point. In reaction to this tendency, a new doctrine, called 'neo-orthodoxy', had made its appearance. It was associated with the two towering figures of American Protestant theology in the 1950s, though some scholars insist that both of them were essentially liberals. One was Paul Tillich, son of a German Lutheran pastor and a professor of philosophy in touch with existentialist ideas. He had emigrated from Germany in 1933 when he was ejected from his Chair at Frankfurt University by the Nazis.

The other, who was to have an abiding influence on Martin Luther King, was Reinhold Niebuhr, an American of German parentage. Niebuhr had started as a Lutheran pastor working with automobile workers in Detroit. He became both a theological and a political liberal. In 1932, however, he published an influential book, *Moral Man and Immoral Society*, in which he challenged many of the assumptions of the Social Gospel and liberal theology. In politics, Niebuhr upset his former liberal associates by denouncing the crimes of Soviet Communism, before most American progressives were aware of them. Later, with Eleanor Roosevelt, Arthur M. Schlesinger Jr and Hubert Humphrey, he was to be one of the founders of Americans for Democratic Action, the influential champions of 'Cold War liberalism'. In theology, Niebuhr shocked pacifists, Tolstoyans and the disciples of the Social Gospel (which he had himself previously professed) with a new, tough-minded insistence on the reality of sin. Twenty years' experience of Soviet Communism and National Socialism made Niebuhr's view of the world, which had seemed unduly pessimistic to many in American academia in 1932, no more than stark realism by the time young Martin Luther King reached theological school.

King was deeply and permanently impressed by Niebuhr, who was perhaps a more profound and lasting influence even than Gandhi, though he talked less about Niebuhr. His strategy was to thread his way through the controversies of his college years by adopting what was known as 'personalist' theology. This school, whose definition in some hands slipped into vague do-what-makes-you-feel-good theory, had been founded by a rigorous, philosophically sophisticated academic, Borden Parker Bowne. It stressed that reality could be perceived only by persons and insisted on God as a divine person or (in Trinitarian Christianity) three persons, as opposed to an impersonal creative force. The details of the argument matter less than the fact that it enabled the young Martin Luther King to find a talisman that could lead him through the theological disputes of mid-twentieth-century Protestantism. It was also relevant that the most eminent living 'personalist' was Dr Edgar S. Brightman, of the Boston University School of Theology.

When King finished, with brilliant grades, at Crozer, he applied to three leading Protestant theology departments, at Yale and at Boston University in the USA, and at Edinburgh. Yale turned him down. Edinburgh University accepted him, but King's parents were not happy at the idea of him going so far away to study. It was his admiration for Brightman that made him choose Boston. Brightman died, however, shortly after King arrived there, and his place as his supervisor was taken by L. Harold DeWolf, a Methodist from Nebraska who shared Brightman's personalist persuasion.

There was another side to King's life at Crozer, besides divinity. From the start, as he recalled himself, he was intent on displaying an elegance that would refute the stereotype of the impoverished southern Negro. He cultivated an elaborate signature and a private language, particularly useful for expressing his appreciation of the finer points of young women. He polished his shoes until they shone, and bought suits from the tailor J. Press in the timeless Ivy League style. (His nickname at Morehouse had been 'Tweed'.) This concern for his appearance went beyond that of the dandy to that of the rake. And to his father's horror, he smoked cigars. On the pool tables in the basement under the chapel at Crozer, young MLK practised and practised until he could display the cool skill of the accomplished pool shark.

Early in his time at Crozer he wrote to his mother that he was seeing a couple of 'chicks'. He presumably did not let his mother in on the detail of later developments. In his last year at Crozer he was taught by a young white professor, Kenneth L. Smith, a strong advocate of the Social Gospel. Smith, a Virginian nicknamed 'Snuffy', was much shorter in stature than King: five foot one inch against King's five foot six and a half (as measured for a medical check-up). Smith's girlfriend Betty was the daughter of a German immigrant woman who worked as a cook in the Crozer cafeteria. Professor and student competed for the affection of this young woman, first in a tone of light flirtation, but increasingly in earnest. King announced to his friends that he was serious, that he meant to marry Betty. His friends, prospective Negro Baptist ministers, warned him that to marry a cook's daughter would be beneath his dignity, or that he would never be able to find a parish that would call a racially mixed family to the pulpit. King continued to protest his undying love for Betty. In the end, after months of genuine unhappiness, the young lover admitted that he could face his father's anger but not 'the pain it would cause his mother'.

Perhaps more equivocal still from a moral point of view was the difficulty in which his closest friend, first at Morehouse and then at Crozer, Walter McCall, found himself. McCall was accused by a white girlfriend of making her pregnant. She was determined to go to court to get him to support her and her child. McCall denied paternity publicly, though he came close to admitting the truth of the charge in a later letter to King. McCall persuaded a Crozer professor to give evidence that he was a theology student of good standing and that it was therefore unlikely that he could be the father. King was not directly involved. But the ethical implications of the case, for his close friend and for his seminary, were not pretty. Given the racial dimension, the issue was a sensitive one for a college like Crozer, which was already under attack in some quarters for its high proportion of black students. Like medieval priests claiming benefit of clergy to get off a felony charge, King's friend and his college had used religion as a cloak for perjury and for the heartless abandoning of a young woman and her child.[8]

In the spring of 1951 Martin accepted the offer of a place at the Boston University Graduate School of Theology. This was not such welcome news for Martin Luther King Sr, who was not convinced of the merits of further graduate study. For one thing, Daddy King was afraid that his son might decide – as he was in fact thinking of doing – to take an academic position somewhere in the North. For another, the father wanted his clever son to come and share the duties of a working pastor at Ebenezer Baptist Church. But young Martin, at twenty-two, knew his own mind. His three years in Boston were to set the compass for his journey, in several ways.

It was there that he deepened and sharpened his thinking about questions that would preoccupy him for the rest of his life. Some of these questions he had already begun to think about at Crozer, even at Morehouse. But now he had broken free from the parochial, if hardly cloistered, atmosphere of the seminary. Now the southern Baptist preacher's son had the freedom of one of the world's intellectual capitals. Boston University was a great urban graduate school, in a city where there were other even more powerful institutions of higher learning. King was to take some philosophy classes at Harvard. MIT and other colleges were down the road or across town. Instead of Crozer's dozen black theology students, most of whom were happy to settle for D grades, King found himself in a bubbling world of ambitious young men and women, black and white.

He played hard, but he also worked hard. He had discovered a deep intellectual curiosity. Sometimes he read all night for the pleasure of it. There were religious questions on which he had to make up his mind. At BU, King committed himself to a theology that rejected the rationalism of the liberal philosophy that had been the prevailing doctrinal fashion at Crozer. He had a dissertation to write if he was to gain a doctorate, and he chose a topic that would enable him to back off from liberal theology, but by no means as far as the traditional fundamentalism of his father's generation of African-American preachers. The title of his dissertation, which he finished with heroic singleness of purpose after he had started work as the pastor of his own church, was 'A Comparison of the Conceptions of God in the Thinking of Paul Tillich and Henry Nelson Wieman'.

The subject sounded dry, and it was, even by the standards of theology. But it was chosen with thought, even with some scholastic cunning. Paul Tillich was one of the towering figures of American Protestant theology. He was also the most prominent figure at the time at the Union Theological Seminary in New York. Wieman was less known outside the world of 'technical' theology, but in the 1930s he had been head of the divinity school at the University of Chicago. He changed his denominational loyalty several times, and in later life passed from Unitarianism to an anguished but sceptical position. Quite early in his research, King made up his mind about the respective weaknesses of his two subjects. 'Wieman', he scribbled on a note card, 'stress[es] the goodness of God while mi[ni]mizing His power. Tillich stresses the power of God while min[im]izing His goodness.'

The details of the thesis need not concern us, but two things are worth recording. The first is that King chose, certainly well knowing what he was doing, a topic that enabled him to distance himself from the modernist subtleties of both his subjects, and to contrast them both with a personalist position. This enabled him also to show himself as au fait with the latest in theological fashion and at the same time to move back to a more traditional position. For Tillich, the German-trained philosopher-turned-theologian who had known Heidegger, God was 'being-itself'. For Wieman, the puzzled refugee from Calvinism, God was 'the source of human good'. For Martin Luther King, God was a 'living' God who could and did answer prayer.

The second thing that has to be said is that in this thesis, as in earlier academic work, King did not observe the academic niceties. He took a course in thesis and dissertation writing from Dr Jannette Newhall, the librarian at the BU theology school, but he continued his bad habit of quoting material in the form he encountered it in secondary sources, not going back to the original. And to quote Clayborne Carson, 'King often appropriated the words of others without attribution. He frequently [made] improper use of Tillich and Wieman. King also borrowed from secondary sources without giving adequate citations.'[9] That is what is called plagiarism. He did compile more than a thousand note cards before he left Boston, and there may be some excuse in the circumstances in which he wrote the thesis – namely, that Montgomery possessed a far from first-rate theological library. His examiners, moreover, one of whom was his supervisor, did not notice the plagiarism. Perhaps King, his eye on other prizes, simply did not think it was important. Yet it has to be said that his handling of sources was not that of a meticulous scholar.

Philosophical, as well as theological, questions absorbed him. He remained fascinated by the thought of Niebuhr, in particular, who had retained a commitment to social justice while rejecting the optimism and meliorism of the Social Gospel. But now too, at last, political questions that no intelligent African-American of King's generation could ignore were beginning to press in upon him.

There was the question of communism which, as noted earlier, King always rejected, and of socialism, which in the form of social democracy he did not reject. This was the age of McCarthyism, of official investigations of 'un-American activities' and agonizing conflicts of personal versus patriotic loyalty. King had read a good deal about communism. During the Christmas vacation of 1949 (when he was still at Crozer), he recalled in a memoir, he decided to spend his spare time reading Karl Marx, 'to try to understand the appeal of communism for many people'.[10] He specifically mentions that he 'scrutinized' *Das Kapital* and the Communist Manifesto, and that he also read some 'interpretive' books about communism. He was emphatic that he was not tempted by the doctrines of Marx and Lenin. He rejected a materialistic interpretation of history that had no place for God. He objected to the ethical relativism of communism that justified murder, lying and violence as means to a millennial end, just as he opposed the political authoritarianism that swept liberty aside and made man a means to an end. However, he admitted that while he thought communism basically evil, he did find it challenging because of its concern with social justice. His reading of Marx, he said, made him more conscious of the gulf in American society between superfluous wealth and abject poverty.

Because of the Cold War, King was also troubled by the related question of pacifism. The Korean War began while he was at Crozer, and the Cold War was at its coldest while he was at Boston. He was not a pacifist. 'While war,' he felt, 'could never be a positive or absolute good, it could serve as a negative good in the sense of preventing the spread and growth of an evil force. War, horrible as it is, might be preferable to surrender to a totalitarian system – Nazi, fascist or communist.' He was, however, to be greatly influenced by pacifists and especially by men and women who had committed themselves to such pacifist organizations as the Fellowship of Reconciliation and the War Resisters' League. He had been impressed by the veteran pacifist A. J. Muste, whom he heard speak while he was at Crozer, and was later to be close to Muste's disciples Bayard Rustin and Glenn Smiley, among others.[11] In a later chapter we shall look into the influence on King of the non-violent philosophy of Gandhi, the 'Mahatma', or 'great soul'. His ideas intrigued King from the moment he first encountered them. They did not harden into an operating political code until later.

A more personal influence came into King's life at Boston in the elegant shape of Coretta Scott. In his first term there, he became a figure of some distinction among the many African-American students in the city. 'He was like a prince,' one friend remembered. 'He wasn't running after the girls,' said another. 'The girls were running after him.' He dated a number of women, and seemed – at least to his worldly father – to be serious about at least one of them, Juanita Sellers, daughter of the wealthiest funeral director in Atlanta. But sometime in his first year at Boston, King asked another woman friend from Atlanta, Mary Powell, if she knew of any girls he might like to meet. She it was who gave him the telephone number of Coretta Scott, a voice student at the New England Academy of Music.[12] King tried out an outrageous chat-up line with her in his first phone call. He was like Napoleon at Waterloo, he said – he was on his knees. She told him not to be absurd, but she did not hang up. One thing he did have in common with Napoleon. Both men were decidedly short, and Scott admitted later that King's short stature worried her until she got used to hearing him talk.

Scott was the daughter of a courageous and determined black farmer from Perry County in the Alabama Black Belt.* By sheer hard work

Obadiah (known as Obie) Scott had accumulated several hundred acres. He had also built a sawmill. When a white man offered to buy it, Scott refused, and the white man burned it to the ground. That was Perry County for you in those days. Coretta went to a segregated but private secondary school, and from there to Antioch College, a famous, and famously liberal, college in Ohio, then to Boston. She had a small scholarship, but she was so poor she had to work as a maid at a boarding-house on Beacon Hill, in the most fashionable Boston neighbourhood, in return for room and board.

King showed up at his first date with her, the day after the Waterloo ploy, in the green Chevrolet his father had bought for him. At that very first meeting he told her she would make him a good wife. She had the four things he was looking for in a woman: 'character, intelligence, personality and beauty'.

It was not long before she was invited to be inspected by the King parents in Atlanta. A later meeting, when his parents travelled up to Boston, was almost disastrous. Daddy King questioned his son in front of Coretta about his other girlfriends. He suggested this was just a college romance, and that her interest in secular music would be inappropriate in a Baptist minister's wife. Finally he asked her directly, 'Do you take my son seriously?' Confused and no doubt annoyed, she said, 'Why no, not really.' At which Daddy King said he was glad, because he knew for a fact that his son had already proposed marriage to several other girls – and he named them – who came from families the Kings knew and respected, and who had much to offer him. Coretta stuck to her guns. She had something to offer, too, she said.

Only after more of this bullying did Daddy King relent. What was his relationship with Coretta doing to his studies? he asked. His son replied stoutly, 'I'm going to get my doctorate, and I'm going to marry Coretta.' At that, the stern father finally gave his blessing, in characteristically aggressive fashion. 'You two better get married,' he said.

---

* So called after the colour of the rich soil, but also the part of the state with the largest black population.

4

Sick and Tired

My feets is tired, but my soul is rested.

Sister Pollard

On 1 December 1955, as everyone knows, a forty-three-year-old Negro seamstress called Rosa Parks boarded the Cleveland Avenue bus at Court Square in downtown Montgomery, Alabama, on her way home from her job in a department store. After one stop, several white passengers got on, filling up the 'whites only' seats. The driver, James F. Blake, asked the four blacks in the next row to move further back. Three moved. Mrs Parks refused, and was arrested.

Two nights later the young pastor of Dexter Avenue Baptist Church, Martin Luther King Jr, made a speech to a mass meeting called to protest against Mrs Parks's arrest. As a result he emerged as the leader of a boycott of Montgomery buses by Negroes, which lasted more than a year. By the time it ended, in a kind of victory, the movement for civil rights and equality for black people in the South was firmly launched, and Martin Luther King had emerged as its most prominent leader.

This familiar story is accurate, as far as it goes. In important respects, though, it gives a false impression of what happened in Montgomery, and of its crucial role in King's career. For one thing, Mrs Parks's rebellion, though extremely courageous, was not unprecedented, even for her. Nor was it altogether spontaneous. There had been bus boycotts before, in Baton Rouge, the capital of Louisiana. Rosa Parks herself had been thrown off a Montgomery bus eleven years earlier for refusing to follow the custom of black people paying at the front of the bus, then going round to the back. The driver had taken her money and ordered her to go to the back; when she refused, he threw her off, kept her money, then drove away. What is more, it was the same driver, Blake. He had form, and so did Mrs Parks. Several leaders of the Negro community in Montgomery had been looking for an opportunity to test the city bus company's segregation practices for some time.

Rosa Parks, too, was something more than the naive woman with tired feet that she has often been portrayed as. She had worked for some years as the secretary of the local chapter of the National Association for the Advancement of Colored People, then the main and virtually the only effective political organization of African-Americans. She continued to work with the chapter's youth council. Only the previous summer she had attended a workshop on civil rights at the Highlander Folk School in the Tennessee mountains. This was an interracial institution, founded and run by a white radical from New York's Union Theological Seminary, Myles Horton, devoted to training Labour union and Negro organizers.

Highlander was widely believed by white conservatives to be a communist school. It wasn't, but it was unapologetically about campaigning for social change. And it had impressive national connections on the left. Reinhold Niebuhr, Norman Thomas, the perpetual socialist candidate for president, and even Eleanor Roosevelt herself had at one time or another been on its board. One of its passionate defenders was Clifford Durr, an Alabama-born supporter of President Roosevelt's progressive 'New Deal' policies, who had once been a member of the Federal Communications Commission. Durr was well connected both in Alabama and in Washington. He came from a patrician family and had studied as a Rhodes Scholar at Oxford. His wife Virginia's sister was married to Alabama's Senator Hugo Black and the Durrs were friends of Senator and Mrs Lyndon Johnson. They had, however, gone too far for many in their defence of radicals of various kinds and were under surveillance by the FBI. Clifford and Virginia Durr were virtually the only outspoken white liberals in Montgomery, and Rosa Parks was a protégée of theirs. She had done some sewing for them, and they had paid her fees at Highlander.

Rosa Parks, in other words, was a well known and politically committed member of the tiny Negro leadership in Montgomery, who were already looking for an opportunity to mount an effective legal challenge. The previous March a young woman called Claudette Colvin had been called on by the driver to give up her bus seat to white passengers. She not only refused – she swore, and she struggled. The driver called a police car, and she was handcuffed and charged with breaking the segregation ordinance along with assault and disorderly conduct.

The most influential African-American, politically speaking, in Montgomery was E. D. Nixon, a union man with the Brotherhood of Sleeping Car Porters and the head of the local NAACP. He was a strong, calm man who had left school at eleven, but had learned how to handle himself and others. Taking advice from Clifford Durr and Fred Gray, one of only two black attorneys in the city, Nixon was looking for a case to test segregation on the bus line, which depended on its 40,000 African-American passengers and could not have survived on the dimes of the 12,000 whites who used the buses. But Claudette was noisy and foul-mouthed. The judge who heard her case cleverly acquitted her of the segregation charge and fined her so lightly on the assault charge that she could not be made a martyr. Worse, unmarried, she was pregnant. She was not right for the part Rosa Parks played so perfectly.

One of the people E. D. Nixon had recruited to the ad hoc committee he assembled for planning the Colvin case was the Revd Martin Luther King Jr, the new pastor of Dexter Avenue Baptist, a Victorian brick church a couple of hundred yards downhill from the imposing Alabama State Capitol, the very building where the Confederacy had been proclaimed in 1861.

In June 1953, after finishing his courses at BU and at Harvard (where he studied secular philosophy), King had travelled to deeply rural Perry County for his wedding to Coretta. The service was conducted by Daddy King, and the young couple spent their first night as man and wife in a local funeral home, the only place of hospitality in that profoundly segregated county where they could have stayed the night safely. They then moved to Atlanta, where King preached at his father's church sermons which, because of the latter's prominence and his own growing reputation, were broadcast on a local black radio station. Later that year he accompanied King Sr to the annual National Baptist Convention, a gathering of fifteen thousand black ministers, already convulsed by divisions between conservatives and younger radicals.

Once he had finished his exams in Boston, the young pastor began to look for a job to support his wife while he finished his dissertation. There were two possible paths open to him. His professors, who had a high opinion of his abilities, put him forward for academic positions, and offers came in from several colleges. The alternative was to be 'called' to the pulpit of a Baptist church. That was what his father wanted for him and it was increasingly what he wanted for himself. Interest was expressed by a church in Chattanooga, Tennessee; then, in January 1954, he was invited to deliver a guest sermon, in effect a trial, at Dexter Avenue, Montgomery. This was not the biggest black Baptist church in the city. That was First Baptist, whose minister was Ralph Abernathy, later to be King's closest friend. It was, however, the most prestigious; closely associated as it was with Alabama State, Montgomery's Negro college. The previous incumbent was a well known preacher, Vernon Johns. King preached a carefully wrought sermon – a 'ladder sermon', no less – on 'The Three Dimensions of a Complete Life'. It was a great success, and he was invited to become Dexter's pastor, and the best-paid Negro minister in the town. He accepted, though it was understood that at first he would have to commute between Montgomery and Boston until he had finished his dissertation.

In May that year he preached his first sermon as Dexter's pastor, on 'Loving Your Enemies'. Knowing from his family background that a new incumbent must take firm control, he presented a set of 'recommenda-tions' for financial and administrative reorganization that would put him firmly in charge, based on the bold theological claim that it was not the elders of Dexter, but God Himself, who had called him to the pulpit there. The congregation accepted his argument and his plans, and in October 1954 he found himself, just twenty-five years old, installed with ceremony, with the support of several busloads of his father's parishioners from Ebenezer and a paternal sermon to send him on his way, as the pastor of the most influential church in Montgomery's restless black community.

Six months earlier, the Supreme Court of the United States had declared its historic judgement in the case of *Brown v. Board of Education of Topeka, Kansas*, with which were joined four other similar cases from different parts of the country. The Court's judgement struck down its opinion in *Plessy v. Ferguson* of sixty-three years earlier. It proclaimed that separate educational facilities were of their nature not equal, and therefore contravened the guarantee of equality made in the Fourteenth Amendment to the Constitution.

By the mid-1870s, the defeated South was able to take advantage of various contingencies in national politics – one of which was the interests of the continental railroads in crossing the South and another the widespread lack of sympathy in the North towards African-Americans – to 'redeem' its racially segregated way of life. By the 1880s, state legislatures in the South passed a host of laws, followed by countless municipal and county ordinances, aimed at depriving blacks of as much as the southern whites dared of their newly won freedom. This new system of segregation, discrimination and subjection, as we have seen, was commonly known as 'Jim Crow'.

In 1890, as part of this movement, the General Assembly of Louisiana passed legislation decreeing separation between whites and blacks on the state's railroads, and two years later a thirty-year-old shoemaker called Homer Adolph Plessy, who claimed to be seven-eighths white, sat in a 'for whites' carriage on the East Louisiana Railway train from New Orleans to Covington. This was a deliberate test of the new segregation law. Plessy was found guilty of contravening that law, and his conviction was confirmed by the state courts. In 1896 the state law was upheld by seven justices of the Supreme Court in Washington. For the majority, Mr Justice Brown said that 'legislation is powerless to eradicate racial instincts, or to abolish distinctions based on physical differences, and the attempt to do so can only result in accentuating the difficulties of the present situation ... If one race be inferior to the other socially, the constitution of the United States cannot put them on the same plane.' Only one member of the court dissented. Mr Justice John Marshall Harlan alone, though a former slave-holder from Kentucky, gave his opinion that Louisiana's 'sinister legislation' was in conflict with the 'broad and sure foundation of the equality of all men before the law'.

By the 1930s Charles Hamilton Houston, a black man with a Harvard law degree who had served as an officer with the American Expeditionary Force in France, was the Dean of the Law School of Howard University, the leading Negro university in the District of Columbia, founded by the head of the Union's Freedmen's Bureau, Yankee General Oliver Otis Howard, appointed by Abraham Lincoln to look after the freed slaves. Houston was soon surrounded by a group of gifted Negro lawyers, led by Thurgood Marshall, who were determined to reverse the

41

Plessy judgement. Houston's strategy relied on his belief that Negro progress would depend on a supply of first-rate lawyers trained at the best white law schools. He also calculated that white judges would find it hard to deny that the quality of law schools mattered, and therefore that the situation did not meet the *Plessy* test of separate but equal facilities. Houston's key perception was that Negroes must focus on the inequality of the provision available.

He and his colleagues won a series of desegregation cases. Their two crucial victories were in *Gaines*, in 1938, and in *Sweatt v. Painter* in 1950. In the first, the Supreme Court held that Gaines, a Negro, must be admitted to the University of Missouri Law School because there was no alternative in the state. In *Sweatt*, the Court found that a separate law school for Negroes in Oklahoma could not be said to be equal.

By the 1950s, the NAACP and the Howard lawyers had broadened their attack on segregated education to primary and secondary schools. Five cases were bundled up as *Brown v. Board of Education*, and tried together by Thurgood Marshall and his team. They were heard on 9 December 1952, re-argued one year less one day later, and decided on 17 May 1954. Marshall and his colleagues focused in their arguments on the proposition that separate education was in itself unequal. They made much of the work of sociologists, especially that of Kenneth B. Clark, an African-American scholar who had produced a telling paper on the effects of discrimination for a 1950 White House conference on children and youth. The Court, speaking through the mouth of its Republican Chief Justice, former Governor of California Earl Warren, fully accepted the argument. 'In the field of public education,' he wrote, 'the doctrine of "separate but equal" has no place. Separate educational facilities are inherently unequal.'

The South was utterly unprepared for this judgement, which knocked down with one massive backhander the whole structure of custom, supported by state law and local ordinance, that had governed every detail of political, social and economic life since the end of Reconstruction in the 1870s. Beginning in the Mississippi Delta, the hardest of hard places, White Citizens' Councils sprang up across the South to protest and, if possible, to reverse the shocking verdict. Though they were later described as respectable versions of the Ku Klux Klan – and supposedly respectable local politicians joined the councils – in the late 1950s no one could be sure that this movement would not sweep the former Confederacy.

In the summer of 1955 the Supreme Court, recognizing that the creation of a uniform school system would present real problems, administrative as well as political, for at least the Deep South, returned to the practical issue. Formally, from the bench, it expressed the hope that southern states would act to implement the *Brown* judgement 'with all deliberate speed', a phrase drawn from the revered former justice Oliver Wendell Holmes Jr that allowed segregationists an argument against prompt or indeed any early action.

Southern legislators in the national Congress now entered the fray. For decades, the South had enjoyed disproportionate power in Congress. There was a simple reason for this: the South had what was essentially a one-party system. (Some southerners voted for the Republican candidate Eisenhower in 1952 and 1956. But in congressional, state and local elections, in all the states of the former Confederacy, the Democrats reigned almost unchallenged.) Congress had a seniority system – the all-powerful chairmanships of committees were acquired by long service. Southerners, their tenure threatened only by contests within their own Democratic Party, were therefore far more likely than legislators from the North or West to serve long enough to rise to chairmanships.

Now the great 'whales' of the Senate, as their leader Lyndon Johnson called them, and their colleagues in the House, rose to denounce the Supreme Court's decision. In March 1956 nineteen Senators (out of twenty-two representing the eleven states of the Confederacy) signed what was known as 'the Southern Manifesto'. So did seventy-seven members of the House of Representatives, from nine southern states – more than one-sixth of all members of the House. They included, in the Senate, the chairmen of the Foreign Relations Committee (Walter George of Georgia), of the Judiciary Committee (James Eastland of Mississippi) and of the Armed Services Committee (Richard B. Russell of Georgia); and in the House the adamantine chairman of the Rules Committee, Judge Howard Smith, and the chairman of Armed Services (Carl Vinson of Georgia), not to mention other men in either Chamber strategically positioned across the paths of legislation and financial appropriations. They included last-ditch reactionaries like John Stennis of Mississippi and Strom Thurmond of South Carolina, but also men with a reputation for national, even liberal concerns, such as William Fulbright of Arkansas and Hale Boggs of Louisiana, proof of the tremendous pressure the issue brought to bear on any southern politician. The manifesto, drafted by Thurmond, was uncompromising. The Supreme Court's decision, it said, was 'unwarranted' and bore 'the fruit always produced when men substitute naked power for established law'. And in a sinister echo of South Carolina's doctrine of nullification of federal law by the state, and the arguments that led to the War between the States, as southerners to this day call the Civil War, it commended 'the motives of those states which have declared the intention to resist forced integration by any lawful means'.

A formidable minority of the national political leadership was determined to disobey the Supreme Court's decision. The White House was then occupied by a great but tired and soon seriously ill soldier, Dwight D. Eisenhower, born in a southern state, Texas, and brought up in the old army with its strongly southern culture and instincts. Eisenhower, however, knew his duty. When tested, by the crisis over school desegregation in Little Rock in 1957, he did that duty. He sent in the 101st Airborne Division from Kentucky to enforce the law and protect nine Negro students at Little Rock's Central High School. But it was with a heavy heart. 'President Eisenhower was very loath to intervene. . .' said his Attorney General Herbert Brownell, 'it was really a great struggle in his mind.'[1]

If, even nationally, it was far from clear how much support there was for the Supreme Court's decision, there was no doubt at all in the minds of most of the citizens of Montgomery. With a population of about 150,000, Montgomery lived essentially off the white-collar jobs provided by the state government. Attitudes in the state capital were not so very different from those in the immobile conservative Black Belt counties – Lowndes and Perry, Dallas and Wilcox – over to the west. Montgomery was a totally segregated city. Hotels, bars, restaurants, schools, buses, lunch counters, sports facilities, toilets, drinking fountains – every place where black and white citizens might have come together – all were strictly segregated. The white citizens of Montgomery hated the *Brown* decision, and were determined to resist it. They thought it was unjust, illegal and plain wrong. Most of them had been brought up to believe that social contact between whites and blacks would lead ineluctably to 'race mixing', 'mongrelization'. Such words were habitually used by ostensibly sane white politicians. A substantial violent minority showed itself willing to bomb, to burn, to lynch. Some understood, but were not inclined to say openly, that racial change would have to come someday. The majority believed with unshakeable certainty that the Supreme Court's decision was bad law, unwise, a reckless invitation to racial upheaval, an insult to decent Americans. Unless this is grasped, the mean tenacity with which Montgomery's white leadership resisted the Negro boycott of the city's buses, as if it presaged revolution, cannot be understood.

This was the broad legal and political climate as young Martin Luther King assumed spiritual, and some degree of political, responsibility over Montgomery's sixty thousand African-Americans at Dexter.

A fortnight before Rosa Parks was arrested, Coretta King had given birth to the couple's first child, Yolanda Denise, known as 'Yoki'. King was, of course, already in contact with the small circle of people in black Montgomery who were actively engaged in the struggle for racial justice. He had already spoken to the Montgomery branch of the NAACP. He knew the black leadership: E. D. Nixon, Ralph Abernathy and Jo Ann Robinson, an Alabama State professor from Ohio who had had her own bruising encounter with segregation and had already complained to the bus company more than once about its behaviour. She was one of the leaders of the Montgomery Women's Political Council.

The morning after her arrest, Rosa Parks was bailed out of prison by Nixon and Clifford Durr. Jo Ann Robinson and some of her friends shut themselves inside offices at the college overnight to avoid detection while using the state's cyclostyle machines for purposes the state would by no means have approved. They had already churned out thousands of leaflets calling for a boycott of the bus company when Nixon called King and other ministers to a meeting to discuss the subject. They met at Dexter, with King in the chair, and decided to call for the boycott. It was still far from clear that King would be the leader. If Nixon had not been away because of his work on the trains, he would have been in the chair. At that first meeting, what was under discussion was a one-day protest, and it was agreed that there should be no one leader.

The next morning, the Kings were up and dressed by 5.30. Black people in Montgomery had to get up early to reach work on time. There was a bus stop on the South Jackson Street line, only a few yards from the parsonage. Normally the line took hundreds of black domestic workers to their jobs. Martin was in the kitchen drinking his coffee when Coretta called out, 'Martin, Martin, come quickly!' He put down his cup and ran into the living-room. Coretta pointed to a bus. 'Darling, it's empty!' So was the next bus, fifteen minutes later. The third held only two passengers, both white.[2]

That Monday, the bus company estimated that 90 per cent of Negroes stayed off the buses. In the afternoon eighteen Negro ministers met and chose King as leader of what was to be called the Montgomery Improvement Association (MIA). That evening, King was to speak to an audience of several thousand at the Holt Street Baptist Church, the biggest in town. A white reporter who was there said later it was the most 'fired up' gathering of human beings he had ever seen.

King had only twenty minutes to think about what he was to say. He was aware that he had to steer a middle course. He must be militant enough to keep up the morale of the boycott movement, yet not so inflammatory as to provoke them beyond 'controllable and Christian bounds'. He proceeded to give one of the speeches of his life – not just that it was powerfully moving, or that it launched his leadership in a movement for civil rights for Negroes, but also because in it he managed to touch most of the themes of his future leadership. He evoked racial pride, the insistent demand for justice, the Social Gospel, and the commitment to non-violence as the method, and he did so in terms of an epic vision.

They were going to stick together, he began, and to work together. Montgomery's Negroes were 'tired of being segregated and humiliated, tired of being kicked about by the brutal feet of oppression'.

'Right here in Montgomery,' he continued, 'when the history books are written in the future, somebody will have to say, "There lived a race of people, a black people, [with] fleecy locks and black complexion, a people who had the moral courage to stand up for their rights. And thereby they injected a new meaning into the veins of history and of civilization". He took care to place the demands of the Montgomery Negroes in the context of American rights and American democratic beliefs, and he did so in soaring rhetoric. 'If we are wrong,' he ended, 'the Supreme Court of this nation is wrong. If we are wrong, God Almighty is wrong. If we are wrong, Jesus of Nazareth was merely a utopian dreamer that never came down to earth. If we are wrong, justice is a lie.'[3]

On 8 December 1955, only a few days after the boycott had established that it was not a one-day wonder, King, fellow leaders of the MIA and its lawyers sat down with the three city commissioners and executives of the bus company. The MIA did not ask for an end to segregation on the buses, or anywhere else. It had three modest demands: an end to rudeness on the part of the white drivers, the hiring of some black drivers, and seating on a first-come first-served basis, with the whites filling up from the front, and the blacks from the back. The city's white leadership made it plain that it had no intention of giving in at the first push. One commissioner announced that black car-pool drivers who charged less than the prescribed fare would be prosecuted, and in other respects too the city made it plain that it meant to get tough. The Negroes responded by organizing an elaborate and highly efficient car pool system. They were also delighted to receive financial help not only from almost every NAACP branch in the country but from all over the world, as far as Tokyo, to a total of $250,000.

The city, or at least segregationists in it, tried a number of tricks, circulating false rumours, either that agreement had been reached to end the boycott or that King and the other boycott leaders had absconded with the MIA's funds and bought themselves Cadillacs and the like. Meanwhile, King was receiving constant ugly, anonymous telephone calls, conveying abuse but also death threats. On 26 January he was arrested for speeding – allegedly at thirty miles an hour in a 25-mile-an-hour area – and sent to jail. Though he was soon released on bail, he now experienced the first serious moral crisis of his career, and surmounted it in a way that would have a permanent influence on his career.

One night he was woken by a particularly nasty call. He hung up, but found he could not get back to sleep. He went down to the kitchen and made himself a cup of coffee. He tried to think how he could remove himself from the picture without appearing a coward. He leant forward at the kitchen table, his face in his hands, and prayed aloud. In an autobiography he would later recall the words of his prayer: 'I am here taking a stand for what I believe is right. But now I am afraid. The people are looking for leadership, and if I stand before them without strength and courage, they too will falter. I am at the end of my powers. I have nothing left.'[4] At that moment, he said, he felt the presence of the Divine as he had never experienced Him before. He heard 'the quiet assurance of an inner voice'. 'Stand up for righteousness,' it said, 'stand up for truth; and God will be at your side forever.' At last he had been granted the direct religious revelation he had told his teachers at Crozer he had never known. Now, he recalled when he described his memory of that night later, he was ready to face anything.

He would need every ounce of the new courage he had been given. Three days later his home was firebombed while he was at a mass meeting at Ralph Abernathy's church, First Baptist. But it was only by sheer chance that neither Coretta nor Yoki was hurt. Once reassured of their safety, King took the news with a calmness that surprised him. The next night, he and Coretta were woken by a soft, repeated tapping at their door. They were terrified. Eventually King went down. It was Coretta's father, Obie Scott. He had come to drive his daughter and her baby to safety. Martin and Coretta were deeply grateful, but they refused his help.

It was a couple of days later that Fred Gray, the MIA's lawyer, filed a suit on behalf of five women, challenging the constitutionality of segregation on the buses. This was something the MIA had hitherto hesitated to do, fearing that it might divide the country against them. Three weeks later, on 21 February, King, twenty-four other ministers and a total of eighty-nine other Montgomery Negroes were indicted on charges of conspiracy to boycott the buses. King was in Nashville, Tennessee, lecturing at Fisk University, having left Coretta and the baby with his parents in Atlanta. When he heard the news he flew to Atlanta, to be met by his father who had gathered together a group of leading Atlanta

Negroes of his own generation in order to persuade his son not to go back to Montgomery. But both King and his wife, backed up by old Benjamin Mays, his president at Morehouse, saw that he had no alternative but to go to Montgomery, and when the decision was made, Daddy King drove there with them.

The case came to trial on 19 March. The MIA produced witnesses who testified that the boycott was the result of no conspiracy, but a spontaneous response to injustice. 'Wasn't no one man started it,' said Gladys Moore in evidence. 'We all started it overnight.'[5] Three days later, nevertheless, King was found guilty of conspiracy and fined $500 plus costs. When he refused to pay he was sentenced to 386 days of hard labour. He appealed, and the immediate impact of the trial was not humiliation and defeat but a kind of coronation. When he went to New York to speak at the biggest black church in Brooklyn, ten thousand people tried to get in and $4,000 was collected for the MIA. He was profiled in the *New York Times* and his fame and likeness flashed around the world.

A prophet, they say, is not without honour, save in his own country. While King was hailed as a Moses in the North and seen around the world as the hero of a sort of independence movement within the body of the great whale itself, in Alabama, as the boycott wore on, it brought envy, hatred and uncharitableness from black and white alike.

White Alabama's hatred did not quickly abate. On 1 June the state's attorney general, John Patterson, persuaded a court to ban the NAACP in Alabama on the grounds that it was 'organizing, supporting, and financing an illegal boycott by Negro residents of Montgomery.' Whether or not this was Patterson's intention, nothing could have been more calculated to divide the world of Negro politics. King was already on uneasy terms with E. D. Nixon, who felt that he had not given him enough credit for political favours. Now the NAACP found itself facing not only a ban on all activities, including fund-raising, in Alabama, but also a fine of $100,000 for resisting an order to hand over its membership lists. So King found himself persona non grata with Roy Wilkins, the powerful head of the NAACP, the biggest, oldest and most respected black organization in the land, who was privately furious that the Montgomery bus boycott was disrupting, in a key southern state, the patient and successful strategy of legal challenges that had already achieved the historic *Brown* victory.

There were other trials and tribulations to be borne, including rumours that the MIA had misspent or even misappropriated large amounts collected to support the boycott. At the worst possible moment its secretary, Uriah Fields, called a press conference to accuse the MIA leadership, and by implication King, of financial corruption. Fields ultimately withdraw his charges, which did contain a grain of truth, and King emerged unscathed.

Still the boycott droned on, with the hurt pride of Montgomery's white politicians undiminished and the righteous fervour of the loyal, patient Negroes as they trudged or queued for lifts to work a little tarnished by the jealousies and human failings of their leaders. The city went to court to ban the car pool and fine the MIA for the taxes the municipality had lost. On 13 November a reporter from the Associated Press broke in on a dreary court hearing and handed King a flash he had torn off the AP wire. 'The United States Supreme Court,' it read, 'today affirmed a decision of a special three-judge panel in declaring Alabama's state and local laws requiring segregation on buses unconstitutional. The Supreme Court acted without listening to any argument; it simply said "the motion to affirm is granted and the judgment is affirmed".'[6]

King, and the patient army of cleaning ladies and other humble workers, had won a great victory. 'My feets is tired,' one of them, seventy-year-old Sister Pollard, had memorably said, 'but my soul is rested.' The hosts of Midian were laid low. It would take five weeks for the Court's judgement to be given effect. But in early December, almost exactly one year after the speech that had made him the leader of the movement, King was back at Holt Street Baptist Church to draw the lessons of the triumph. There were six of them, he said:

'We have discovered that we can stick together for a common cause;

'Our leaders do not have to sell out;

'Threats and violence do not necessarily intimidate those who are sufficiently aroused and nonviolent;

'Our church is becoming militant, stressing a social gospel as well as a gospel of personal salvation;

'We have gained a new sense of dignity and destiny;

'We have discovered a new and powerful weapon – nonviolent resistance.'

This last proposition requires some explanation, which will be the subject of the next chapter.

5

The Little Brown Ghost

The little brown ghost of Mahatma Gandhi
stalks this town tonight.

Daily Express, report from Birmingham, Alabama, 1963

One day in late February 1956 a visitor to the Dexter Avenue Church
parsonage, at 309 South Jackson Street, was about to lower himself into
a chair when his friend barked a warning. He had almost sat down on
a loaded firearm. Martin Luther King, disciple of Gandhi, future prophet
of non-violence and Nobel peace laureate, had applied to the Montgomery police for a permit to carry a weapon, which they, predictably
but unconstitutionally, turned down. His self-appointed 'bodyguard',
Bob Williams, an old friend from Morehouse days and a music professor at Alabama State, had brought a shotgun with him into the Kings'
house and sat up at night with it in the tense days after the firebombing.
Two New York pacifists, the Reverend Glenn Smiley of the Fellowship
of Reconciliation, and Bayard Rustin, now of the War Resisters' League,
were both shocked by the casual attitude of the Kings and their friends
to guns, which southerners, both white and black, were very comfortable with. Smiley wrote to a friend that they had a veritable 'arsenal' in
South Jackson Street.

Smiley later stated that when he had said to King that he assumed
he was familiar with Gandhi's thought, King had replied, 'I know very
little about him.'[1] King's commitment to peace and non-violence was
real, but at the time of the bus boycott it was neither absolute nor
long-established. As an undergraduate at Morehouse, he tells us, he
read Henry David Thoreau's essay 'Civil Disobedience' (1849) more
than once and was 'deeply moved'. He also tells us that when he was
at Crozer he found a lecture by Dr Mordecai Johnson, the president
of Howard University and a serious student of Gandhi's life and philosophy, so 'electrifying' that he went out and bought half a dozen
books on Gandhi. One was an admiring biography by a British

clergyman, Bishop Frederick Fisher, *That Strange Little Brown Man Gandhi*.

It has been pointed out that after the Montgomery struggle King had every reason to present himself in colours that would reassure northern intellectuals that he was on the same wavelength as they were.[2] His early autobiography, *Stride Toward Freedom*, first published in 1958 and written at the encouragement of New York friends, is full of such touches, including the statement that Donizetti's *Lucia di Lammermoor* was his favourite opera as well as erudite references to Hegel, Shakespeare and Nietzsche, even a disquisition (later to become a staple of his sermons) on the difference between the three words for love in Plato, *eros*, *agape* and *philia*. There was nothing phoney in this. King was a highly educated man and a serious and gifted intellectual. At the same time, precisely because of his intelligence, he understood that he needed both to stay in touch with the Negro masses who looked to him for leadership and to draw on the ideas, the strengths, the contacts and the experience of the American left.

Over the five years after the Montgomery victory, Dr Martin Luther King Jr would become, thanks to the assistance of the news media, a national political figure. He was often described as a Moses leading his people out of Egypt, even as a Messiah. He was occasionally courted both by Vice-President Richard Nixon and by the Democratic candidate, John F. Kennedy. He would visit Ghana, identifying with its first president, Kwame Nkrumah, and other leaders of the anticolonial movement that was sweeping the world as Britain, France and the other colonial powers found they could no longer afford to maintain their dominance in the face of dwindling resources, rising nationalism and American disapproval. He would visit India, briefly.

King was never, however, a leading American Gandhian, either as a scholar of Gandhian doctrine or as one who shared Gandhi's personal austerity. Several African-Americans of the generation older than his, including Mordecai Johnson and Bayard Rustin, and some of his own contemporaries, notably James Lawson, had spent substantial periods in India studying the principles and practice of satyagraha, Gandhi's policy of non-violent political action. It was those two pacifist visitors from New York, the white Texan Methodist minister Glenn Smiley, and

Bayard Rustin, singer, socialist, homosexual, heroic activist and brilliant political strategist, who helped him most to see the appropriateness of Gandhian non-violence to the situation in which African-Americans found themselves in the 1950s. For a people who confronted a near-monopoly of state power in the hands of those who resisted their progress, non-violent action was not just intelligent, it was indispensable.

The second half of the 1950s has been described, and not unfairly, as a fallow period in King's life. It was not, however, uneventful. It was the time when he became a leader of national stature. He published his first book, travelled abroad for the first time, and came within millimetres of being stabbed to death. Above all, it was the time when he was able to put himself at the head of a political organization of his own, the Southern Christian Leadership Conference. Those years also saw a welling-up of black protest over which he had little or no control, in the sit-in movement and the Freedom Rides.

'There go my people, I must follow them, for I am their leader.' The mot has been attributed to many, including the nineteenth-century French radical Alexandre Ledru-Rollin, Benjamin Disraeli and Mahatma Gandhi. To none of them did it apply more appositely than to Martin Luther King.

King's transition from a local and regional leader into a national figure was helped by a whole vortex of political forces, but also by a quartet of remarkable, and remarkably diverse, personalities: Bayard Rustin, Ella Baker, Stanley Levison and James Lawson. Crucially, they not only taught him the theory and practice of non-violent resistance; they also put him in contact with the American left – battered, but not extinct, as it was during that decade of frustration and reaction. By the time the Supreme Court reached its *Brown* decision, the New Deal was over. The Cold War was freezing hard. Red scares, loyalty oaths and every other manifestation of collective paranoia had stigmatized political radicalism, and many who had once shared radical instincts now kept their heads safely below the parapet.

The least sympathetic to King of his four new allies was Ella Baker. Middle-aged when she met King, she had spent her life up to that point as a New York radical organizer. Born in 1905 (or 1903), she was educated at Shaw University in North Carolina, and was briefly, and unhappily, married to a minister. She went to New York in 1927 in the days of the 'Harlem Renaissance', and worked for the Young Negro Cooperative League and the New Deal's Works Progress Administration (WPA) before taking two executive posts, first as national field secretary and then as director of branches, with the NAACP. She worked closely on voter education with Septima Clark in the Low Country of South Carolina, among some of the most deprived black people in the South. Before the end of the 1950s, somewhat disenchanted with King and his allies among the black clergy, Miss Baker – it was a sign of her immense personal dignity that she was always called 'Miss Baker', never by her first name – had transferred her loyalty to the young radicals of the Student Nonviolent Coordinating Committee, and helped them learn the basics of political activism.[3]

In December 1957 she was sent to Atlanta by Rustin and Levison, who did not bother to consult her first. There, working initially without an office or a telephone, and receiving a miserable salary, she got the Southern Christian Leadership Conference (SCLC) off the ground. She found it hard to work with King and with the SCLC. She was irritated by the disorganized style of the southern preachers, whom she had left behind in her personal life, and she found King self-absorbed and – though the word had not yet come into vogue – sexist. She also felt that there was too much emphasis on him, and not enough on less prominent members of the movement.

Baker and Rustin had both worked briefly for a New York charity called In Friendship, which existed to help victims of racism in the South and had sent money to the Montgomery Improvement Association. There they had worked with a powerful and in some respects mysterious figure who was to have immense influence on King's life and on the civil rights movement as a whole. This was Stanley Levison, a wealthy New York lawyer who had business interests both in New York real estate and in Ecuador.[4]

Levison was both a skilful man of business and a wholehearted man of the left. He was good at raising money, and good at managing and controlling it, qualities that Martin King's entourage badly needed. The

FBI had been told as early as 1952 by the Childs brothers, Morris and Jack, informers collectively known by the code name 'Solo', that Levison was a member of the Communist Party of the United States and had played an important part in managing its financial affairs. In 1962 the FBI passed this suspicion on to Robert Kennedy, then the Attorney General. Shortly afterwards Levison was subpoenaed by the international security subcommittee of the Senate, chaired by the arch-conservative Senator James Eastland of Mississippi. Levison began by saying, 'I am not now and never have been a member of the Communist Party', and thereafter refused to answer their questions. He pleaded the Fifth Amendment (which protects Americans against self-incrimination). It seems probable that he had been close to some Party members, but was never actually a member himself. At any rate, as a man of the left he was generous with his time and money in supporting causes he believed in. He became involved in helping King, first, at the time of the Montgomery bus boycott. Later, it was he who not only arranged the contract for King's first book, *Stride Toward Freedom*, but organized a team of ghost writers and editors to make sure that it came out on time. He was the object of the deepest suspicion to the FBI, who tapped his telephone. But he was a loyal friend to King and a worldly-wise counsellor, not only in business matters but also on political questions in the widest sense.

If Stanley Levison was an intriguing figure in his way, he could not compete for sheer exotic oddness and originality with Bayard Rustin.[5] This was a man with half a dozen strikes against him: he was black, he was gay, he had been (briefly) a communist and then a Trotskyite, and he spoke with what many Americans found an irritatingly British accent. (His mother married a Barbadian, and some said he acquired his accent from him; or perhaps it was simply an early sign of Rustin's desire to stand out from the crowd.) He was illegitimate – the woman he was told was his mother was really his grandmother, and he was told his real mother was his sister. He was a proud and difficult man. A lifelong pacifist, in the late 1960s he shocked his friends by finding arguments to justify the Vietnam War. Yet his commitment to peace and racial justice and his sheer courage were exemplary. He served almost three years in jail for refusing military service, and then twenty-two days on a

Georgia chain gang for his part in a challenge to segregation on southern buses. He puzzled 'Captain Jones', the gang boss, whose experience of life had not led him to expect such things, by his willingness to be shown how to use his shovel to better effect. After he served his time, he 'heaped coals of burning fire' on the captain's head by thanking him for his kindness and hoping that a cold that was troubling him would soon clear up.

Rustin, whom I was privileged to know, was a tall and handsome man, an athlete in his youth, with a beautiful singing voice and a wonderful sense of humour. He sang professionally and hung out with Josh White, Maya Angelou, Dylan Thomas and Norman Mailer in the bars and jazz clubs of Greenwich Village. He was a protégé at different times both of A. J. Muste, the veteran pacifist, and of A. Philip Randolph, the leader of the Brotherhood of Sleeping Car Porters. He had been convicted in Pasadena, California, on a charge of homosexual behaviour, a fact that made his superiors in various radical organizations acutely nervous – understandably, given the climate of 1950s America. But he brought great talents to King, and he spent them without stint.

The last of this remarkable quartet of comrades, James Lawson, was King's age, and their friendship lasted to the very end of King's short life. He was in Memphis to help Lawson, as the leader of a strike by the local dustmen, when he was assassinated. Lawson was born in Ohio and became a pacifist in his teens. Like Rustin, he was sent to prison for refusing military service. Released early, he was ordained a minister and then went to India, where he spent three years studying Gandhian ideas and techniques at Hislop College, an Anglican college in Nagpur, Maharashtra state. He came back to the United States in 1956, and enrolled first at Oberlin (Coretta King's alma mater), then at Vanderbilt University in Nashville, from which he was expelled for taking part in a sit-in protest in March 1960. Before that, he taught a workshop in nonviolence that was also attended by students from Fisk University and the local Baptist theological seminary. These included John Lewis, later chairman of SNCC, and a Congressman from Georgia; the erratic but charismatic James Bevel; Diane Nash, later married to Bevel, and others who played leading parts in the civil rights movement.[6]

Lawson became a very close colleague and friend of King's. In April 1960, the two spoke at a conference at Shaw University in Raleigh, North Carolina, organized by Ella Baker, which founded SNCC. But whereas King gave a relatively benign talk, Lawson's was what Mary King, a young white recruit to SNCC, called 'ringing and militant'. He sharply criticized the NAACP's 'overreliance on the courts', and called for a 'nonviolent revolution'.[7]

The Supreme Court had ended the need for the Montgomery boycott in December 1956, after thirteen months of political and legal conflict, and ordinary black people doing their best to get to work without using the buses. In the following January, sixty black leaders, almost all of them ministers, met at Ebenezer Church in Atlanta. The result of their discussions was the formation of the Southern Christian Leadership Conference. It was exactly a year later that Ella Baker was sent to Atlanta to organize an office for the SCLC there. This was to become the vehicle for Martin Luther King Jr's political progress, but it was not intended for that purpose, or not for that purpose alone.

By 1957 there was in every sizeable city in the South a movement for change that went beyond the essentially law-related activities of the NAACP. To some extent, because these movements received funding that would otherwise have gone to the NAACP or to its tax-exempt wing, the Legal Defense Fund Incorporated, known as the 'Inc. Fund', they were in competition with the NAACP. They were certainly seen as a potential threat by Roy Wilkins and his colleagues at NAACP headquarters in New York and all the more so because many of the local black leaders were also officers in the local branches of the NAACP. So not just King, who moved to Atlanta in 1959, but also clergy such as Ralph Abernathy in Montgomery, Fred Shuttlesworth in Birmingham, C. K. Steele, who had led a bus boycott in Tallahassee, the capital of Florida, and T. J. Jemison, who had done the same in Baton Rouge, Louisiana, felt the need for an organization that would encourage and coordinate direct action for civil rights.[8]

These were the cream of the African-American leadership in the South, highly educated, more radical and politically active than most of their fellow preachers, and based in the larger and more important southern cities. This was the first, so to speak, of the armies whom King could not command, but who would follow him.

Early in 1960 four young black students at the Agricultural and Technical Institute in Greensboro, North Carolina, set off a second wave of direct action that appealed especially to students and other young people, and so brought into the field a second army that was even less under King's command. Ezell Blair Jr, Franklin McCain, Joseph McNeil and David Richmond sat down at the lunch counter in the local Woolworth's and ordered coffees. (Blair said later that he had been inspired by hearing King speak sometime earlier.) They were refused service, so the next day they came back, and by the fifth day hundreds of young black people were demanding to be served at what had previously been whites-only counters in Greensboro. The protest spread across the South, and by the end of the year no fewer than seventy thousand black students had sat in at a lunch counter, and about 3,600 had been arrested.

By 1957, King was well enough known to be invited by Kwame Nkrumah to attend the celebrations of that country's independence from Britain. Among the other guests were such prominent American Negroes as the Harlem Congressman Adam Clayton Powell, Charles Diggs, a Congressman from Michigan, and the Under-Secretary General of the United Nations and winner of the 1950 Nobel Peace Prize, Ralph Bunche. In Ghana, King also met Vice-President Richard Nixon, who responded in a friendly way, though he had previously ignored King's letters. King was greatly and in some way naively moved by his visit to Ghana. He was uncritical in his admiration for Nkrumah, who did not take long to become a dictator, flanked by a praetorian guard of Communist soldiers from East Germany and even China. He was particularly struck by the fact that the Duchess of Kent, who was present at the celebrations as the Queen's representative, danced with her African host.

The Ghana visit did give King a new, international perspective. He saw now that the struggle of the Negroes of the South was part of a broader movement that was destroying empires and liberating people of colour across the world. On his return to America he preached a powerful sermon at Dexter Avenue, in which he described what he had seen in Africa and drew some spiritual lessons from it. 'Not some white and not some black,' he ended, 'not some yellow and not some brown, but all flesh shall see it together. They shall see it from Montgomery. They shall see it from Ghana. They shall see it from China.'

That summer King preached powerfully at the Lincoln Memorial in Washington, to be the scene of his greatest speech six years later. This was part of a 'prayer pilgrimage', intended to encourage the Eisenhower administration to become actively involved in destroying segregation. The event was a disappointment. No more than twenty-five thousand people turned up, in part because of jealousies between different civil rights organizations.

Then, in 1959, after months of invitations, postponements and nego-tiations, Martin and Coretta King, accompanied by their friend the his-torian L. D. Reddick, visited India. The trip began badly. Reddick persuaded the Kings to slip over from London to Paris to meet his friend Richard Wright, famous as the author of *Native Son*. They missed their plane and were still stuck in Bombay when they were due to be dining with the Prime Minister, Jawaharlal Nehru. They finally did meet Nehru, with his daughter Indira Gandhi acting as his hostess, the next day. The other guests at dinner were Edwina, Lady Mountbatten, and her daughter Pamela. Again, King was impressed that the wife of the British colonial master should be on such good terms with the independence leader. He may not have realized that the easy relationship between their host and Lady Mountbatten was not primarily the result of political tol-erance. They were, or had been, lovers.*

The Kings were in India for only four weeks, from 9 February to 9 March. They visited Bodh Gaya and other holy places in the north-east associated with the life of the Buddha. They met several leading disci-ples of Gandhi (who had been assassinated in 1948), including Jayaprakash Narayan, who opposed Nehru's drive to bring India into the modern industrial world, and Vinoba Bhave, the farouche but

---

* So, at least, it has been widely reported, for example by the novelist, journalist and politician Khushwant Singh, *Truth, Love, and a Little Malice*, New Delhi, Viking, 2002, p. 134, and many others, though this has also been denied by admirers of Lord Mountbatten. The London *Daily Herald* is said to have published a large photograph of Lady Mountbatten opening her front door to Nehru in her négligée.

impressive 'walking saint'. Bhave spent his life criss-crossing India, in apostolic poverty, to persuade the rich to give up their land to landless peasants. They visited the ashram from which Gandhi launched his famous 1930 Salt March to the coastal village of Dandi, to protest against the British salt tax. At a press conference just before his departure King tried to argue that India should set an example to the United States and the Soviet Union by disarming, but the Indian journalists would have none of it.

King was fascinated by India. Like many first-time visitors from the West, he was shocked by the ubiquitous contrast between poverty and luxury. When he got home to Montgomery, he commented on the half-million people who were sleeping in the streets of Bombay. He was also aware of the human qualities, including compassion and spirituality, that coexisted in India (as elsewhere) with cruelty and indifference. King admitted that he found the sub-continent confusing. In the radio talk he gave the evening before he left India, he called non-violent resistance 'the most potent weapon available to oppressed people in their struggle for justice and human dignity'. But he had little opportunity, driven as he was by the 'improving' itinerary arranged for him by the American Friends Service Committee, to go at all deeply into the theory, still less the practice, of Gandhian non-violence.

On the way home the Kings visited Egypt, Greece and the Holy Land. King was profoundly moved to stand where Paul had preached on the Areopagus in Athens,[9] and to walk where Jesus had been taken to his crucifixion. On his return, on Palm Sunday, he preached one of his greatest sermons on a text from St John's gospel: 'I have other sheep, who are not of this fold.' He seemed to be saying that Gandhi was the greatest of the spiritual heirs of Jesus. 'It is one of the strange ironies of the modern world,' he said, 'that the greatest Christian of the twentieth century was not a member of the Christian Church.' In that same sermon King reflected on Gandhi's assassination, and perhaps showed that he understood what might be his own end. 'The world doesn't like people like Gandhi,' he concluded. 'That's strange, isn't it? They don't like people like Christ. They don't like people like Abraham Lincoln. They kill them.'

In the immediate future, the only threat to King's life was to come from a crazy member of his own race. In September 1958, while signing copies of *Stride Toward Freedom* at a bookstore in Harlem, he was stabbed in the chest with a paper-knife by a mentally deranged forty-two-year-old black woman called Izola Ware Curry. She was later diagnosed as a paranoid schizophrenic. It was not clear what her motive was. She mentioned that King had undermined her Catholic faith and her strong anti-communist feelings. The wound was nearly fatal. King was told later by one of the surgeons that if he had sneezed, it would have killed him.

On 3 September 1958 he was also arrested in Montgomery, in bizarre circumstances.[10] A well-known local black footballer and low-life character called 'Big Two' Ed Davis turned up at the office of King's friend and colleague Ralph Abernathy waving an axe and a pistol, and accused the minister – quite plausibly – of having had an affair with his wife. He then chased the straying preacher for two blocks down the street until pursuer and pursued were stopped by a police cruiser. When Dr King arrived at the courthouse to give evidence, a policeman, addressing him as 'Boy!', arrested him for 'loitering'. Two cops twisted King's arm painfully behind his back. After a night in jail he was tried, convicted and sentenced to pay a fine of $14 or serve fourteen days in jail. He decided to go to prison. Copies of a statement explaining his reasons, founded on conscience, were circulated. Then King found that he was denied this small martyrdom. Someone had paid his fine.

This arrest was no more than the casual prejudice of a boorish policeman. King was a smartly dressed, well-spoken man with a PhD, but according to the conventions of the white South in the 1950s this did not protect him from being rudely and roughly treated by white officials. Furthermore, it was to be made plain that there were those in the white power structure in Alabama who were determined to destroy King, and none too squeamish about how they would go about it.

In February 1960 an Alabama grand jury – all white, of course – indicted King for tax evasion and perjury.[11] Two Georgia sheriff's deputies showed up at Daddy King's Ebenezer Church in Atlanta with a warrant for the younger King's arrest on a felony charge of perjury in signing tax returns that were said to be untrue. It was a blatantly political charge. King had already paid the higher tax assessment – it amounted to the modest sum of $235.16 – and even if he had not, he would normally have been charged only with a misdemeanour. He was the first person in the history of Alabama ever to be charged in these circumstances with a felony. On 28 May, however, to general astonishment, he was pronounced 'not guilty' by the all-white jury. King said it showed that there were hundreds of thousands of white people of good-will in the South. The judge thought otherwise. It was, he said, the 'most surprising thing in my thirty-four years as a lawyer'.

King had been worried about how he could pay his legal costs. Levison and Rustin, working with the singer Harry Belafonte, organized fund-raising events in New York on behalf of a 'committee to defend Martin Luther King and the struggle for freedom in the South'. They paid for an advertisement in the *New York Times* which was to have an unexpected consequence. The ad alleged that Dr King's arrest for perjury was part of a campaign to frustrate his efforts to integrate public facilities and to encourage African-Americans to vote. One of the Montgomery city commissioners, L. B. Sullivan, sued for libel, claiming that the ad defamed him personally.

In the Alabama court, Sullivan won a judgement for $500,000. But the Supreme Court held unanimously that the First Amendment of the US Constitution protects the publication of all statements about the conduct of public officials, even false ones, unless the statements are made with 'actual malice'. That is defined as meaning that the statement was made either in the knowledge that it was false or with reckless disregard for whether it was true or not. By this test, Sullivan's case collapsed. The case went on to transform the libel law of the United States so far as public officials were concerned. After *New York Times v. Sullivan*, any serious attempt to investigate misconduct on the part of public officials in the United States was in practice protected from libel suits.

Alabama's white politicians, police and prosecutors were still determined to punish King for his challenge to the code of segregation. So far, since the bus boycott, King had been imprisoned only for a single night, in the aftermath of the 'Big Two' farce. It was in his home state of Georgia that real trouble came. On 19 October 1960 he was arrested with five dozen other demonstrators 'sitting in' to desegregate the lunch counters at Rich's, Atlanta's premier department store. King was sentenced to four months' hard labour in the state prison at Reidsville. He was woken roughly in his police cell, handcuffed and shackled, then driven more than two hundred miles to Reidsville. En route he was seriously worried, as he had been when first arrested in Montgomery, that he might be on the way to a lynching. He was allowed only one call from the jail, which he made to Coretta to say where he was, before being put into striped prison clothes. Six months pregnant, she was uncharacteristically but understandably close to panic.

By this time the 1960 presidential election was reaching its climax. Kennedy was at O'Hare Airport in Chicago, waiting for a flight after a session with powerful businessmen, when he learned what had happened to King.[12] The news came from Harris Wofford, perhaps the most liberal member of Kennedy's election staff and himself both a serious student of Gandhi and a personal friend of the Kings. He had been upset when Coretta King called, in obvious distress. It was Wofford who suggested to the candidate that he should intervene to protect King. Both aide and candidate were of course well aware that this could be a good campaign move with black voters. Wofford waited until the more hardboiled politicos on the staff had left Kennedy's suite then suggested that he intervene. He briefed Kennedy's brother-in-law, Sargent Shriver. When Kennedy went into the bedroom, Shriver followed him.

'I think you should give her a call, Jack,' he said.

'What the hell!' he said, sitting on the bed. 'That's a decent thing to do. Why not? Get her on the phone.'

Shriver, who had been given Coretta King's number by Wofford, dialled, then handed the phone to his brother-in-law. Kennedy just said to Mrs King, 'I know this must be very hard for you. I understand you're expecting a baby, and I just wanted you to know that I was thinking about you and Dr King. If there is anything I can do to help, please feel free to call on me.'

The candidate's brother, known to his enemies as Bobby and to his friends as Bob, was not yet the crusader for civil rights he was to become. He was furious. He summoned Wofford and the campaign's top Negro aide, the tough Chicago newspaperman Louis Martin. He tore a strip off them both, and ordered them never to do anything of the kind again. But Shriver, Wofford and Martin mounted a subtle campaign to publicize John Kennedy's gesture in the Negro press, while downplaying it in the white media to avoid a backlash.

For a hundred years, mindful of Southern Democrats' responsibility for Jim Crow and the persistence of segregation, most southern blacks had continued to vote Republican, if for no other reason than that Abraham Lincoln, their emancipator, was a Republican. That one phone call changed the loyalty of many. The story soon faded in the white press, but not in the African-American papers. The *Pittsburgh Courier* for example, quoted someone as saying: '"These white folks have now made Dr Martin Luther King, Jr., the biggest Negro in the United States"'. In so doing, they won the hair-trigger 1960 presidential election for John Fitzgerald Kennedy.

6

Between Two Fires

Blessed are the peacemakers,
for they catch hell from both sides.
Assistant Attorney General Burke Marshall

A telephone call from the soon to be victorious presidential candidate might have made Martin Luther King 'the biggest Negro in the United States', but at the beginning of the 1960s new developments were threatening King's status as the most exciting American Negro leader. For the rest of his life, King and the SCLC would have new competition from the left as well as from long-established organizations to the right.

Starting in Greensboro, the sit-in movement led to the emergence of a new, radical black organization, the Student Nonviolent Coordinating Committee, which, while ostensibly allied to King's SCLC, was to become a serious competitor for the loyalty of younger, more impatient, blacks. King might be the best-known and, for whites, the most reassuring of the black leaders. But in 1962, as he settled down to grapple with the financial and administrative problems of getting the SCLC into gear, for the time being he was no longer pre-eminent.

Now, the Freedom Riders were challenging segregation. Black and white protesters alike were riding the Greyhound and Trailways interstate buses, which were governed by federal law, and at each stop exposing the petty discrimination, the law and custom in the South, backed as it was by public opinion – and, where flouted, by murderous violence. The suicidal courage of the Riders, sponsored by the Congress of Racial Equality (CORE), made King and his fellow ministers seem cautious by comparison[1]. Nevertheless King and his associates fell under the suspicion of the FBI, whose wily, reactionary chief J. Edgar Hoover was convinced, in part by the unreliable testimony of informers, that King must be a communist. The Kennedy administration itself, for all it owed to John F. Kennedy's impetuous but shrewd gesture to the Kings, became suspicious too. As we shall see in the next chapter, King's next major initiative, the Albany movement of 1962, would be little better than a defeat. It was not until 1963, when he wrote from Birmingham jail describing the police brutality there, followed by the culminating glory of the march on Washington, that he would emerge once again as the Negro Moses, leading his people out of Egypt.

Seven years after the *Brown* judgement, progress for black people was still frustratingly difficult. To be sure, although the white South, or at least most of its leaders in the Deep South, had said 'Never!' to school desegregation, schools had begun to desegregate, especially after President Eisenhower's reluctant decision, mentioned earlier, to send in the 101st Airborne Division to protect nine black children admitted by court order to Central High School in Little Rock, Arkansas. Around the edges, the segregated South was shrinking. Yet in the core itself – South Carolina, Georgia, Alabama, Mississippi, Louisiana, and pockets of plantation culture in the other six states of the former Confederacy as well as in parts of Kentucky, Missouri and Oklahoma, even in parts of Maryland's Eastern Shore, close to Washington – the Jim Crow system survived.

Most schools across the former Confederacy were still segregated by race. Most cities, in the North as well as in the South, were almost completely residentially segregated. Overall, fewer blacks than whites voted, and in the core very few blacks voted at all. Those who sought to register to vote in such regions as the Mississippi Delta were subjected to crude violence both by white extremists and by the public authorities. Blacks were treated with prejudice and discrimination as they went about their daily lives and not least in their encounters with the courts and the police; and they were systematically excluded from most, and in the Deep South from all, 'public accommodations' such as hotels, restaurants and lunch counters. It is hard to imagine all the practical implications of this code, let alone the psychological damage it inflicted. A cross-country journey, say, from Washington to New Orleans, which would be a pleasure for white families, was for blacks a desperate venture. They must sleep in their cars and relieve themselves in the woods or risk assault. As writers such as Ralph Ellison, Richard Wright and James Baldwin graphically described, the Jim Crow code was intended to undermine the self-esteem of African-Americans, and all too often it succeeded.[2]

There were no 'Whites Only' signs in northern cities (in this respect Washington, as late as the 1950s, was not a northern city), but by most statistical measures, whether in relation to employment, income, health, housing or in their treatment by the criminal justice system, northern Negroes were worse off, much worse off, than whites. To an extent that was scarcely admitted in 1960, many northern whites, while priding themselves on their freedom from southern prejudices, shared the view that Negroes were socially, even congenitally, inferior.

There was therefore, as John Kennedy marched his men to the New Frontier, no strong determination in the Democratic Party, or even in the Kennedy White House, to move decisively to change the status of the Negro, either in law or in fact. Kennedy himself had little empathy for the civil rights movement: the only African American he knew at all well was his valet, George Thomas. It took months for his administration to take a step to which in theory it was already committed, to issue an executive order banning discrimination in federally owned or funded housing. (Much housing benefited from federally guaranteed mortgages.) Even less was there by now any enthusiasm for civil rights in the Republican Party, traditional defender of Negro rights since the days of Abraham Lincoln and the Radical Republicans, though individual liberal Republicans such as Nelson Rockefeller, the Governor of New York, supported the civil rights movement.

Indeed, one feature of the politics of the period was the veto power over many areas of national policy held by what came to be called the 'conservative coalition'. This brought together on the one hand conservative Republicans led by Senator Robert Taft of Ohio, men of the stamp of Senator Bourke B. Hickenlooper of Iowa, an obstinate opponent of racial equality, or Senator Homer Capehart of Indiana, known as the 'Indiana Neanderthal', and on the other conservative southern Democrats like Richard Russell of Georgia, Jim Eastland and John Stennis of Mississippi, and many more, some of whom (like Russell himself), justifiably prided themselves on their civilized behaviour in other respects but did not see that it should be extended to Negroes. The difference between such Republicans and southern Democrats was not that the former disagreed with the latter about racial issues, so much as in the matter of priorities. In the former Confederacy, race came near the top of the conservative agenda. Northern and Middle Western conservatives were on the surface more concerned about economic issues and anti-communism, but still saw no need to do anything at all urgently about racial injustice.

For blacks, of course, segregation, discrimination and racial injustice had always been the highest priority. In the North, the Roosevelt administration and the labour union movement had worked for certain measures to help blacks. At the time it was widely believed, both by those who were in favour of progress and by those who bitterly opposed it, that the New Deal was a powerful force for racial change. More recent scholarship has shown that to be a considerable exaggeration. One recent scholar, for example, has written that the 'conflicted and sclerotic alliance between southern conservatives and northern liberals that was the mid-century Democratic party . . . denied blacks their fair share'.[3]

While liberal Democrats intended the social reforms of Roosevelt's New Deal and President Truman's Fair Deal to apply to everyone, there were many reasons why poor blacks did not benefit as much as poor whites from the GI Bill, the Federal Housing Agency, and even Social Security and Aid for Dependent Children. Federal aid for mortgages, in particular – available mostly to whites – from 1934 on, contributed to the spread of housing segregation to the north and helped to create vast black ghettos on the South Side of Chicago, in Washington, Philadelphia, Cleveland and other northern cities. 'Could the limitations of the New Deal racial state,' the same writer asked, 'ever be surmounted?' This was the largest challenge of the 1960s. Not without a political revolution in the South, many liberals and the labor–civil rights coalition concluded.

The Kennedy administration was in many respects, and consciously, the heir of the New Deal and the Truman Fair Deal. Civil rights for black Americans was by no means the most urgent item on the agenda. Kennedy was not personally a racist, though he had grown up in an upper-class world where black people were encountered mainly as servants. He often showed his instinctive sympathy with blacks and their aspirations. But those aspirations, for him, must be limited. They must not jeopardize the administration's other goals. Negro leaders who became too insistent in demanding justice tended to be seen as unrealistic, or annoying, or both. 'Kennedy's presidential campaign in 1960,' wrote Nicholas Lemann, 'operated on the assumption that blacks in the North were machine voters who could be reached through businesslike dealings with their political bosses – not people with special problems and a unique moral claim on the government's help.'[4] The fact that, in his eloquent inaugural address devoted to the challenge of combating communism, the President made no reference whatever to domestic questions, let alone to race, gives a telling indication of the real Kennedy priorities. The civil rights division in the Justice Department, led by the Assistant Attorney General Burke Marshall, had a strategy for gradually bringing lawsuits so as to spread Negro voting in the South. He even had a large map with eighty pins, showing where the government was supporting suits. He also had a wry sign on his desk saying 'Blessed are the peacemakers, for they catch hell from both sides.' But until 1963 there was no special urgency about civil rights within the administration.

By the early 1960s, nonetheless, the structure of Negro politics was changing fast. Since the 1920s the premier black organization had been the NAACP. Under Walter White it had campaigned, sometimes heroically, against lynching. More recently it had put many of its eggs into the legal basket, and with the *Brown* judgement, in 1954, it looked as though that strategy had been triumphantly vindicated. But southern states and cities dragged their feet and schools and neighbourhoods remained segregated, and as individual Negroes continued to be humiliated by being denied access to lunch counters, motel rooms, public toilets and drinking fountains, a head of steam began to build up. Younger black men and women, especially, were yearning for change. The question was which organization could most effectively express that yearning.

The background to the racial politics of the 1960s and 1970s was what has come to be called 'the Great Migration'.[5]

Though all black people suffered to a greater or lesser degree from discrimination, there were already quite sharp differences in the circumstances, and therefore in the political agendas, of different sections of the black population. In part, this was a matter of geography. Many hundreds of thousands still remained on the plantations of the rural South. It was not uncommon, even in the 1960s, for the grandchildren of slaves to be living in what had been the slave 'quarters' of planta-tions before Emancipation.* The rural population was shrinking quite rapidly, however. Cotton was still the main plantation crop, though there were others: sugar in Texas, rice in Louisiana, indigo in South Carolina and tobacco in North Carolina and Kentucky. But the impor-tance of cotton was declining, for several reasons: as a result of the depredations of the boll weevil, competition from India and Egypt, the mechanization of cotton-picking, and the relocation of much Amer-ican cotton-growing to Arizona and the Imperial Valley of southern California.

As a consequence, starting as early as the second decade of the twen-tieth century, and accelerated by the growth of the war industries during the First World War, black people began to move from the rural South, first into southern towns and cities and then in growing numbers to the North. From the Carolinas and Virginia they moved into Washington, Baltimore, Philadelphia and New York, while from Alabama and the Mississippi Delta they travelled north to Chicago, Cleveland and Detroit to work in the booming steel, automobile and engineering industries. At least three million African-Americans moved from the South to the North between 1910 and 1940, and the movement continued at an increasing tempo in the next two generations.[6]

This migration was an event of unfathomable emotional as well as economic and cultural significance in the lives of millions of people. What had once been a strong, if desperately impoverished, rural cul-ture in the South now had to compete with the seductive but also in many ways destructive life of great northern ghettos, with their fragile employment, dazzling but corrupt entertainment districts and insecure family structure. The Great Migration was one of the cardinal facts – arguably the cardinal fact – setting the terms for American national pol-itics in the 1960s, 1970s and 1980s.

In 1962 two black sociologists, Selz Mayo and Horace Hamilton, drew together some of the threads of this demographic and cultural cataclysm

---

* The beautiful 'freedom quilts', now eagerly collected by museums in New York and California, were produced in the 1970s by the Pettways and other families in the former slave quarters at Gee's Bend, Alabama.

while it was still happening and before its profound implications for both black and white people, North and South, had been fully understood.[7]

They showed that while over the two decades 1940–60 the white population of the South grew by 39 per cent, the non-white population (more than 98 per cent Negro) grew by only 9.4 per cent. This had nothing to do with fertility: it resulted solely from the fact that a million and a half Negroes had moved from the eleven states of the Former Confederacy to the North. The proportion of blacks in the population of the Deep South states dropped over the two decades from 49.3 per cent in Mississippi to 42.3 per cent, and from 42.9 per cent to 34.9 per cent in South Carolina. Moreover, since black people were moving off the land into the towns and cities, adult Negroes were in short supply in the rural South. Astutely, Mayo and Hamilton picked up another trend. 'Are there large numbers of Negro children remaining in, or being returned to, farm families while parents are living, or employed, in urban centers or even in communities outside the Southeast?' they asked. Indeed there were. Delta communities were full of black children being looked after by their grannies while their parents worked in Chicago or Detroit.

Southern politics since Emancipation had developed on different lines in the cities from in the country; and in the 'white counties' – for example, in the Appalachians, the Ozarks and other hill-country zones in northern Alabama and the western Carolinas – from the way they had evolved in the plantation districts of the Mississippi Delta, the Alabama Black Belt, the Low Country of South Carolina and the Virginia Tidewater. In the latter areas, and in comparable parts of East Texas, Louisiana, Georgia and North Carolina, blacks formed a far larger proportion of the population than in the hill country and 'piney woods', where the poorer whites congregated. There were counties in South Carolina, central Alabama and above all in the Mississippi Delta where blacks outnumbered whites by two and as many as four to one – a very different world from the cities of the New South, such as Atlanta. Rural areas were also, until long after a Supreme Court decision that tried to restore the balance (*Baker v. Carr* in 1962), grossly overrepresented in both state legislatures and Congress.

Black migrants moved north to improve themselves, and to an extent they succeeded.* In the growing manufacturing industries of the North-East and the Middle West wages were high, at least before and after the Great Depression of the 1930s. Many of them joined unions, some of which, especially the powerful United Auto Workers, campaigned energetically for the economic interests of their black members and lobbied within the Democratic Party on their behalf. Other unions, especially in the building trades, covertly perpetuated racist working practices, such as dual promotion ladders for white and black workers, or openly discriminated against black workers. Even where unions were sympathetic to black interests, their advocacy had mixed results.

Some black politicians were elected to office. In New York, a number of them came to power in the city's component boroughs. But politicians like Richard Daley, Mayor of Chicago, and similar leaders in Pittsburgh, Philadelphia and elsewhere used patronage to organize black political support for themselves and their urban political machines. They were not, though, willing to act effectively to prevent residential segregation and the creation of ghetto slums. For African-Americans economic prosperity, even when and where it did happen, did not translate into anything like real social equality.

In southern cities like Atlanta or New Orleans, blacks were able to exert some pressure for improvements in conditions. In a border city like St Louis, with strong Middle Western traditions, school desegregation came quite early and without much opposition. In the Deep South, resistance to change was more engrained. In cities such as Memphis, Houston and Jackson, that resistance was highly effective. In Birmingham, little or nothing had changed by the beginning of 1963, and the white leadership was determined that nothing *should* change.

Yet – and this is an underlying explanation of the civil rights movement second in importance only to the migration itself – the mentality of African-Americans, in the South and in the North, *had* now changed. A people still largely tied to the soil, mostly working on the land and under the eyes and often the guns of white masters determined not to

---

* They also moved south, to Florida. Florida's situation was exceptional. It gained 1.6 million people, more than 100,000 of them Negroes.

allow them to leave a condition of subservience, had turned into a mobile, restless people. The plaintive dignity of Delta blues was being replaced by the driving insistency and chromium-plated urban sophistication of rhythm 'n' blues. Some had prospered. More than a few were now well educated. Almost all had come to the conclusion that they were as good as the white man or woman. Many had served in the armed forces in both world wars, and in the second war many had travelled enough, at home and overseas, to see how anomalous and out of tune with the new age their status was. As the 1960s dawned, the Negroes of the United States were hungry for change. Their minds, as the songs of slavery reminded them, were set on freedom. Some were bolder, some more impatient, than others. If ever a whole people was looking for leadership it was the Negroes of the United States, North and South, at the historic moment when John Fitzgerald Kennedy, largely unaware of the greatest challenge of his political life, entered the White House.

A number of organizations offered Negroes competing strategies. They shared long-term goals, and most of them cooperated with each other most of the time. But they disagreed on style and method, and on the relative effectiveness of different strategies. They competed for members and money. Some favoured legal action, some voter registration, others mass direct action. Some oscillated between different courses, or tried to combine them in different political packages. As time went on, and under the pressure of stubborn resistance from the white majority, differences and jealousies between them grew wider.

The NAACP, as the oldest, largest and richest Negro organization, had branches, some of them strong, in many communities in the South and in northern and western cities. Roy Wilkins was a devoted, if cautious, leader, supported by a remarkably able and dedicated team of lawyers. Their strategy remained the pursuit of equality through legal action. In this they could count on some support from white politicians and lawyers, and at least a sympathetic hearing from the courts.

The most conservative of the black organizations was the National Urban League, which dated back to the second decade of the twentieth century when a number of philanthropists got together to try to alleviate the problems of the hundreds of thousands of black people who were moving out of the rural South. The League's traditional emphasis had been on local action, in cooperation with white power structures. It was energized, and its focus shifted to the national political scene, by an able new director, Whitney Young, appointed in 1961. He put the League's resources and prestige behind many of the initiatives of the next ten years.

The Southern Christian Leadership Conference found itself, almost immediately after its foundation, the third major Negro organization. It was southern, it was dominated by ministers, especially but not entirely Baptists, and it had the advantage of being led by someone as gifted, as dynamic and as well known nationally as Martin Luther King Jr. It lacked the membership and financial strength of the two older organizations, as well as suffering from less obvious disadvantages. King was an inspiring leader and, if pointed in the right direction, an effective fundraiser. But he was neither a particularly good administrator, nor especially interested in administration. At first, such organization as there was came from Ella Baker and from Stanley Levison and his friends in New York, including the young Harry Belafonte.[8] They mounted two highly successful fund-raising concerts at Carnegie Hall in April 1959, starring such names as Frank Sinatra and Sammy Davis Jr. Levison also hired Jack O'Dell, a young Negro member of the Communist Party, to put the fund-raising on a systematic basis.

In August 1960 Miss Baker was replaced as the executive officer at the SCLC's Atlanta office by Wyatt Tee Walker. Brought up poor in New Jersey, the son of a Baptist preacher, Walker was educated in Virginia. He became the pastor of one of the oldest black churches in the South, in Petersburg, Virginia, and became known to King. He worked with both the NAACP and with CORE. He was able, energetic and impatient.

The Congress of Racial Equality was, or at least was widely seen to be, more radical than the SCLC. Its origins were in the North, and it was close to elements of the pacifist left. It had been founded in 1942 by a group of students in Chicago, among them Bernice Fisher and George Houser, who were white, and James L. Farmer, who was black. They were members of the Fellowship of Reconciliation (FOR), and CORE was influenced by the Gandhian pacifist, Krishnalal Shridharani, author of *War without Violence*, as well as by Bayard Rustin, then working for the FOR. (It was CORE that mounted the 'journey of reconciliation' in the South that led to Rustin's spell on a chain gang.) In 1961 Farmer returned after a long absence to become the head of CORE, and revived the idea of what became the famous Freedom Rides.

More recent than King's SCLC and the most radical of the national civil rights institutions was the Student Nonviolent Coordinating Committee (SNCC), universally known as 'Snick'. It emerged in 1960 from the need to coordinate the rapid growth of the sit-in movement, and, as already noted, took shape under the leadership of Ella Baker two months after the Greensboro sit-in, at a conference at Miss Baker's *alma mater*, Shaw University in Raleigh, North Carolina. SNCC can be seen as a stepchild of the SCLC. While the two organizations never definitively split apart, SNCC was a constant critic – more aggressive, less patient – and irritant vis-à-vis its more cautious parent. SNCC gradually became more and more attracted to the somewhat nebulous concept of 'black power'. This was misunderstood by white people, and sometimes presented by some of its partisans as a revolutionary, anti-white ideology. Essentially it was more a device to 'raise the consciousness' of the mass of black people, encouraging them to take responsibility for their own liberation. SNCC attracted a number of committed and charismatic leaders, including John Lewis, chairman from 1960 to 1966, then Robert Parris Moses, the inspiration of the Mississippi Freedom Summer of 1964, Marion Barry (later Mayor of Washington), Diane Nash and James Bevel.

Not surprisingly for such an energetic and morally engaged young organization, SNCC people went on to play very diverse and important roles. John Lewis became a highly respected Congressman. Bob Moses, after a spell of schoolteaching in Tanzania and teaching mathematics at Harvard, now runs the Algebra Project, a scheme for teaching underprivileged students who have difficulty with language through the culturally neutral techniques of mathematics. Two of SNCC's early women members, Casey Haydn and Mary E. King, played a key role in creating the new radical feminism of the 1960s. Some of the most impressive members were brave and devoted activists like Charles Sherrod and Bob Mant, who shunned personal publicity; others, such as Stokely Carmichael and Hubert 'Rap' Brown, were avid self-promoters.

Although non-violence featured in the organization's title, many SNCC field secretaries found themselves obliged in the dangerous circumstances of their work to carry weapons.

On 4 May 1961 thirteen activists, some black, some white, left Washington in two buses, one owned by Greyhound, the other by Trailways, for Atlanta. They intended to repeat the 'journey of reconciliation' taken by Rustin and his friends in 1947. This time their venture was to be a Freedom Ride. The people who took part had little in common except their resolution. They included a retired white professor from Michigan, James Peck, who in 1933 had taken a Negro date to a Harvard freshman dance, Albert Bigelow who had sailed his yacht *Golden Rule* into an atomic test site as a protest, three white women and seven Negro men. James Farmer, CORE's executive director, was not able to take part: his father, the first Negro PhD from Texas, died just before the buses were to set out, and James went to his father's funeral.

The journey was a calculated provocation, intended to bring out and display the character of southern racism and the ruthless violence with which it was maintained. James Farmer wanted to put the new Kennedy administration in a spot, where it would be shamed into challenging its segregationist supporters in the southern congressional delegations and obliged to take a stand against segregation. 'What we had to do,' Farmer said, 'was to make it more dangerous politically for the federal government not to enforce federal law than it would be for them to enforce federal law.' It was perhaps both a reckless and a naive tactic. It was certainly extraordinarily brave, and it depended on the superlative courage of those who consented to test the mood of the South. It was also, incidentally, presenting Martin Luther King and his fellow ministers in the SCLC with an agonizing set of decisions. 'We felt we could count on the racists,' Farmer said, 'to create a crisis so that the federal government would be compelled to enforce the law.' If Farmer was naive about the Kennedy administration's probable reaction, he was under no illusions about how dangerous the Freedom Rides would be for the Riders. 'We were prepared,' he recalled later, 'for the possibility of death.'

The Freedom Rides passed through Virginia without upset and through the Carolinas without major trouble. The Riders reached

Atlanta, where they had dinner with Dr King. But on 14 May they ran into serious trouble in Anniston, Alabama. The first bus was set on fire and its occupants beaten up so badly they had to go to hospital. Birmingham was even worse. Jim Peck was so severely beaten that he had to have fifty-three stitches.

The federal government, in the person of the President's brother the Attorney General, became locked in futile negotiations with Alabama officials. Meanwhile, after many hours of intense debate, the non-violent civil activists in Nashville, led by the fragile-looking but fiery Diane Nash, insisted on joining the fray. When they arrived in Birmingham, they were attacked by hundreds of thugs from the Ku Klux Klan. In the end the city's police commissioner, the fearsome Eugene 'Bull' Connor, handcuffed the activists and dragged them off to the city jail. A second busload of Nashville students arrived, and met the same fate. Abruptly, Bull Connor changed his tactics. He released the demonstrators from jail, and personally escorted the young activists to the Tennessee border and dumped them there. The nearest black farmer was too scared to let them in, and they had to call from a pay phone to Nashville to be rescued.

A second wave of Riders from Nashville took their place. Now they arrived in Montgomery. Both future black Congressman John Lewis and a white Kennedy aide, John Seigenthaler, who was later the editor of the *Nashville Tennessean*, were severely beaten. In Montgomery the Freedom Rides reached a Wagnerian climax. The Riders, Martin Luther King and many of the leaders of the southern civil rights movement holed up in Ralph Abernathy's First Baptist Church, surrounded by at least a thousand Klansmen and other violent segregationists. The Negroes were protected from a baying mob of white racists only by a thin line of hastily improvised federal 'marshals', who were mostly retired policemen and revenue agents, scratched together by Attorney General Kennedy's staff. The segregationists hurled rocks and Molotov cocktails over the marshals' heads and several times came close to rushing the church. In the end, the Kennedy administration called the Alabama National Guard, the segregationist governor's private army, into the federal service, and the Freedom Riders and Dr King were saved.

After further negotiations, in which the federal government always seemed to have one hand tied behind its back because of the Kennedy brothers' reluctance to break finally either with potential southern voters or with the South's all-powerful representatives in Congress, it was agreed that the Freedom Riders would be escorted to the Mississippi state line. Mississippi's powerful and rabidly segregationist senator, Jim Eastland, promised that there would be no violence, and he was obeyed. Instead, once the Freedom Riders reached Jackson they were summarily marched off to prison and thence to the dreaded Mississippi state prison farm, Parchman, for sixty days. They were taken by night, in closed trucks. When they arrived, the prison governor welcomed them with a little speech. 'We have bad niggers here,' he said, 'niggers on death row that'll beat you up and cut you as soon as look at you.'[9] Some of them were forcibly dragged to the shower rooms. All were stripped and made to shower under the guards' shotguns.

The Freedom Rides represented a new and hard test for Martin King. More than once the SNCC demonstrators raised, directly and in the most personal terms, the question of his personal courage. He argued, and Wyatt Walker argued for him, that he must stay out of jail to raise money, to direct the movement and to lead his people. He was on probation, he said. They said they were on probation too. They expected him to go with them. When, on 27 May in Montgomery, he refused to join them on the bus to Mississippi, he said he must choose 'the when and where of his own Golgotha'. They accused him flatly of cowardice. King had already shown, and would show again and again, that he was no coward. But he did not want to be told when and where he should risk his liberty and his life by a group of passionately committed but somewhat unfriendly students.

The Freedom Rides not only marked a widening gap between King and the students, which grew into institutional rivalry between the SCLC and SNCC and raised deep and dangerous disagreements about the tactics and the strategy of the movement; they also prefigured the way the struggle would develop over the next five years, and set the course for the rest of his life.

Moreover, the Rides showed how far many whites in the Deep South were willing to go to defend their cherished 'way of life'; they revealed the visceral rage brought out by a determined challenge to that code. They made it clear how ostensibly dignified white politicians were either the servants of violent extremists or intimidated by them. They showed that, although at every level from federal judges like Skelly Wright in New Orleans and Frank Johnson in Alabama down to honest policemen, there were exceptions, the whole structure of government, law and public order in the South could be put at the service of segregation and blatant racial supremacy. Almost routinely, southern policemen delayed coming to the aid of black protesters and their hated white allies, known as 'nigger lovers'. They deliberately left them for ten minutes or longer to the mercies of Klansmen armed with clubs, iron bars and pipes before lifting a hand to help them. Sometimes southern hospitals even turned badly wounded victims of violence away.

The Freedom Rides also revealed all too clearly the limits of the Kennedy administration's sympathy with the civil rights movement. With great courage individual young white Justice Department officials – John Doar, Joe Dolan, John Seigenthaler – did what they could to protect the Riders. The head of Justice's civil rights division, Burke Marshall, did what he could to enforce the *Brown* decision. But the Kennedy brothers themselves were deeply ambivalent. They just didn't understand the emotional and historical resonances of the struggle. Sometimes they suggested to the grandsons of slaves that their exclusion from the opportunities of American life was to be compared to the casual insults and social snubs encountered by their own Irish ancestors. When Dr King pressed his demands in moralizing language, they stood on their dignity, as if their personal as well as their official superiority had not been properly acknowledged.

Both were men of subtle political insight, and later both – especially Bob – came to understand that they were confronted not by tiresome, even impertinent, Negro preachers, but by the great challenge of their generation. They did not use, nor did they consider using at this stage, the overwhelming superiority of the federal government, by sending in the army. They negotiated with southern officials as if with the agents of a sovereign power. They had no love for racist southern governors and senators, but they treated them sometimes as social inferiors, sometimes as if they were the antique Roman dignitaries of their own imaginings. In the spring of 1961, to use the slang phrase, the brothers Kennedy 'didn't get it'. By the summer of 1963 President Kennedy had come to see that he must come out for a strong civil rights bill, but the relationship between King and the Kennedys was nonetheless at all times edgy and ambiguous. This was due in part to the ceaseless bombardment of information from the FBI, accusing King of everything from communist allegiance and financial dishonesty to diverse sexual transgressions.

The Deep South's response to the Freedom Rides also exposed the limitations of King's (and Bayard Rustin's) Gandhian tactics. The British Raj might have yielded to Gandhi's non-violent protests, but the Raj never had more than a few tens of thousands of soldiers, many of them Indian, to control hundreds of millions of Indians; and it was ultimately subject to the political authority of governments in London that were under strong anti-imperial pressures throughout the twentieth century. So while some in the civil rights movement believed that it would be enough to confront the conscience of white southerners and the walls would come tumbling down, others, contemplating the ruthlessness and political intransigence of the white South, believed that only political power for Negroes, only the vote, could win what they sought.

Even before the Freedom Rides, the young activists were already debating the rival merits of direct action – sit-ins, Freedom Rides, marches, protests, every other kind of non-violent demonstration – as against efforts to increase pressure on segregationist southern politicians at the grass roots by increasing the proportion of blacks who voted in their states and districts. With extraordinary courage, as early as 1963 Bob Moses and others were working in the most dangerous backwoods of Mississippi to register black voters.

After the Freedom Rides, the Kennedy administration used its influence to promote voter registration drives. These would have the not so incidental advantage of improving the national Democratic Party's electoral prospects in the South. (Although in congressional and local elections the South was still solidly Democratic, in recent presidential elections it had delivered growing numbers of votes to the Republican, Eisenhower.) Wealthy white philanthropists duly channelled substantial sums to voter registration drives. A Voter Registration Project was set up in the offices of the liberal Southern Regional Council in downtown Atlanta, where Vernon Jordan, later the golf partner and adviser of President Bill Clinton, got his first political experience.

In the event, the civil rights movement found that the issue as between direct action and voter registration was a distinction without a difference. If a young activist went to teach Mississippi sharecroppers how to read and write so that they could register to vote, then as far as the county and state officials were concerned, they were just as much upsetting the racial apple cart as if they sat in at a local lunch counter or moved to the front of the bus. Still, for the rest of Martin Luther King's life, the tension between social and political goals was a tactical factor he had to consider.

From the spring of 1961, King found himself between two fires. He had to deal, now, not only with the intransigence of southern white segregationists, but with the impatience and suspicion of young Negroes who wanted to go faster than he was yet ready to go. These tensions could no longer be hidden when Dr King, his followers and his rivals came face to face with the situation that had arisen in the city of Albany, among the fruit and nut orchards of south-west Georgia.

From Albany to Oxford

We killed them with kindness. Apparently it was a condition
M. L. King and the other outsiders had never encountered before.
White official in Albany, Georgia

On Wednesday 11 December 1961 Martin Luther King received a phone
call from a Negro osteopath, Dr William Anderson, in Albany, Georgia.
Anderson, deeply religious and highly strung, had been a student at Alabama State with Ralph Abernathy, and through Abernathy had been put
in contact with King. His message was peremptory. King must come to
Albany as soon as possible. A situation had developed there that only
King himself could resolve.

Martin had just emerged from a period of travel and public speaking
so demanding that it had taxed even his robust constitution. He disappeared into hospital for tests and bed rest. He had visited in quick succession London, Montgomery, Seattle, Minnesota and Cleveland and
spoken to one or more audiences in each place. Then he had been the
keynote speaker at the annual convention of the AFL-CIO, the newly
combined American Federation of Labor and the Congress of Industrial Organizations, at Bal Harbour, Florida. This was the biggest date
in the calendar of American trade unions. So the invitation constituted
the most promising opportunity yet for King to bring his campaign to
a national stage.

The AFL-CIO was then only seven years old, and still a somewhat
awkward amalgam of two very different traditions. The AFL was made
up of craft unions representing workers with particular skills, many of
them in the building trades, such as the Bricklayers, the Hod Carriers
(later Laborers), the Carpenters, Plumbers, Plasterers and so on. Their
traditions went back to the cautious unionism of Samuel Gompers, a
cigar cutter who said there was no reason for Negro workers to be
'petted or coddled'. There was little socialism left in the AFL by 1961.
Its boss, George Meany, was an Irish Catholic, tough, conservative and

not known for his sympathy with African-American aspirations, either at work or in politics. Though the AFL-CIO was supportive of civil rights, many of the craft unions, and especially many of the elite building trade unions who traditionally dominated the policies of the AFL, had few black members. Some of them, in practice, actually excluded blacks. Meany's deepest conviction, and the policy of the AFL in his forty years of union leadership, was of the need for cooperation between labour and capital. He had never, he liked to say proudly, walked on a picket line in his life.

The CIO, on the contrary, set out to organize all the workers in a given industry. They were brought together in giant industrial unions like Walter Reuther's United Auto Workers and the Steel Workers. Its politics were those of the New Deal, where they were not to the left of it. Reuther and his brother Victor started out sympathetic enough to communism that they actually went to work for a time in a factory in the Soviet Union. Though Reuther himself was now staunchly anti-communist, the CIO still cherished the radical traditions of the mass demonstrations and sit-ins of the 1930s, in which communists had played a leading part; in the 1940s many organizers were still communists. Many of its leaders were sincerely committed to black equality, and many of its constituent unions had substantial Negro membership. Indeed, the very day of King's speech in Bal Harbour, black trade unionists had been confronting the more conservative leaders of the AFL in sharp exchanges.

For King, the Bal Harbour speech offered the prospect of support from an organization with millions of members, deep financial resources and cadres of experienced organizers in every state. This was an entrée to national politics on the grand scale. Indeed, it opened the prospect of progress towards that strategic alliance between black and white working people that was, and remained to the end, one of King's lifelong dreams.

His speech that day had been largely drafted by Stanley Levison, but certainly expressed King's own instinct: that decisive progress for Negroes could only come about if they became part of a broad coalition of radical and working-class movements. Starting in what were for him relatively quiet, restrained tones, he argued that Negroes and the union movement shared vital interests, and must therefore work together. Negroes could help white working people press for better wages and conditions, while defensively the unions had a common interest with the civil rights movement in preventing repression and the abuses of citizens' rights:

> This unity of purpose is not an historical coincidence. Negroes are almost entirely a working people. There are pitifully few Negro millionaires and few Negro employers. Our needs are identical with labor's needs: decent wages, fair working conditions, livable housing, old age security, health and welfare measures, conditions in which families can grow, have education for their children and respect in the community. That is why Negroes support labor's demands and fight laws which curb labor. That is why the labor-hater and Negro-baiter is virtually always a twin-headed creature, spewing anti-Negro epithets from one mouth and anti-labor propaganda from the other mouth.

The importance King attributed to this occasion is suggested by the stem-winding peroration he gave it, in biblical periods that owed nothing to the lawyer-like persuasion of Stanley Levison. He ended by evoking a new day and a new America, when the brotherhood of man would bring secure and expanding prosperity for all. Swinging into his Old Testament vein, he ended with the very words with which he was to close the best-remembered of all his speeches: 'This will be the day when all God's children, black men and white men, Jews and Gentiles, Protestants and Catholics, will be able to join hands all over the nation and sing in the words of the old Negro spiritual, "Free at last! Free at last! Thank God Almighty, we are free at last!"' This was not mere biblical boiler-plate. Martin Luther King really did believe, in the fibres of his being, that black men and women would not be free until white men and women felt a sense of shared destiny with them.

The speech was well received, and when the speaker got home to Atlanta he had reason to be pleased with what he had achieved. Then he saw on television images of long lines of black people marching patiently in the rain in Albany, marching and being carted off to jail in their hundreds by dozens of policemen in raincoats.

Dr Anderson's call to Abernathy came on the Tuesday. Anderson spoke to King on the Wednesday. There was a formal invitation, which King asked for, on the Thursday, and by Friday evening he was preaching at Shiloh Baptist Church in Albany, Georgia.

One consequence of the Great Migration, the first phase of the epic movement of black people, pushed by the collapse of the cotton kingdom in the South and pulled by the hope of prosperity in the North, was a sharp growth in the Negro population of southern towns.[1] Negro tenants and sharecroppers and their families left the farms in their tens of thousands: their total across the South declined from 282,000 in 1940 to 72,000 in 1959. Although there was a tiny increase in white-collar jobs, from 4.8 per cent to 6.8 per cent, most Negro men were in manual jobs, and more than two-thirds of those Negro women who were employed were either domestic servants or in public service jobs.

Albany was in this respect a typical Deep South town.[2] It was the business centre of a region of south-west Georgia that had once grown cotton and was now diversifying into peaches, pecans and a number of light industries. Once bywords for racial repression, including lynching, the surrounding counties, known to black people by nicknames like 'Bad Baker' and 'Terrible Terrell', were still a notoriously hard district for blacks, few of whom voted. The population of Albany itself had grown from 31,000 in 1950 to 56,000 in 1960, of which two-fifths were black. Job opportunities for them were limited. Decent jobs in the new pharmaceutical factories were largely reserved for whites. As in many Deep South towns, the best jobs for less skilled Negroes were at the newly desegregated army bases nearby, procured by the political clout of congressional magnates.

There was, however, a small black bourgeoisie in town, including Dr Anderson the osteopath. So far its most ambitious demand was for the paving of the streets of Lincoln Heights, the neighbourhood where the better-off black families lived. The Clennon King family (no relation to the Ebenezer Kings) had prospered modestly, building up substantial holdings of real estate. Clennon King's five sons, one of whom was a professor in Australia, included Slater King, an accountant, and Chevene

B. King, the only black lawyer in the whole of south-west Georgia. The historically black college Albany State, with 650 students, offered good jobs to educated blacks, starting with the college's very conservative president, William H. Dennis. There was a NAACP chapter in the town, run by its secretary Marion Page, and a dentist, E. D. Hamilton. The most prominent minister in Albany, politically speaking, was the Revd Samuel Wells of Shiloh Baptist Church.

The white mayor, Asa Kelley, was keen to attract federal funding to the town, and to that end had started tentative talks with Page and Hamilton, which discredited them with some of the more radical young Negroes as Uncle Toms. One of the strongest personalities in white Albany was the police chief, Laurie Pritchett, a physically imposing former football player. He proved to be intelligent, wily and professional to a degree unusual among his contemporaries in southern law enforcement. Both Mayor Kelley and chief Pritchett were able to exploit sharp divisions within the Negro community.

In October 1961 two SNCC members, Charles Sherrod and Cordell Reagon, arrived in Albany. They had previously worked in south-west Georgia, which they regarded as 'the most dangerous place in the region, second only to Mississippi'.[3] Three SNCC workers had been kept in jail there for two years on capital charges, dating back to slave codes, of 'inciting to insurrection'. Teenage demonstrators were imprisoned there in appalling conditions. Sherrod was then twenty-two, Reagon eighteen. Reagon was later, with his wife the former Bernice Johnson, one of the founders of the Freedom Singers. Sherrod, bespectacled and owlish, was a man of strong Christian faith, a graduate of the Union Theological Seminary in New York. Because he wore sandals, some in Albany thought he must be 'a kook or a commie'.[4]

The situation in Albany was already delicate for the SNCC missionaries. An Albany chapter of the NAACP already existed, though it was unaggressive. Sherrod and Reagon began by simply practising with a basketball on public courts. Young people with 'hoop dreams' gathered round them. Before long, virtually the whole of the NAACP's youth project defected to SNCC.[5] Tom Chatmon, a successful Negro businessman and unsuccessful gambler who was the supervisor of the youth project, was particularly suspicious of Sherrod and Reagon and did his best to keep them away from his flock.[6] Nonetheless, by late October the two SNCC men had set up a committee with eighteen members, and on 1 November they organized their own Freedom Ride. When Sherrod and Reagon arrived on a Trailways bus at the segregated bus station, nine of Chatmon's students were supposed to meet them. Instead, they were met by a dozen of Pritchett's police. As demonstrations go, it was a flop. But teenagers had dared to confront Pritchett's myrmidons.

During that month things heated up in Albany's black community. There were two big rallies. There were also increasingly obvious divisions. The authorities at Albany State and the local NAACP both did what they could to thwart SNCC. The Georgia state NAACP leaders, Ruby Hurley and the young Vernon Jordan,[7] locked horns with Sherrod and Reagon. On 17 November, at a meeting in the garden of Slater King's house, all but one of the local civil rights organizations agreed to come together to form the Albany Movement.

The big test was planned for Thanksgiving. Sherrod called James Forman, the new executive director of SNCC, in Atlanta. They agreed to test Albany's compliance with the desegregation orders from the Federal government's Interstate Commerce Commission. Forman pulled together a job lot of nine Freedom Riders, including a visiting Danish journalist and some office workers, as well as the newly married Casey and Tom Hayden (future husband of Jane Fonda). He had to persuade Wyatt Walker of the SCLC to come across with the train fares. The nine Freedom Riders, four black and five white, sat together in the 'white' carriage, under protest from the conductor but without serious objection. When they pulled into the Albany Union railway terminal, police chief Pritchett allowed two SNCC workers to meet them. But when hundreds of supporters broke into cheering, Pritchett uncharacteristically lost his cool and arrested the nine riders and the reception committee of two.

Now came the trial of strength. The morning after the scene at the station, the Riders went on trial. Hundreds of Negroes marched. Hundreds more crowded around as bystanders. Chief Pritchett, instead of picking out the ringleaders, herded the marchers into an alley behind the police station and arrested them all. Now, to Sherrod's delight, the jails were full. What was less welcome was that Pritchett sent hundreds of prisoners to the noisome and frightening jails in the surrounding counties. By 13 December there were no fewer than 471 students in jail. It was at that point that Eliza 'Goldie' Jackson, Sherrod and Reagon's landlady, sent a wire to Dr King, inviting him to come to Albany, and Dr Anderson got hold of him on the phone. On the 14th, King, Abernathy and Wyatt Walker drove down there. King spoke to a congregation of about a thousand at Shiloh Baptist. The next day King, Anderson and Abernathy led 250 marchers to City Hall, where chief Pritchett duly arrested them. King refused to post bond, and vowed to spend Christmas in jail.[8]

At this point things went badly wrong. King and Anderson had been driven to the jail in Americus, an hour's drive north in Sumter County. There, Sheriff Fred Chappell addressed Anderson as 'boy'; in jail, he fell apart, hailing Martin Luther King as Jesus and keeping his cellmates awake with noisy religious enthusiasm. He became delusional, and King worried that he might do himself harm. It was imperative, he thought, to get the man out of jail. He thereby exposed himself to charges of hypocrisy or cowardice, or both. He had boasted he would stay incarcerated, and he could not explain why he had changed his mind without destroying Anderson's reputation.

In the meantime the Albany Movement, too, fell apart. A six-man commission of three black and three white citizens had negotiated a fragile settlement. But now the seething suspicion and jealousy between the Albany Negro leaders and the incomers burst into the open. The spark that caused the explosion was a story in the *Atlanta Constitution* saying that Wyatt Walker would 'take over the leadership'. That infuriated Marion Page, the NAACP secretary, who called a press conference and said that the Albany Movement was 'by and for local Negroes'.[9] Even the Revd Wells of Shiloh Baptist seemed to resent the prestige of Dr Martin Luther King.

By Christmas it was plain that the city had no intention of conceding the modest reforms negotiated by the unofficial six-man commission. The local paper, owned by a friend of the Kennedy family, James Gray, a Dartmouth graduate who had married the daughter of the previous owner, denounced King as a professional agitator who had 'learned that martyrdom can be a highly productive practice for the acquisition of a buck'. The national press was not so nasty, but the feeling was unanimous that King had sustained the worst defeat of his career to date: the Republican New York *Herald Tribune* called Albany 'a devastating loss of face' for him. *Time* magazine quoted Roy Wilkins of the NAACP attacking SNCC, and anonymous SNCC leaders accusing King of 'meekly' getting out of jail.[10] Claude Sitton, the *New York Times*'s lead reporter on the civil rights story, contributed a long piece for the paper's Sunday magazine about the ill-feeling between the SCLC and SNCC, headed 'Rivalries Beset Integration Campaign'.

Albany was in fact not only the worst setback Martin King had encountered so far; it was arguably the worst political setback of his entire career. It was partly the result of bad luck. No one could have predicted Dr Anderson's psychotic reaction to prison. Part of it was due to Wyatt Walker's apparent arrogance. Much of it was caused by haste and a lack of understanding of local conditions on the part of the SCLC, and by a consequent lack of preparation. King, already exhausted by weeks of travel and speaking, plunged headlong into a situation without any reconnaissance. He was in no state to handle an exceptionally awkward set of relationships, which were in fact managed by chief Pritchett and the Albany city fathers with more finesse than their counterparts in either Montgomery or Birmingham would show.

Having said all that, Albany revealed some troubling truths about the civil rights movement itself. It was not just split into different organizations with different styles, different tactical preferences and to some extent different goals. These organizations were riven by personal jealousies and also over real issues: political support, money and power. Albany did not wholly disappear from the scene after the humiliations of late 1961. Twice in the course of the next year King had to confront the situation there again. Both he and the Albany Movement did their best to recover from apparent disaster, while Albany's white leadership, led by Pritchett, did their stubborn best to preserve the city's segregated way of life by stealth, and even with a certain legalistic subtlety. To some extent, the segregationist city fathers of Albany, compared to their opposite numbers in Birmingham and elsewhere, were converts to non-violence.

In early January 1962, Martin King and the SCLC staff in Atlanta held an informal two-day brainstorming session to review the fall-out from Albany. They decided to put a new emphasis on voter registration, and to that end hired five new field secretaries in addition to Harry Blake, the sole existing one. Jack O'Dell took charge of administering the voter registration drive. King was warned that O'Dell had been a communist. His response was that he didn't mind what a man had been if he was willing to say that he was no longer a communist.

For much of 1962 King was preoccupied with matters other than Albany, and in particular with his shifting and complex relations with the Kennedy administration. It was at this time that J. Edgar Hoover and the FBI first began to suggest to the President and his brother the Attorney General that King, if not himself a communist, was under communist influence. On 8 January the FBI director sent them the first warning to this effect. Robert Kennedy decided that King should be told of the FBI's suspicions about Stanley Levison, mentioned earlier. It appears to have been established that Levison did have some connection with the financial side of the CP's activity in the early 1950s, but that his connection, whatever precisely it was, came to an end in the middle of the decade. Indeed in 1960, Levison was approached by the FBI and asked to work with them as an informant. He refused. Two of Kennedy's aides, the Nashville newspaperman John Seigenthaler and the head of the civil rights division Burke Marshall, were now ordered to pass the FBI's warning on to King. Seigenthaler duly did so, and Marshall asked Harris Wofford, the Justice Department aide with a long history of personal commitment to civil rights, to talk to King. Martin's prescient response was that he had far more reason to trust Levison than to trust the FBI.

In July King and Ralph Abernathy were due to appear in court in Albany, charged with marching without permission. They arrived the night before the trial and were greeted at a huge rally at Shiloh Baptist. On 10 July Judge A. N. Durden sentenced them to forty-five days in jail or fines of $178. They chose prison. Two days later, they were told that the fines had been paid by a 'well-dressed Negro'. It is a reflection of relations between the civil rights organizations in Albany that there was immediate speculation that King had paid his own fine in order to get out of jail. In fact, the well-dressed Negro was almost certainly imaginary. Probably Mayor Kelley, anxious to get the ministers out of jail, ordered their release.

Little more than a week later, on 20 July, Martin King faced another legal hurdle. Federal judge J. Robert Elliott, a recent Kennedy appointee, issued an injunction banning a list of named persons, including Martin Luther King Jr, from leading demonstrations in Albany. After furious activity, the Movement found a more senior judge, Elbert P. Tuttle of the Appeals Court, to reverse the injunction. But by this time the Albany Movement was running out of steam. While some five hundred demonstrators were imprisoned that month, the numbers were down on the previous year. It was getting ever harder to persuade Albany's black citizens to suffer the unpleasantness and indignity of jail when it seemed that so little was being achieved. Some, too, were not sure that nonviolence was effective. At a big rally the day before Tuttle's reversal, angry Negroes threw rocks at the police, enabling chief Pritchett to ask the visiting reporters, 'See them nonviolent rocks?'

In early March J. Edgar Hoover had sent Robert Kennedy a formal request for a wiretap on Levison. It was returned with Kennedy's signature a few days later, and on the night of 15–16 March FBI agents broke into Levison's office and installed first a microphone and later a wiretap. Now the FBI could listen to his conversations, including Martin Luther King's intimate private discussions of tactics and strategy with his most important financial supporter and closest adviser. From now on, Hoover, never sympathetic to the civil rights of Negroes in general or to Martin Luther King in particular, was able to feed to the Kennedy administration and to journalists titbits carefully chosen to put King in the worst possible light. Later on, when he was able to bug King's phones too, Hoover's capacity for mischief became exponentially greater.

In 1962 it was already dangerous. Albany and the FBI director's hostility came together in an unfortunate way. That November, King preached at John D. Rockefeller's magnificent Riverside Church in New York. After the service, a *New York Times* reporter came up and asked him what he thought of a report written for the Southern Regional Council by the radical historian Howard Zinn, then teaching at Spelman College in Atlanta. It noted that there was considerable hostility among Albany Negroes towards the FBI, pointing out that in spite of a pattern of violations against them by local police 'the FBI has not made a single arrest'. King said he agreed, and added that it was a problem that FBI agents in the South were influenced by the mores of the community and also by the perceived need to keep in with the local police.

The FBI reacted swiftly and furiously. The Atlanta bureau protested that of the five agents in the Albany office, only one was a native southerner. (The one, however, Martin Cheek, was not only a native southerner and the dominant figure in the office, but a notorious racist.) It was true that FBI agents in the South, wherever they happened to have been born, generally shared the contempt and resentment of local law enforcement men for civil rights protesters. It was decided, however, that Cartha 'Deke' DeLoach, one of Hoover's top men, should call King to put him right. Loach called. King was out and did not return the call. He was to pay dearly for the omission. Hoover bore a lasting grudge about what he saw as an unwarranted slur on the impartiality of his men. He was able to find ways to punish a man whom he already saw as little better than an agent of communist subversion.

In 1962 and 1963 the most important political process, so far as Martin King's hopes of improving the lot of southern Negroes were concerned, was the struggle within the Kennedy administration. We have seen that the Kennedy brothers started with no great moral commitment to racial equality. They did, however, have a powerful interest in the reputation of the United States in so far as that affected the prospects for the country in its worldwide competition with the Soviet Union. They were aware that increasingly the world was noticing the gap between American protestations of commitment to democracy and the reality of life for African-Americans in the South. They were also highly sensitive to the importance of keeping good relations both with black voters and with the liberal constituency, whose good opinions must be balanced against the suspicions of the southern Democrats, powerfully ensconced in the Congress and elsewhere. The President's vague goodwill towards black politicians had allowed him, moreover, to call Coretta King when her husband was in prison in 1960. Again, in 1962, when King was jailed in Albany, Burke Marshall had called Coretta to assure her that the federal government was concerned about her husband's safety.[11]

Martin Luther King was deeply frustrated by the Kennedys' reluctance to take a clear stand on behalf of civil rights. At the time of the Freedom Rides, Robert Kennedy had taken it very badly when King attempted to expound the non-violent philosophy. 'That is not going to have the slightest effect on what the government is going to do in this field or any other,' he replied, with some heat. When King, assuming that he was being helpful to an end Kennedy shared, suggested bringing hundreds of thousands of students south to demonstrate against segregation, Kennedy responded, as he sometimes did, like a bar-room brawler whose self-esteem had been impugned: 'Don't make statements that sound like a threat. That's not the way to deal with us!' King, likewise, was furious with the Kennedys' inaction when two churches were burned by white racists in south-west Georgia late in the Albany conflict. 'No president can be great,' he said – and compounded the offence by saying it at a dinner in the presence of the probable Republican presidential candidate, Nelson Rockefeller – 'if he attempts to accommodate to injustice to maintain his political balance.'[12]

By the spring of 1962 the Kennedy brothers, their top domestic adviser Kenneth O'Donnell* and Burke Marshall were all listening to the FBI's charges that King was under communist influence. (O'Donnell was especially reluctant to put political relationships at risk by proposing executive action on behalf of civil rights.[13]) They authorized the wiretaps, and were influenced by the FBI's jaundiced interpretation of what they revealed. In Montgomery, as noted earlier, the President had been willing to call the Alabama National Guard into the federal service to protect the Freedom Riders, after rejecting the idea of doing what President Eisenhower had done to protect black children at Little Rock – to call in regular federal troops.

---

* Early in 1962, when I asked O'Donnell in an interview why the President did not sign the order desegregating federal housing, O'Donnell's response, delivered in a tone of weary political sophistication, was 'Where do these people' – meaning Negroes – 'go?'

The logic of events, in the shape of rising white intransigence, now forced President Kennedy to do what he had not been willing to do the previous year: in Oxford, Mississippi, in November 1962, he called out the 101st Airborne Division from Fort Campbell, Kentucky.

The circumstances were not directly connected to King or to the SCLC. They arose out of the determination, brave to the point of fool-hardiness, of a black air force veteran called James Meredith to register as a student at the University of Mississippi in Oxford. This was not any old college as far as southerners were concerned. It had been the home, until his death in July that year, of William Faulkner. (The great nov-elist's attitude to race, miscegenation and the southern way of life evolved in a progressive direction, but his position, to the end of his life, was at best conflicted, at times confused.) The university was venerated by white southerners as 'Ole Miss', and feared and despised by many blacks as one of the proudest citadels of Confederate nostalgia and modern racism.

In late September the SCLC was holding its convention in Birm-ingham. Privately, King and his colleagues had already decided that the toughest city in the South would have to be the scene of their next major effort. The convention passed off without political incident, but King was punched in the face repeatedly by a member of George Lincoln Rockwell's American Nazi Party, visiting from suburban Washington. King was not seriously hurt, and the incident was chiefly remarkable for his reaction, which was totally and spontaneously non-violent. Old Septima Clark, veteran of civil rights struggles for decades, said he dropped his hands 'like a newborn baby'. Wyatt Walker jumped between King and his assailant. 'Don't touch him,' King shouted. A circle of preachers then leapt in to protect him, and it was not long before Jim Bevel had calmed the black audience down and got them singing 'I'm on My Way to Freedom Land'.

The incident was hardly reported, because more stirring events were happening in Mississippi. James Meredith was determined to register at Ole Miss, and the Kennedy administration had no alternative but to support him. The Governor of Mississippi, Ross Barnett, however, was determined to prevent this desecration. Meredith was escorted only by young, elegant John Doar of the Justice Department and by a veteran federal marshal, an armed but civilian official. Three times Meredith and his two escorts tried to register, and three times they were turned away. Meanwhile Robert Kennedy joined with Barnett in a more than slightly cynical telephone negotiation. In the end they were virtually helping each other to script, in detail, the scenario for a bogus confrontation.

A starker reality was now injected into the situation. Hundreds of diehard segregationist thugs were converging on the Ole Miss campus with its classical red-brick buildings and handsome magnolias and oaks. They raced up the highway from Jackson, rifle in the rear windows of their pickup trucks and Confederate flags blowing out of the windows.[14] From as far away as Florida, Klansmen offered their support. That Saturday afternoon, as ever uglier crowds appeared in Oxford, the President himself came on the line. 'Go get him, Johnny!' muttered his pugnacious brother. But the President merely exchanged politically anodyne greetings and agreed to wait for an 'A-1 lawyer' to come to Washington to talk things over. The governor chose that moment to thank the President for his support for Mississippi's poultry industry.

By now it was plain that Meredith would need more serious protection. Surly youths in jeans and T-shirts were stalking the campus with steel reinforcing bars in their hands and plenty of beer and bourbon inside them. Kennedy wondered whether the Mississippi National Guard, if drafted into federal service, could be relied on. The President suggested that Meredith might retreat from Oxford and be clandestinely registered away from the university; the governor offered to send his highway patrol, unarmed, to defend him. Some government officials believed they had a deal with Barnett. Others feared they were walking into a political trap. The governor, meanwhile, went off to watch the Ole Miss Rebels play the Kentucky Colonels at football in Jackson, going down to the touchline and delivering an emotional harangue to the fifty thousand fans present. 'I love Mississippi!' he shouted. 'I love her people! I love our customs!' The crowd went wild with more than sporting emotion. Hundreds of cars and pickups streamed north from Jackson towards Oxford.

That night Robert Kennedy returned to drafting the script for what was nothing less than a political pantomime. Now Barnett was suggesting that three hundred Mississippi troopers would confront three hundred Guardsmen, called by the Kennedys into federal service. The President even proposed to announce the deal on national television at eight o'clock that Sunday evening. Long before then, the leafy campus was crowded with students and rougher reinforcements, all in an ugly mood and many with firearms of their own. They were encouraged by one Major General Edwin Walker, a Korean war veteran who belonged to the anti-communist John Birch Society. As the crowd gathered and lethal violence loomed closer, Barnett reneged on his deal. He withdrew his patrolmen and left Meredith, defended only by a small force of marshals, to the mercies of the mob.

At two minutes to eight, the President went on television to announce that the court's order to register Meredith was being carried out. But that was easier said than done. By then, the crowd around the Lyceum in the middle of the Ole Miss campus were throwing stones, and soon they started shooting. Tear gas did not disperse them. At one point they launched a driverless truck and a bulldozer at the marshals. It was a full-blooded riot. Two were killed, one of them a London reporter, Paul Guihard of the *Daily Sketch*.

Finally, President Kennedy stopped joking ('We've had riots like that at Harvard!') and sent in first military police from a nearby base, the 101st Airborne, who had been moved into the area in readiness. The riot was over. Very reluctantly, the Kennedy administration had been forced by events to cross a line. How reluctantly only became fully apparent when the history books were written, years later. The instincts of the President and his brother had been entirely political. They were prepared to go a very long way indeed to parley with a cynical and unreliable segregationist, to agree to almost anything to avoid taking a stand, because they were desperate to avoid losing votes in the South. That hesitation cost two lives, and might have cost many more. (Twenty-eight marshals had gunshot wounds.) Yet in the end they had taken a stand, on behalf of the equal rights of a black man to enter a university, and on behalf of constitutional law.

There were to be more hesitations before the Kennedy administration threw its weight without equivocation on to the side of equality.

That would not happen until after a sequence of events in Birmingham, Alabama. For it was to Birmingham that Martin Luther King and his allies were now headed, to put behind them the divisions, the frustrations and the near-defeat at Albany.

8

In the City of Vulcan

> For years now I have heard the word 'Wait!' ...
> This 'Wait' has almost always meant 'Never'.
> Martin Luther King Jr in a letter from Birmingham jail

On 4 May 1963 the *New York Times*, along with many other newspapers across the world, published a photograph that was to be one of the abiding images of the 1960s. A white Birmingham policeman, wearing a military cap and dark glasses, grasps in his right hand a young black man's shirt, while from his left he releases the leash he is holding just enough to allow his German shepherd dog to lunge at the young man's belly, fangs open. Uncut, the picture reveals other dogs and their handlers. That day the same paper showed firemen firing water from special high-powered hoses at black children demonstrating in the same city.

In Birmingham itself those images, and the casual oppression, at least, that they seemed to reveal, were decisive in reviving the campaign, led by Martin King and by the local leader Fred Shuttlesworth, to break the reign of segregation there. Many in the city, including Negroes, had questioned the wisdom of taking on Birmingham's stubborn white leadership directly. The Kennedy administration thought King did not know what he was doing and, in Burke Marshall's opinion, did not even know exactly what he wanted. The sheer ruthlessness of Birmingham's resistance, led by the infamous Bull Connor, outgoing head of the city's government but still in control of the police and their fancied 'K-9' dog squad, looked like defeating King's non-violent assault on the city's rigid racism.

The dogs and the water cannon changed everything. The pictures went around the world, epitomizing the ferocity with which the American South was resisting change. They transformed American public opinion, too, causing many in the North to demand robust action from an administration that had claimed to be unable to act effectively to give southern Negroes their rights as American citizens. Finally, they helped

to persuade the President and the Attorney General that it would neither be good for America's image in the world, nor clever politics at
home, to stay aloof from the struggle in the South.[1]

A couple of years later another picture became an icon, this one sym-
bolizing the cruelty of the American bombing in Vietnam. It was the
famous photograph of a naked child, Kim Phuc, burning napalm stuck
to her skin, running down a road. Most of the world assumed that she
was moments from death. But she did not die. After seventeen operations, she survived. Later she was allowed to train as a doctor in Cuba.
Arriving in Canada on her way home to Cuba from her honeymoon,
she defected and became a Canadian citizen.[2]

In the case of the equally iconic picture of the Birmingham police
dog, too, there were ironies and complexities that were not immediately
evident. The young man was Walter Gadsden, son of an African-American newspaper publisher, whose papers had done their best to ignore
the civil rights movement in Atlanta as well as in Birmingham. Far from
being a non-violent victim, he owned a big dog himself and had kneed
officer Dick Middleton's Alsatian, Leo, rather forcibly. Far from being a
committed activist or a demonstrator, young Gadsden was simply a spec-
tator unlucky enough to have been picked out by the K-9 officer. His
reaction afterwards was to say he regretted having got into the bad company that talked him into going to watch the demos. He intended to
steer clear of politics and concentrate on his career in college, and that
is what he did.

By the standards of a twentieth century that began with the Somme
and ended with Tiananmen Square, Bull Connor's violence was comparatively low-key. No one was killed by the forces of order in Birmingham, and fewer than a dozen were bitten by the dogs. (There were
eventually deaths, among them those of four young black girls killed by
a bomb in a church, but they were not Bull Connor's direct responsibility.) Plenty of demonstrators were drenched and some bruised by fire
hoses, but there were no machine-guns. Pictures went around the world
with captions like 'They Fight a Fire that Won't Go Out'. They certainly
revealed the ugly side of Birmingham's determination to resist. But they
were far from the worst that city, let alone embattled oppressors elsewhere, had to show.

If, in Albany, the black people were divided, and local black leaders resented first SNCC and then Martin Luther King and the SCLC getting involved in the affairs of their town, in Birmingham both blacks and whites were divided, fearful and full of inveterate resentments. The city had an appalling reputation – as hard, people said, as the steel it produced, and as black as the coal on which it depended. Its brutally enforced racial code was all of a piece with the harsh regime imposed on white and black workers alike for almost a century by its coal owners and iron masters, known as the 'Big Mules'. They had gone to whatever lengths they thought necessary to keep unions out of their mines and mills, and to keep in power politicians who would defend their interests at any cost. If that meant flirting with the Klan and defending bullies and bombers, so be it.

Long before King and the SCLC decided to make Birmingham the site for their 'Project C' – for 'confrontation' – the city's black people had been offered radical leadership by a thin, intense Baptist minister called Fred Shuttlesworth and his Alabama Christian Movement for Human Rights. Shuttlesworth grew up poor in rural Alabama. He worked as a labourer and truck driver before graduating from a black college in Selma and becoming a preacher. Few other jobs, in his generation, were open to an educated Alabama Negro without money. At one stage a friendly college professor gave him a cow. Once he had supplied the college, the rest of the milk went to feed his family.

Shuttlesworth was the bravest of the brave. When he and a group of friends tried to imitate what Montgomery had done and integrate Birmingham's buses, he won the unrelenting hatred of white segregationists. So on Christmas Day 1956 they put sixteen sticks of dynamite under his bedroom window. He survived. In 1957 he and his wife tried to register their child at a smart white Birmingham high school. White thugs beat him with a knuckle-duster, whips and chains. He survived. In the 1963 demonstrations firemen turned a high-powered hose on to him which threw him against a brick wall so hard that he spent several days in hospital. Then, too, he survived.

Shuttlesworth was one of the original group of ministers who founded the SCLC, and it was he who invited Martin King to come to Birmingham in the first place. But compared to the highly educated, mellifluously eloquent Dr King, Fred was a rough diamond. He didn't like King's 'flowery speeches', as he called them. He resented King's assumption of leadership, and he made that plain. Nor was he the only prominent black man in Birmingham who thought King's campaign was a mistake. So too did the Revd J. L. Ware, chairman of the black Baptist Ministers' Conference. And so did A. G. Gaston, the millionaire owner of the Gaston motel where King and his ministers made their headquarters, and the richest black man in the city. King was far from being accepted as the undisputed leader of a united Negro people. To many blacks, as to almost all whites, he appeared a tiresome troublemaker who was showing up at the worst of times. After Albany, his coming to Birmingham seemed to many, among both those who would resist desegregation to the death and those who supported it, a desperate move whose predictable failure would set back the whole cause of civil rights.

In 1963 Birmingham had a little under 350,000 inhabitants, 40 per cent of them African-American. Over the 'mountain', past the great statue of the smith god Vulcan, fifty feet high, and built for the 1904 St Louis World Fair, Birmingham's 'Big Mules', the rich white men who controlled its industries, lived in lily-white suburbs with their tennis courts and their azaleas, their country clubs and golf courses, well outside the city limits. Birmingham's main industry, indeed its *raison d'être*, was steel. It was perched on rich deposits of everything you needed to make steel: iron ore, coal and limestone. The first primitive iron-making dated back before the Civil War, but it was not until the 1880s, when the metallurgists had figured out how to make steel with Alabama ore, which is rich in phosphorus, that Birmingham became the biggest centre of heavy industry in the whole South and, after Pittsburgh, the second most important centre of steel-making in the United States. In 1907 Tennessee Coal & Iron (TCI), the company that united the Alabama ore- and coal-mining, blast-furnace and rolling-mill industries, was taken over by J. P. Morgan's United States Steel.

Birmingham was always a hard town, a fact touchingly acknowledged in a whole discography of blues from Bessie Smith, who spent a lot of time in its bars and burlesque houses. Until 1928 the TCI works were still partly manned by convict-lease labour. Throughout the 1930s and

1940s the steel industry resisted unionization with systematic and ruthless violence. One recent historian has argued that the resistance to desegregation in the 1960s was simply a continuation of the tactics the Big Mules had used to break the unions.[3] The city's racial politics were controlled by an unacknowledged alliance between the respectable Big Mules, segregationist politicians and their agents, and uncouth vigilantes and Ku Klux Klansmen. The latter administered beatings and on occasion unofficial death sentences to union organizers or to insubordinate black men, as the case might be.

In the 1950s, southern politics were about the conflict between relatively moderate New Deal Democrats, many from upper-class backgrounds, like Senator Hugo Black, once a member of the Ku Klux Klan but later a liberal justice of the Supreme Court on the one hand, and an anti-New Deal Right-wing coalition on the other. This brought together big industrialists who wanted to keep out the unions and professional anti-communists with white supremacists and racists of various degrees of viciousness, plus some ugly anti-Semites. In 1948, many of the anti-New Deal persuasion bolted from the Democratic Party to back feisty South Carolina Senator Strom Thurmond's 'Dixiecrat' party in an insurgency against the mildly progressive policies of the Truman administration.

Birmingham had the autocratic commission system of municipal government. By the late 1950s its commission was dominated, as we have seen, by Bull Connor, a sadly typical figure from the southern politics of the time. He had never graduated from high school but picked up the skills of radio telegraphy from his father, worked in radio and – like Ronald Reagan in the Middle West – became a sportscaster, adept at turning the bare facts of a news wire into artificial excitement. He started out running errands for a segregationist lawyer-politician called 'Sunny Jim' Simpson before launching into politics on his own.

Connor was only one of the ambitious politicians who navigated the shoals and storms of Alabama's 'Gothic politics'. He eventually became notorious across the South, from South Carolina to Texas, for his brutal and cynical enforcement of segregation. Fred Shuttlesworth was not the only man to have had his house bombed by segregationist thugs: there had been several dozen bombings in the course of the past ten years, especially in the pleasant, previously all-white neighbourhood of College Hills, into which middle-class black families were moving. There were so many bombings there that the district became known as 'Dynamite Hill'. Indeed, already known as the murder capital of America, the city earned the further nickname of 'Bombingham'.

Alabama's comparatively liberal Senator, Lister Hill, was not alone in his suspicion that 'the Alabama Klan is unquestionably and undoubtedly directed from tall buildings'.[4] He hinted broadly that it was directed from one particular tall building, the local corporate headquarters of United States Steel on First Avenue. The Big Mules were careful to distance themselves from the night-riders and the bombers, but the two faces of the segregated system, the dignified and the violent, were conveniently bound together by two deep fears – of communism and of black radicalism. Fear of communism was shamelessly used to maintain both the exclusion of trade unions and the ruthless subjection of the local Negroes.

As Martin King and Fred Shuttlesworth prepared for confrontation in Birmingham in the spring of 1963, however, many of the city's white citizens were already hoping for reform. Connor was being challenged by a number of white candidates, and on 5 March an election was held. It had no decisive result, leaving the new office of mayor to be decided in a run-off election between Connor and a 'moderate' segregationist, Albert Boutwell, Lieutenant Governor of the state of Alabama. The election was held on 2 April, and on that day Boutwell became mayor. But Bull Connor was still in charge of public order. In readiness for trouble, he had acquired a K-9 unit of eight fierce police dogs and their handlers, and the wicked 'monitor' hoses that joined two pumps, thereby doubling the force of the water jet so that, with a rattle like a machine-gun, it could skin the bark from a tree at a hundred yards and knock a strong man flying.

King and Shuttlesworth and their team had planned to launch their campaign – Project C – on 6 March, the day after the original special election. That deadline was missed because the result was inconclusive, and so too was another deadline on the 14th. In late March Stanley Levison met an old Communist Party acquaintance, Lem Harris, to pass the word formally that he and his friends, including the communist former merchant seaman Jack O'Dell, wanted to have no more to do with the Party. On the last day of the month Martin King and Ralph Abernathy were in New York for a big party at the Belafontes', and sat up all hours drinking Bristol Cream sherry, King's new favourite drink, and talking over their hopes, and fears, for Birmingham. Coretta was in hospital in Atlanta, having just given birth to their second daughter, Bernice. On 2 April the new father picked up his wife and baby from the hospital, then flew into Birmingham, largely unnoticed because of the excitement about the election.

'NEW DAY DAWNS FOR BIRMINGHAM,' blared the headline in that day's *Birmingham News*. There had been negotiations with representatives of the five major department stores in town about desegregating their lunch counters. The failure of those talks, King, Abernathy and Shuttlesworth announced, made demonstrations inevitable. Burke Marshall, Assistant Attorney General for civil rights, tried to persuade King to allow more time for negotiations. But the fact was that the Negro leaders were committed to a campaign of demonstrations. With the memory of Albany ever present in their minds, they could not afford to back off. On 3 April, the first Negro marchers set out from the Sixteenth Street Baptist Church towards City Hall. The big brown brick church, the rallying-place for hundreds and in the end thousands of marchers, and from which they set out bravely to meet Bull Connor's men, was across a small city block of greenery called Kelly Ingram Park. The other side of the park was the Gaston Motel. The civil rights leaders held their councils of war in King's room, number 30.

That first day, a few demonstrators were arrested and sent to jail. It was on Saturday 6 April, however, that the first real test of strength took place. Fred Shuttlesworth led forty-odd demonstrators, who were stopped by Connor's policemen, arrested and jailed. That day Martin King appeared accoutred as no one had ever seen him before. He was no longer 'Tweed', the nattiest student at Morehouse or Crozer. He was wearing jeans, rolled up at the bottoms, though admittedly brand-new and visibly ironed, and an equally pristine work shirt. He was sending a signal. He meant business. He meant to go to jail.

The next week, however, was something of a phoney war, or the tactical manoeuvring for position on the eve of battle. On the Sunday,

Martin's brother A. D. King led a small march. Connor showed, but did not unleash, his dogs. On Monday, Martin King spoke to the black ministers, and the next day the Revd Ware came out in favour of the campaign, as did A. G. Gaston. On the Wednesday Martin King announced prophetically that he couldn't think of a better day than Good Friday to go to jail. That same day the city's attorneys went to a state judge and secured an injunction against King, Shuttlesworth and Abernathy to keep the peace. The next day King led a mass meeting, but it was discovered that there were no funds to pay bail bonds.

Sure enough, on the Friday King led a small demonstration, was arrested, taken in a paddy-wagon to the city jail, then found himself in solitary confinement – 'the hole', as prisoners call it. At the best of times Martin did not like jail. Now he found it frightening and depressing. 'You will never know the meaning of utter darkness,' he wrote later, 'until you have lain in such a dungeon, knowing that sunlight is streaming overhead and still seeing only darkness below.'

On Saturday, 12 April the *Birmingham News* carried a long letter signed by eight of the city's most prominent white clergy, including Episcopalians, Methodists, a Baptist, a Presbyterian, a rabbi and a Roman Catholic bishop. Most of them were men with reputations for being relatively liberal where segregation was concerned. (Some of them allowed Negroes to stand in a roped-off area at the back of their church; Episcopalian Bishop Coadjutor George Murray had spoken out courageously on racial issues.) They were led by the senior prelate of the American Anglican Church, Bishop C. C. J. Carpenter of Alabama.*

The letter called King's demonstrations 'unwise and untimely'. 'White Clergymen Urge Local Negroes to Withdraw from Demonstrations,' read the headline in the *News*. 'Recent public events,' they wrote, presumably with Mayor Boutwell's election in mind, gave 'opportunity for a new constructive and realistic approach to racial problems.' Now Birmingham was confronted by demonstrations 'led in part by outsiders' – a comment that both reflected and played on resentments as old as the

---

* The initials commemorated his great-grandfather, the Presbyterian C. C. Jones, who had led the southern Presbyterians out of communion with their abolitionist northern brethren on the eve of the War between the States.

Post-Civil War Reconstruction, of interfering Yankee 'carpetbaggers'. Hatred and violence were to be deplored, the clergymen argued. But so too were 'such actions as incite to hatred and violence, however technically peaceful those actions may be'.

King did not see this pompous and uncomprehending defence of the status quo for many hours after his arrest. His hours in solitary confinement were, he said later, 'the longest, the most frightening and bewildering ... I have lived'. Unbeknown to him, Wyatt Walker had been swift to turn his arrest to political advantage. An attorney tried to see King, but was told a visit could take place only in the presence of guards, something the lawyer would not accept. Late on Friday night, Walker called Burke Marshall to ask the federal government to help, and followed this up with a telegram: 'WE ASK YOU TO USE THE INFLU-ENCE OF YOUR HIGH OFFICE TO PERSUADE THE CITY OFFICIALS OF BIRMINGHAM TO AFFORD AT LEAST A MODICUM OF HUMANITY.'

On the Sunday morning Walker spoke to Coretta. She first suggested that she make a statement herself. Walker had a better idea: she should call President Kennedy. At first she was reluctant to do so before she had talked to Martin, but that proved impossible. In the event, the famously resourceful White House switchboard connected her to Pierre Salinger, Kennedy's press secretary, in Florida. Three-quarters of an hour later Robert Kennedy called back, promising that the Justice Department would make sure King was being properly treated. Late on Sunday and again on Monday, King was able to see lawyers. Without warning his jailers told him to call Coretta. She said she had just had a call from the President, but then the children came on the line and it took a few moments for her message to sink in. When it did, King's priority was to let Walker know, and that evening Walker was able to announce to the nightly mass meeting in Birmingham that the President had called. The national reporters filed the story immediately. Slowly, but inexorably, the Kennedy administration was being sucked into doing what it had been so reluctant to do hitherto.

When Coretta King and Juanita Abernathy finally visited their husbands on the Tuesday, they learned that Martin had been indignant at the white clergymen's criticism and had been replying. At first, the only paper he had to write on was a copy of the *Birmingham News* containing the clergy letter, a copy brought in by one of the lawyers. Soon the lawyers brought him paper, and as he scribbled furiously they took his nearly illegible script away – 'that chicken scratch,' Wyatt Walker called it – and gave it to Walker's secretary Willie Pearl Mackey, to be typed up and sent back to the jail to be edited. Sometimes, when Mackey was so tired that she fell asleep at the typewriter, Walker would type some pages himself.

What emerged from this intense and unconventional production line was the most cogent and passionate document of Martin Luther King's career, and one of the most revealing of his character with all its strengths and weaknesses. It is the only one of his major utterances that was not delivered in his magnificent voice. It must stand or fall by the sheer power of argument, and by that test it succeeds unquestionably, while at the same time revealing what may be considered a fault, King's desire to be accepted as an equal in learning and intellect by his white contemporaries. The letter speaks to fellow clergymen as a scholar and spiritual leader, correcting and reproving his peers. Indeed, it comes close to talking down to them. He seems at once to be sharing with his critics firm and fully formed conclusions, and to be thinking his way through his own dilemmas.

The letter begins by addressing the white clergy's complaint that he has come to Birmingham as an 'outsider'. He comes, he contradicts them, as the head of the SCLC, an organization of Christian leaders with no fewer than eighty-five branches, one of which was Birmingham's own Alabama Christian Movement for Human Rights. He comes by invitation, and he comes to Birmingham 'because injustice is here'. Like the Hebrew prophets and like the apostle Paul, he must respond to the call. He does not need to remind this readership what that call was: 'Come over into Macedonia and help us.'[5]

Moving on, he demolishes as 'narrow and provincial' the idea that he is an 'outside agitator'. 'We are,' he says, 'caught in an inescapable network of mutuality ... Anyone who lives in the United States can never be considered an outsider anywhere within its bounds.' The white clergy deplored the demonstrations, but failed 'to express a similar concern for the conditions that brought [them] about. Fred Shuttlesworth and his colleagues had agreed to a moratorium on demonstrations. But 'as in so many past experiences, our hopes had been blasted, and the shadow of deep disappointment settled upon us'.

But why 'direct action'? 'The purpose of our direct action program,' King explained, 'is to create a situation so crisis-packed that it will inevitably open the door to negotiations.' But why now? Why not give the new city government time to act? 'Lamentably,' King replied, 'it is an historical fact that privileged groups seldom give up their privileges voluntarily. Individuals may see the moral light . . . but as Reinhold Niebuhr has reminded us, groups tend to be more immoral than individuals.' Frankly, King went on, 'I have yet to engage in a direct action campaign that was "well timed" in the view of those who have not suffered unduly from the disease of segregation. For years now I have heard the word "Wait!" . . . This "Wait" has almost always meant "Never".'

'Before the Pilgrims landed at Plymouth, we were here. Before the pen of Jefferson etched the majestic words of the Declaration of Independence across the pages of history, we were here.' We have waited for more than 340 years, he said, for our constitutional and God-given rights. The nations of Asia and Africa are moving with jet-like speed towards gaining political independence, 'but we still creep at horse-and-buggy pace toward gaining a cup of coffee at a lunch counter . . . When you find yourself stammering as you try to explain to a six-year-old daughter why she cannot go to Funtown, or answer a five-year-old son when he asks, "Daddy, why do white people treat colored people so mean?"' – piling one humiliation on another, he then slings his rhetorical haymaker – 'there comes a time when the cup of endurance runs over, and men are no longer willing to be plunged into the abyss of despair. I hope, sirs, you can understand our legitimate and unavoidable impatience.'

Then he turned to the question of obedience to the laws. 'One has not only a legal but a moral responsibility to obey just laws. Conversely, one has a moral responsibility to disobey unjust laws. I would agree with St Augustine that "an unjust law is no law at all".' Citing Aquinas and Paul Tillich, he asked how one could tell the difference between a just and an unjust law. 'I can urge men to obey the 1954 decision of the

Supreme Court,'* he concluded, 'for it is morally right; and I can urge them to disobey segregation ordinances, for they are morally wrong.' A law is unjust, he went on, if it is inflicted on a minority that is denied the right to vote. He himself was in prison for parading without a permit. Nothing wrong with such an ordinance in itself, but it becomes wrong when it is used to maintain segregation and deny citizens their First Amendment privilege of peaceful assembly.

So he continued, citing the very texts and authorities that would be most persuasive to white ministers of religion who were also, according to their lights, men of good will. He quoted Paul and Luther, John Bunyan and Abraham Lincoln, until he reached the most deadly paragraph of his whole argument, a condemnation from which moderation has never wholly recovered its reputation among those who have read his words. 'I must confess,' he told his 'Christian and Jewish brothers',

> that over the past few years I have been gravely disappointed with the white moderate. I have almost reached the regrettable conclusion that the Negro's great stumbling block in his stride toward freedom is not the White Citizen's Councilor or the Ku Klux Klanner, but the white moderate, who is more devoted to 'order' than to justice, who prefers a negative peace which is the absence of tension to a positive peace which is the presence of justice . . . Shallow understanding from people of good will is more frustrating than absolute misunderstanding from people of ill will. Lukewarm acceptance is much more bewildering than outright rejection.

He did not condemn all white people. He commended those 'white brothers' and sisters 'who have grasped the meaning of this social revolution and committed themselves to it'. He congratulated, even patronized, some of the authors of the ministers' letter: 'I am not unmindful of the fact that each of you has taken some significant stands on this issue.' Yet he was disappointed in the Church. 'There can be no disappointment where there is not deep love. Yes, I love the church. How

* In *Brown v. Board of Education*

could I do otherwise? I am in the rather unique position of being the son, the grandson and the great-grandson of preachers.' He had hoped to hear the Church say that integration was right and the Negro is your brother. Yet 'in the midst of blatant injustices inflicted upon the Negro, I have watched white churchmen stand on the sideline and mouth pious irrelevances and sanctimonious trivialities.'

In his letter Martin King staked out a proud position, one that has since triumphed. Yet, at the time, victory was not obvious. The Birmingham campaign was coolly received in the national press. It risked alienating the Kennedy administration. Indeed, the campaign itself, King's campaign, as he conceived it, failed. It ran out of adult demonstrators willing to be arrested and imprisoned. It was only by means of desperate measures, initiated by others and opposed by him, that defeat in Birmingham was turned into victory, resounding and decisive.

On 26 April Judge Jenkins found King, Shuttlesworth, Abernathy, Wyatt Walker and a few others guilty of criminal contempt and sentenced them to five days in prison, suspended pending appeal. By now, the campaign was in danger of petering out. Fewer Negroes were willing to go to jail, and there was less money to bail them out, though Harry Belafonte had raised $50,000 at the beginning of the campaign. 'We had run out of troops,' said Wyatt Walker, 'we needed something new.'[6] They needed it, especially, because if they didn't come up with news the reporters would leave town.

At this point Martin Luther King's whole career was rescued by the actions, which he opposed, of a man of whom he disapproved. Jim Bevel was a tall figure, ostentatiously dressed in the bib overalls of a poor Negro labourer. Improbably, he habitually wore a yarmulke on his head. Bevel came out of the Nashville movement, centred on the campus of Fisk University there and led by King's friend James Lawson. Bevel had recently married the beautiful and passionate Diane Nash. At this height of the Birmingham crisis she was away, leading a 'freedom march' across the dangerous back roads of Alabama and Mississippi to commemorate a half-crazy Baltimore postman, William Moore, who had been shot down by Klansmen as he marched with a sandwich board reading, subversively, 'Eat at Joe's Both Black and White'. Bevel was a notable womanizer, even by the relaxed standards of black ministers, a wildly charismatic preacher and at times only tenuously connected to reality. But now he had an inspiration. As a preacher, he was familiar with Jesus's injunction: 'Suffer little children to come unto me, and forbid them not: for of such is the kingdom of God.' King disapproved of exposing children to the tender mercies of Bull Connor's men, but Bevel forbade them not. And he knew how to get to the kids. He persuaded two disc jockeys from the radio station popular with Birmingham's black teenagers, Shelley Stewart and 'Tall Paul' Dudley White, to preach his message on air. 'Fight for freedom,' was the word, 'then go to school.'

On 2 May, the little children marched and sang freedom songs, sang and marched, and were put in jail. A policeman asked Shuttlesworth, 'Hey, Fred, how many more have you got?' 'At least a thousand,' was the answer.[7] And by the end of two days close to a thousand of them were in prison. That first day, some of the children were as young as seven. One, asked by a policeman what she wanted, lisped 'F'eedom!' The next day was the climax of the whole campaign; the demonstrators were older, high school students – this was the day of Walter Gadsden's encounter with the dog Leo, and of the monitor fire hoses.

On 4 May the pictures were on the front page of every newspaper in the nation, and indeed in the world. On the Saturday the celebrities moved in, led by the black comedian Dick Gregory, along with the white pacifist Dave Dellinger and the folksinger Joan Baez, come to sing at the local churches, her straight hair covered to fool the segregation ordinances. The heavy hitters in the movement came too, starting with James Forman of SNCC and Ella Baker, the inspiration of SNCC. Now neither the Kennedy administration nor the white power structure of Birmingham could ignore what was happening. Burke Marshall, too, and another Kennedy aide, Joe Dolan, arrived in town.

Negotiations began with a group of white businessmen. Desegregation of the stores, mostly owned by Jewish businessmen who were themselves by no means accepted by the Big Mules 'over the mountain' and their wives, proved negotiable. But the white intermediaries baulked at releasing the hundreds of demonstrators in jail. Fred Shuttlesworth was furious with Martin King for reaching this agreement without him, and threatened to go home. 'You're mister big,' he shouted, 'but you're going to be mister S-H-I-T!'[8] The Negro side was mollified after trade unions in the North guaranteed a big sum to bail out the demonstrators. A second agreement was reached, and at a press conference on 7 May Martin King, careful to nudge Fred Shuttlesworth forward as leader, was able to claim it as victory.

Throughout the crisis, both blacks and whites had dreaded the Klan. The men of violence were capable of anything. On the Saturday King and Abernathy returned to Atlanta to preach at their respective churches, promising to be back on Monday to tidy up the loose ends of the agreement. On Saturday night the Klan showed its hand. A large bomb destroyed A. D. King's house in Birmingham. Another went off outside Martin's room at the Gaston motel. By an added stroke of luck, the friend King had allowed to stay in the room that night had decided to go home. No one was killed. But the riot everyone had feared now broke out. Crowds of furious black men hurled bricks and bottles at Connor's men. And there was a new and troubling presence. Governor George Wallace, cunning and contemptuous of civil rights demonstrators and national Democratic politicians alike, sent in his Alabama state troopers, commanded by Colonel Al Lingo. As the rioting took hold, Lingo pulled out his men, only to send them back in, swinging their billy clubs.

Over the weekend, a precarious order was restored. The city fathers tried to welsh on their agreement, maintaining that they had agreed to hire only one black salesman for just one of the city's half-dozen department stores. Powerful white businessmen pressed Wallace to pull Lingo's men out. By now, both John and Robert Kennedy were concerned about the situation in the South, though not yet convinced they would have to take action to support Negro demands. King reassured a nervous President that if there was no further Klan violence, he could control Birmingham's Negroes. Kennedy went on television on the Sunday night, warning that if there was further trouble he would call the Alabama National Guard into the federal service and station regular US army troops near Birmingham.

Kennedy was still hesitating about whether to commit himself to national civil rights legislation. The political risk was obvious of asking the southern Democrat committee chairmen on Capitol Hill to support legislation that banned the system they had spent their life defending. What was less clear to the Kennedy brothers was that the dangers, both political and in terms of civil disorder, of inaction were at least as great. So it would take one more turn of the wheel in Alabama to drag John Kennedy off the fence he had been sitting on since he took office. This time the focus of the drama was not Montgomery, nor Birmingham, but the quiet college town of Tuscaloosa, home of the University of Alabama and its legendary football team, the Crimson Tide.

9

The Tide Turns

I still believe that we shall overcome.

Martin Luther King Jr's Nobel Prize acceptance speech

On 11 June 1963 a strange little scene was acted out in front of the Foster Auditorium on the leafy campus of the University of Alabama at Tuscaloosa. Its two principal actors neatly symbolized the conflicts, as old as the United States, between North and South, city and country, populist and patrician. They embodied, in their contrasting physiques, accents and personal styles, sharp differences of social class, culture and political ideology.

One of them, George Wallace, Governor of Alabama, his back to the auditorium's southern portico, was short, feisty, a former chicken farmer, truck driver and amateur boxer, aggressively conscious of representing the plain people of the South and their passionate commitment to a way of life under threat. That threat was personified by the tall, bald, elegant Nicholas deBelleville Katzenbach, a posh Yankee if ever a southerner saw and instantly resented one. He was born in Philadelphia, educated at Phillips Andover, at Yale, at Balliol College, Oxford, and again at the Yale Law School; he was a corporate lawyer, and now he was the representative here in southern fields of the detested Kennedy brothers.[1]

Wallace had vowed that he would 'stand in the schoolroom door' before a black student was admitted to the university. 'Bama' was the beloved focus of the state's pride, not least because of the feats of its football team. Number one in the nation in 1961 and again in 1964 and 1965, the Tide was schooled by its coach, Paul 'Bear' Bryant – so called because he was said to have once wrestled a bear – to pray to God for victory in the locker room before inflicting mayhem on its opponents. Seven years earlier, two black women, Pollie Anne Myers and Autherine Lucy, had attempted to register as students at Tuscaloosa. Myers had been cruelly but casually disposed of when it was discovered that she was pregnant and unmarried when she applied, though she married before her child was born. To get rid of Lucy was more difficult. Her counsel, none other than Thurgood Marshall, later the first African-American justice of the Supreme Court, charged the university with 'conspiracy', but that enabled the university's lawyers to expel Lucy on the ground of 'outrageous, false and baseless accusations'.

Now two more brave young Negroes, Vivian Malone and James Hood, had plucked up the courage to try. They were represented by the only two black lawyers in town, Orzell Billingsley and Arthur Shores, and advised by Birmingham's most formidable white liberal, Chuck Morgan.[2] The Kennedy administration, still hesitating on the brink before plunging into the turbulent waters of southern racial politics, had committed itself to the extent of sending Deputy Attorney General Katzenbach to escort Hood and Malone to registration. As at Ole Miss, however, what looked like a trial of strength was really a pre-scripted comedy. Wallace earned political points by defying the might of the federal government. Katzenbach asserted federal authority, then withdrew. But later the bayonets of the Alabama National Guard, the governor's army, called into federal service by the President, could be seen glinting through the campus trees as they marched up to enforce the federal court's order. Both sides had won something, and each avoided humiliation.

Martin Luther King was not involved in these theatricals. Yet his political career was decisively affected. The background was growing violence across the South. A black reserve officer in the US army, Colonel Lemuel Penn, was murdered on a Georgia road; the Baltimore postman, William Moore, was murdered; black activists, helping Mississippi Negroes to vote, were shot at and wounded. In prison, especially in Mississippi, civil rights workers were subjected to appalling conditions, amounting in some cases to torture. Yet demonstrations still spread like a rash of optimism across the South.

The evening of the face-off at Tuscaloosa, John Kennedy, habitually so cautious, made a sudden decision. At six, Eastern time, he decided to go on national television at eight. He was listened to in the bar of Tuscaloosa's main motel by an audience that included reporters from the national and international media,[3] civil rights lawyers, and Robert

Shelton, a local man who gloried in the title Imperial Wizard of the Alabama Knights of the Ku Klux Klan. At long last, Kennedy slid off the fence. He announced that he would present before Congress a civil rights bill which would include provision for abolishing segregation in housing and 'public accommodations' such as lunch counters.

King was delighted by Kennedy's speech. He fired off a telegram calling it 'one of the most eloquent, profound and unequivocal pleas for justice and the freedom of all men ever made by any president'. Since Lincoln's death almost a hundred years earlier, indeed, there had not been much competition. Still, now Kennedy was committed to legislation. King immediately spotted that the thrust of the march on Washington he was already discussing with A. Philip Randolph, Bayard Rustin and other Negro leaders must now shift, from putting pressure on the President to send legislation to Capitol Hill, to helping him accumulate votes for that legislation.

That night, something happened that showed not only how far there was to go before the South would accept the end of segregation, but also how divided Negroes and their representatives still were. Medgar Evers, the leader of the NAACP in Mississippi, was murdered by a white man called Byron de la Beckwith. King immediately proposed that he and Roy Wilkins, national head of the NAACP, should jointly announce a national day of mourning and a fund to commemorate Evers. Wilkins, concerned about the SCLC's inroads into the NAACP's sources of funding, told King to mind his own business. When the two men met at Evers's funeral, Wilkins brusquely warned King off.

The Birmingham settlement was a victory in national politics, but it did little enough for the city's black people at the time. The Big Mules and their lawyers and politicians stalled on some of their commitments, and simply welshed on others. They continued to argue that they had only agreed to one black salesman for all the downtown stores, and no black policemen were recruited. Meanwhile, the SCLC was involved in a whole series of other campaigns across the South, from Danville in 'Southside' Virginia to Plaquemines and Iberia parishes in Louisiana. In several cities, hundreds of black demonstrators went to prison. In Danville, a tough judge frustrated desegregation, but some five hundred black voters were registered. In Gadsden, Alabama, 685 blacks were arrested on a single August day, but their demonstrations achieved nothing.

These campaigns did for the most part without Martin Luther King. He was consumed by the preparations for what would be his crowning moment, the march on Washington. He found, too, that the more closely he worked with the Kennedy brothers, the more intense was the suspicion he encountered, dispensed by J. Edgar Hoover and his Federal Bureau of Investigation. The Kennedys, in their political way, did not refuse to deal with him because of this: instead, they sent endless messages warning King that the FBI had evidence that there were communists – meaning Stanley Levison and Jack O'Dell – in his entourage. King seemed not to care. The truth was that he had no intention of depriving himself of Levison's advice or, for that matter, of his capacity to raise funds for the SCLC. While the Kennedy brothers embraced King without much sympathy but rather out of political necessity, as they calculated it, after the march they could not afford to alienate him.

On 15 September, eighteen days after the march, when Martin had dreamed of the day when 'little black boys and black girls will be able to join hands with little white boys and white girls as sisters and brothers', four young black girls left Sunday School at Sixteenth Street Baptist in Birmingham and went down to the church basement to primp before singing in a Youth Day service. Denise McNair was eleven; Cynthia Wesley, Carole Robertson and Addie Mae Collins were all fourteen.

Sixteenth Street Baptist, the wealthiest and most imposing of Birmingham's black churches, had been at the heart of the confrontation four months earlier. It was across the street that the Alsatian dog Leo lurched at Walter Gadsden. The church was a block from Martin King's command post in room 30 at the Gaston motel and across from Kelly Ingram Park, where angry crowds of black people had gathered night after night. It was from Sixteenth Street Baptist that the endless waves of children emerged to cram Bull Connor's prison, and it was into the church basement that Fred Shuttlesworth was knocked by the jet of water from the monitor hose. Yet Sixteenth Street Baptist was far from being a hive of black revolutionaries. It was the favourite church of Birmingham's black bourgeoisie, such as it was. Its members, as a group, were made uncomfortable by demonstrations, by Martin Luther King, and even more so by rough-and-ready Fred Shuttlesworth.

That did not save Denise, Cynthia, Carole and Addie Mae. At 10.22 a.m. nine sticks of dynamite exploded. The blast blew the clothes off the girls, killing them stone dead and hurling their bodies across the basement. One of them was decapitated. The killers were Klansmen, members of a clique of bombers from the Birmingham suburbs. Many in Birmingham, especially in the police, knew who they were. But it was years before any of them were brought to trial.*

King rushed back to Birmingham. He was deeply angered by President Kennedy's response, which was, first, to send eighty-three-year-old General Douglas MacArthur to represent him, and then to send the West Point football coach Earl 'Red' Blaik and another retired general, the white North Carolinian Kenneth Royall, in MacArthur's place. Transparently, Kennedy was more concerned with the good opinion of white Birmingham than with the feelings of its grieving, angry blacks. For King, not for the last time, triumph had turned to disaster. He preached at the funeral of three of the dead girls at Sixth Avenue Baptist, but it was not one of his best sermons. He cited the text, 'A little child shall lead them'. As always, he tried to turn tragedy into a Christian message of optimism. 'The death of these little children may lead our whole Southland from the low road of man's inhumanity to the high road of peace and brotherhood.'

It was Chuck Morgan, white liberal and hard-headed lawyer, who for many said what more urgently needed to be said, not in sorrow, still less in hope, but in cold anger. Morgan was infuriated by the continued pious talk about how the trouble had been caused by 'outside agitators' and how most of Birmingham's white citizens were 'innocent victims'. Not so, Morgan told the Young Men's Business Club, which happened to be holding its usual meeting in a downtown hotel. 'Who did it?' he asked, and answered his own question. The guilty included everyone who talked about 'niggers', and every 'crude oaf whose racial jokes rock the party'.

---

* Robert 'Dynamite Bob' Chambliss was convicted in 1977 and died in prison in 1985. In 2001 Thomas Blanton Jr and Bob Frank Cherry were convicted of murder and sentenced to life imprisonment. Cherry was found mentally incompetent and sent to a mental hospital.

They were 'all the Christians and all their ministers who spoke too late' against violence. 'What's it like living in Birmingham?' he ended. 'No one ever really has and no one will until this city becomes part of the United States. Birmingham is not a dying city. It is dead'.[4]

Just over two months after the Birmingham bomb, John Kennedy was murdered in Dallas and Lyndon Johnson succeeded him as President. To the surprise of many northern liberals, who associated Johnson with the southern grandees he had led in the Senate and therefore assumed that he would be more conservative than Kennedy, Johnson turned out to make racial justice his priority, far more than Kennedy had done. He pressed ahead and by the summer of 1964 he had persuaded Congress to pass the Civil Rights Act. At long last the executive and legislative branches of the federal government of the United States had declared social segregation unlawful.

The implications for Martin Luther King Jr's public life were immense. As the leader of a southern crusade for equality, he understood that the trumpet had at last sounded and the walls of Jericho had fallen. There was a further battle to be fought over voter registration, which was still being denied to blacks more or less systematically in the Deep South and especially in its rural areas. But now King had to adjust his policy towards what had always been his ultimate concern, social justice and equality for all, white as well as black, and in the North as in the South.[5]

There was, however, a very direct and painful personal impact of the Kennedy assassination. King had always understood that by putting himself at the head of a movement to change the racial mores of the South he was inviting his own violent death. No African-American could be unaware of how many black men who had stood up had been cut down. This had been the fate, not only of acknowledged leaders – most recently, for example, of Medgar Evers – but also of obscure martyrs, shot, bombed or lynched, and forgotten.

King was far too intelligent not to have been aware of this from the earliest days of the Montgomery bus boycott. He was a reluctant martyr, but in the end a cheerful one. At that time, when Coretta said she was afraid he would be killed, he admitted: 'If anyone had asked me a year ago to head this movement, I tell you very honestly that I would have run a mile to get away from it.' But, he went on after a pause, as he became involved, and as other people became inspired, 'I realized that the choice leaves your own hands.' A little later, on 14 January 1957, before the bombing of his own house, he had to be helped to his chair when he shouted out in the middle of a prayer, 'Lord, I hope no one will have to die as a result of our struggle for freedom in Montgomery. Certainly, I don't want to die. But if anyone has to die, let it be me!'[6] He was at home watching television when the news from Dallas appeared on the screen. He called, 'Corrie, I just heard that Kennedy has been shot, maybe killed.' When they finally heard that he was dead, Coretta recalled later, Martin said, 'This is what is going to happen to me. This is such a sick society.' In Memphis, in the very last hours of his life, he would tell an audience, 'I'm not afraid of any man.' 'I'd rather be dead than afraid,' he used to tell his aides. 'You've got to get over being afraid of death.'[7]

King was enabled to cope with the ever-present fear of violent death in part through the strength of his Christian belief in the afterlife. But he also turned for comfort to the company, and the sexual solace, of women. 'I'm away from home twenty-five to twenty-seven days a month,' he told a friend. 'Fucking's a form of anxiety reduction.'[8] This filled him with guilt. It was also one of three aspects of his life that exposed him to the suspicions and, in effect, to blackmail by the FBI and its legendary director J. Edgar Hoover. The least damaging, because evidently untrue, was Hoover's belief that King was financially dishonest, that – like many another religious leader, black or white, in American history – he was siphoning off large sums for his personal use and living it up on the donations he attracted.

The second, as already mentioned, was Hoover's conviction that King was surrounded and controlled by communists to the extent of being an agent of the Soviet Union, which was keen to take over the Negro civil rights movement. (After King came out strongly against the Vietnam War, another informant sought to convince the CIA that he was a 'Peking-line' communist.) Hoover and his tight coterie of senior agents tried repeatedly to persuade first President Kennedy and his brother the Attorney General and key Justice Department officials, then President Johnson and his White House staff, that King was a communist agent.

As noted earlier, they tapped the telephones of his confidant Stanley Levison and others; they bugged his hotel rooms when he travelled. They passed information, true or false, about King's alleged sexual behaviour to these senior government officials and to journalists.

It was in December 1962, as we have seen, that King first incurred Hoover's public fury.[9] The Southern Regional Council, a liberal organization in Atlanta, published a report which claimed that the authorities, from President Kennedy down to the local police but specifically including the FBI, had not protected Negro citizens' rights in Albany. Two years later a group of women reporters, led by the conservative Texan Sarah McLendon, was ushered into Hoover's office. In the course of a rant that went on for more than twice the scheduled hour, Hoover called King 'the most notorious liar in the country' and more in the same vein. In public, King responded smoothly in a brief public statement: 'I cannot conceive of Mr Hoover making a statement like that without being under extreme pressure ... I have nothing but sympathy for this man who has served his country so well.' In private King told both his secretary and a colleague that Hoover was senile. His remarks were duly recorded by an FBI wiretap and did nothing to calm Hoover's mountainous rage.

In retrospect, Hoover can seem a tragicomic figure, even a figure of fun, a secret cross-dressing homosexual who cast himself as the guardian of the nation's sexual morality, and a public figure of whom the kindest thing Lyndon Johnson could say was that it was 'probably better to have him inside the tent pissing out than outside the tent pissing in[10]'. Yet since 1919 Hoover had been very far from a figure of fun: in that year, as an assistant to Attorney General A. Mitchell Palmer, he had played the leading part in the 'Palmer raids' on political leftists, several thousand of whom were rounded up and deported to Russia in the middle of the Russian civil war.

Hoover grew up in a lower-middle-class home on Capitol Hill in Washington, a neighbourhood then (as now) full of black people, and he was a lifelong racist. He became an accomplished bureaucrat, a toady to the powerful and ruthless. He specialized in blackmailing the powerful, including Richard Nixon, whom he claimed to have caught in a secret relationship with a Chinese bar girl in Hong Kong. He built up

'Justice will rush down like waters, and righteousness like a mighty stream.' (AP/PA Photos)

Rosa Parks is fingerprinted after refusing to move to the back of the Montgomery bus after her confrontation with her old antagonist, driver James F. Blake, 1 December 1955. Parks's action led to the Montgomery Bus Boycott, which was led by Martin Luther King.
(Gene Herrick AP/PA Photos)

Dr King and his friend Ralph Abernathy (centre), following their arrest on 24 February 1956 during the Montgomery Bus Boycott.
(Gene Herrick AP/PA Photos)

A cop with a bullhorn controls a demonstration in Albany, Alabama, where police chief Laurie Pritchett mostly used brains rather than brawn to outwit King's supporters, December 1961.
(AP/PA Photos)

Dr King is arrested in Birmingham, 12 April 1963. From jail, he sent his famous 'Letter', rebuking Birmingham's clergy for urging Negroes to be patient.
(AP/PA Photos)

Many pictures showed King as passive, yet in the heat of his powerful rhetoric, as here, he could be formidable and severe.
(AP/PA Photos)

Police dog Leo, handled by 'K-9' dog squad officer Dick Middleton, lunges at Walter Gadsden. AP photographer Bill Hudson's iconic shot was taken in Birmingham on 3 May 1963 during a demonstration by black schoolchildren.
(Bill Hudson AP/PA Photos)

By the end of April 1963, King's Birmingham campaign was running out of adult demonstrators, but an army of schoolchildren took their place. Pictures such as this, taken on 3 May 1963, went round the world and doomed white supremacy. 'Let 'em have it!' ordered Birmingham's police commissioner, 'Bull' Connor. Double strength fire hoses could strip the bark from a tree and the shirt from a boy's back. (Bettmann/Corbis)

King waves to participants in the Civil Rights Movement's March on Washington from the Lincoln Memorial, 28 August 1963. It was from this spot that he delivered his famous 'I Have a Dream' speech.
(Hulton-Deutsch Collection/ Corbis)

On 2 July 1964 President Johnson signed the Civil Rights Act with 75 pens, which were handed to the senators and congressmen who had helped to pass the legislation. One of the pens was given to Dr King.
(AP/PA Photos)

King follows the hearse carrying the body of Jimmie Lee Jackson, shot by a state trooper in Mack's café in Marion, Alabama, 18 February 1965. Jackson had intervened to help his 82-year-old grandfather, who had been beaten by the troopers. (AP/PA Photos)

Brown's Chapel in Selma, Alabama, the African-American church where King preached to demonstrators before they set off to cross the nearby Pettus bridge, Sunday 7 March 1965.
(AP/PA Photos)

Marchers climb the steep Pettus bridge at Selma, Alabama, while police and state troopers wait for them with horses, tear gas and cattle prods.
(AP/PA Photos)

From the air, hundreds of marchers made the bridge at Selma look like a dark stripe of humanity, singing on their way to the confrontation with Governor George Wallace's state troopers. (AP/PA Photos)

Coretta Scott King with her husband at Selma. (AP/PA Photos)

James Meredith set out on his 'March Against Fear' from Memphis, Tennessee, to Jackson, Mississippi, on 5 June 1966. Near Hernando, Mississippi, Aubrey Norvell stepped out of the woods and shot him three times with a shotgun. Meredith survived the attack, and Dr King, Stokely Carmichael and others continued the march in his name.
(AP/PA Photos)

At Greenwood, Mississippi, on 16 June, Carmichael – to Dr King's annoyance – began to preach the rhetoric of 'Black Power'.
(Bob Adelman/Corbis)

'A time comes when silence is betrayal.' On 2 April 1967, at the huge Riverside church in New York, Dr King finally came out openly against the Vietnam War, infuriating President Johnson.
(AP/PA Photos)

Dr King and his friends on the balcony of the Lorraine Motel in Memphis, 3 April 1968. Moments later he was dead.
(AP/PA Photos)

The view of the Lorraine Motel through James Earl Ray's scope from the bathroom window of Bessie Brewer's rooming house.
(Bettmann/Corbis)

Coretta King and her children, Yoki, Martin Junior, Dexter and Bernice at her husband's funeral, Atlanta, 9 April 1968.
(Flip Schulke/Corbis)

After King's assassination, there was rioting in every large city in America. Some of the worst disturbances took place within a few blocks of the White House in Washington, DC.
(AP/PA Photos)

Bayard Rustin – homosexual, athlete, musician, pacifist, communist then socialist – with Dr King, whose trusted *consigliere* he was.
(AP/PA Photos)

Dr King's assassin, James Earl Ray. He confessed to murdering Dr King, then withdrew his confession. Ray survived being stabbed by black inmates in 1981, and died in prison in 1998.
(AP/PA Photos)

President John F. Kennedy; J. Edgar Hoover, director of the FBI; and Robert F. Kennedy. The Kennedy brothers didn't know what to make of Dr King. (Henry Burroughs AP/PA Photos)

the FBI as a top-down organization, 'with its rigid hierarchy, its ide-ology, its insularity, its mystique of secrecy, its insistence on internal loy-alty'.[11] He also built up its legend, boasting shamelessly of its triumphs in tracking down such criminals as John Dellinger and Al Capone, and in saving the nation from communist subversion and Soviet sabotage.

In January 1962 Hoover received the first FBI report that King was close to Stanley Levison, in whom, as we have seen, the FBI had long taken an interest. Before the end of February headquarters had ordered 'complete background data' on King, and on 6 March the director sent over a formal request for both a 'bug' in Levison's office and a tap on his telephone. By 20 March both had been installed. It was not until the middle of June that this surveillance hit pay dirt of a kind. The wiretap picked up a conversation between Levison and Jack O'Dell about the latter moving to Atlanta to replace Wyatt Walker in the SCLC office.

After Albany, Hoover's relationship with King deteriorated, especially after he failed to return two phone calls from Hoover's assistant DeLoach. During the first half of 1963, from the SCLC's preparations for going into Birmingham until President Kennedy's televised address on the night of the stand-off at Tuscaloosa, the FBI kept hinting that Levison was King's communist Svengali, and the Kennedy brothers, through various intermediaries, passed on broader and broader hints to King that he should cut his links to Levison. The normally cool Burke Marshall went so far as to compare him to Colonel Rudolf Abel, the Soviet master spy. Eventually the President himself took King into the White House rose garden to make the same point, warning him that he might be brought down by Levison just as Kennedy's old friend Harold Macmillan had been by John Profumo's sharing a mistress with a Soviet diplomat. Finally, in July, Levison, in this as in everything else remark-ably free from self-interest, volunteered to step down 'for the good of the civil rights movement'.

A couple of weeks later the FBI asked for a wiretap on Clarence Jones, a successful black entertainment lawyer who had helped raise money for the SCLC and had acted as a channel of communication between King and Levison so as to allay the government's suspicions. Hoover's chief expert on domestic communism, William C. Sullivan, then shocked him by producing a report arguing that the Communist Party had almost wholly failed to exploit the racial situation – then changed his mind within a couple of days.

The context of tension between the FBI, the civil rights leaders and the Kennedy administration was the growing struggle over the civil rights bill in Congress. Senator Richard Russell of Georgia, the much admired spokesman for thoughtful southerners, inquired about the FBI's information on King's communist contacts, then explained that he was determined to keep such questions from interfering with the debate on civil rights legislation. The conflict intensified. As 1963 ended, an internal FBI conference openly discussed how to 'expose' King. The FBI asked for, and was given, permission by the Justice Department to tap King's phones in Atlanta and at the SCLC office in New York. It was not these devices, however, that gave director Hoover what he wanted and added an ugly new twist to his persecution of the man he called 'the burrhead'.

In the New Year, *Time* magazine chose Martin Luther King as its 'man of the year'. Hoover was outraged. Bill Sullivan was already convinced that King was 'an immoral opportunist who is . . . exploiting the racial situation for personal gain'. On 5 January King and Ralph Abernathy were due to check in to the Willard, the massive Victorian hotel two blocks from the White House. The FBI bugged their suite, and on the Sunday night the agents were rewarded. Their microphone picked up the sounds of a party. Martin, Ralph and SCLC colleagues were entertaining two lively young black women who worked at the naval yard in Philadelphia. The agents claimed to have heard sounds of drinking, raucous laughter and love-making. The tapes were quickly transcribed, and eight pages of edited transcript rushed off to the White House, where President Johnson and his confidential aide Walter Jenkins, who had himself several times been caught by police picking up men in the lavatory of a nearby club, were greatly titillated. One of Hoover's senior officials claimed to be able to tell that 'eight, ten, eleven' men, naked, were watching King having sex with one of the young women, though it is not clear how he could tell how many men were there, let alone that they were undressed. The agents also claimed to have heard Martin exclaiming, 'I'm fucking for God.'[12]

Delighted and excited, as well as duly shocked, by what they had heard, Hoover's top officials changed the focus of their investigation from communism and possible financial peculation to King's sex life, referred to inside the Bureau as 'entertainment'. Bugs in hotels in Milwaukee and Honolulu were disappointments, but when King and his companions checked into a Los Angeles motel the FBI listeners were rewarded by what from their point of view was the most valuable material turned up in the whole sordid operation. They recorded this group of Baptist ministers in richly bawdy conversation, giving each other sexual nicknames. They claimed to have heard King tell a supremely tasteless sexual joke about the dead President Kennedy and his wife. At first J. Edgar Hoover jibbed at sending this to Robert Kennedy, but he allowed himself to be persuaded by his colleagues to do so.

Throughout 1964, the FBI did what it could to interest journalists in what Hoover's men saw as evidence of King's immorality. Several, including Ben Bradlee of the *Washington Post*, Ralph McGill and Eugene Patterson of the *Atlanta Constitution* and reporters from the *New York Times*, *Los Angeles Times* and *Chicago Sun Times* were offered material. All refused to touch it. Nelson Rockefeller, the Governor of New York, who was thinking of making a large contribution to the SCLC, and senior officials of the Baptist Church and the World Council of Churches were also approached with dirt on King's private life.

There were, as we shall see, more scandalous incidents involving King's SCLC colleagues, including his brother A. D. King, on a trip to Europe in late 1964, from which King returned in a depressed state – the FBI's listeners twice overheard his wife admitting her concern about him. Meanwhile, Sullivan had concocted a psychological bomb intended to destroy King just as surely as if he had been blown up in the Birmingham church. The FBI laboratory was charged with splicing together the spiciest extracts of the Willard hotel tape. With it, Sullivan himself drafted, on unwatermarked paper, a cruel letter purporting to come from a black man.

King, look into your heart. You know you are a complete fraud and a great liability to all of us Negroes . . . You are no clergyman and you know it . . . you are a colossal fraud and an evil, vicious one at that. You could not believe in God . . . Clearly you don't believe in any personal moral principles . . . King, there is only one thing for you to do. You know what it is . . . There is but one way out for you. You better take it before your filthy fraudulent self is bared to the nation.

King's staff knew that Coretta liked to listen to tapes of her husband's speeches. So when what looked like a box containing a tape arrived at the SCLC's offices, they put it aside for Coretta. She listened to some of the tape and read the letter. Then she called her husband, who summoned Ralph Abernathy, Andrew Young* and a couple of other close friends to listen. He had no doubt where it had come from. And the effect was as Sullivan had intended. King was distraught. He was ashamed, and guilty. His wife said later that he was in general a man plagued by guilt. He was also, as anyone would be, afraid of the sheer malice the package displayed. He told a friend, 'They are out to break me.'

This very real crisis in his personal life exacerbated existing tensions with Coretta. She was already hurt that he had what would come to be called a sexist attitude to her and to marriage. He expected her not to get involved in his work, and to stay at home and look after the children. Now he could not sleep. The FBI's Atlanta office picked up his response. Their reaction was, first, sadistically, to send a fire engine increase his alarm; and second, to send messages to the White House and to the Attorney General, now Nick Katzenbach, reporting King's distress, without explaining the reason for it. Andy Young and Ralph Abernathy bearded Deke DeLoach, who lied: he and the Bureau, he said, knew and cared nothing about King's finances or his private life.

The whole question of the FBI tapes and what they prove, and do not prove, about King's private life must be handled with great care. There is no doubt that he had at least two serious relationships with women other than Coretta, one in Atlanta and one in Los Angeles, which perhaps threatened his marriage, and in addition he had numerous brief, casual affairs. He himself did not seriously deny it, and many of his friends have confirmed it.[13] Many observers noticed that he was surrounded by beautiful young women. He introduced them as secre-

---

* A rising SCLC staff member and later President Carter's ambassador to the United Nations.

taries, but their duties were clearly not exclusively secretarial. Others pointed out that he had extraordinary opportunities. Everywhere he went, from black churches in the South to white fund-raising events in the North, women were attracted by his celebrity and his personality, and made it very plain that they were available. At the same time, one has to keep reminding oneself that the salacious detail on the tapes is known only from accounts by men who did not bother to conceal their contempt and dislike for him. The general proposition that King had a number of extramarital affairs, that he and his friends gave wild parties, and that he sometimes paid prostitutes, is beyond doubt. The detail, on the other hand, and especially those titillating details that could be used to prove his unworthiness, to destroy his reputation and to turn Presidents Kennedy and Johnson and other high officials against him, must be taken with shedloads of salt.

What these episodes do show is that Martin Luther King, though a leader of rare moral vision and courage, was no saint. His conduct, however, easily stands comparison with that of J. Edgar Hoover, William C. Sullivan and the others who set out to destroy him. They coldly used information, true or false, about his private life to frustrate the great public causes he stood for. Their own conduct, especially Hoover's but also that of Lyndon Johnson and especially of John Kennedy, could no more stand malicious exposure than could his.

Hoover, Sullivan and other enemies saw King as merely a hypocrite, and tried mightily to present him to the nation as such. And it is true that there was a genuine contradiction between what he practised and what he preached. This was not just a matter of a cynically philandering Baptist minister. It was all very well for him to say, as he did, 'What I do is only between me and my God.' At some level King knew that he was diminished by the contrast between his conduct and his principles. 'Sex,' he told one interviewer, 'is basically sacred when it is properly used . . . Sex must never be abused in the loose sense in which it is often abused in the modern world.' In a sermon at Ebenezer Baptist Church he once said, 'Each of us is two selves. And the great burden of modern life is to always try to keep that higher self in command . . . There is a civil war going on within all of us.'[14]

*

As Lyndon Johnson swept towards the most decisive electoral victory in American presidential history,* King threw himself into equally obsessive travel and speaking engagements to raise money for the SCLC, and also to urge Negroes to go out and vote for Johnson, though he avoided using the President's name. After six speeches in three days in mid-October he was close to collapse. He checked in to St Joseph's Infirmary in Atlanta with a virus, but essentially for bed rest. The very next morning Coretta called with great news: Martin Luther King Jr had been awarded the Nobel Peace prize.

Earlier in 1964, King had made a brief European tour. He was the guest of the Mayor of Berlin and future German Chancellor Willy Brandt (he, too, eventually to be charged with sexual misbehaviour), and spoke at a church behind the Iron Curtain in East Berlin. In Rome he had an audience with Pope Paul VI, no mean tribute to a black Baptist minister. (The FBI, through Francis Cardinal Spellman of New York, moved heaven and earth to prevent King being granted an audience.) The Nobel Prize took him to an even higher pinnacle of fame. Few have ever more clearly exemplified the biblical axiom that 'a prophet is not without honour, save in his own country, and in his own house'.[15] The honour was to infuriate his enemies – it may have been the last straw that caused Sullivan to send his poison letter – and it brought additional tension in his marriage. It marked the triumphant end of one phase in his journey and the beginning of another, stonier, stretch.

The King party left for Europe on 5 December. Originally they had planned to be a party of six. It proved hard to turn away all those who wanted to join in the celebration, and in the end they flew in two planes, the men in one, the women plus Daddy King in the other. The next day Martin preached at St Paul's Cathedral in London: he was said to be the first non-Anglican to do so. For the first time, he spoke publicly of his strong feelings about apartheid in South Africa. He was beginning to understand that the struggle he was engaged in was part of a world conflict against racism and white supremacy, but also – and the realization

---

* On 3 November Johnson won with 61 per cent of the vote, higher than FDR's 60.8 per cent in 1936 or Nixon's 60.7 per cent in 1971. Ronald Reagan's victory in 1984 was impressive, but because a third-party candidate was in the race Reagan won only 59 per cent of the popular vote.

would affect the whole later course of his life – against war. During his brief London visit he met the great Trinidadian writer, Marxist and former professional cricketer, C. L. R. James, as well as many other peace campaigners, anti-apartheid activists and Indian friends. The experience strengthened his new, broader conception of his mission.

Then on to Oslo.[16] On 9 December Martin and Coretta were formally received by King Olav V of Norway at the royal palace, followed by a dinner at the American embassy that verged on the riotous. One CIA official[17] complained afterwards that he had been asked by no fewer than five members of the King party where they could meet Norwegian girls. That was nothing compared to the scenes later that night in the Grand Hotel. Bayard Rustin, asked by one of the accompanying women to put a stop to what was going on outside, opened his door to see 'two guys come running down the hall chasing a woman [who were] stark naked'. One of them was Martin's brother, A. D. King. Several prostitutes attempted to steal watches and money. Rustin had to ask the hotel's security men not to take them into custody, or it would reflect badly on the Norwegian government. The visit was also marred by an unseemly scene when Ralph and Juanita Abernathy attempted to get into the leading car when the Kings were being driven to the university for Martin to make his Nobel Prize acceptance speech.

The speech was brief but characteristically eloquent. He accepted the prize as a trustee, he said; it was given not to him personally, but to honour the ground crew whose work and sacrifices made possible the 'jet flights to freedom'. He reminded his European listeners that the struggle was not yet won in the American South, but he also broadened his focus to embrace a world dimension, speaking both of South Africa again and of the threat of thermonuclear war. As ever, he found biblical language to clothe his vision – here, of the day when 'the lion and the lamb shall lie down together and every man shall sit under his own vine and fig tree and none shall be afraid'.

He was not free from fear himself; indeed, throughout the visit he was deeply depressed. 'Only Martin's family and close staff members,' said Coretta, 'knew how depressed he was during the entire Nobel trip. It was a time when he ought to have been happy . . . But he was worried that the rumours might hurt the movement and he was concerned about what black people would think. He was always worried about that.'[18] He was shaken by the FBI's enmity and in fear of what they might do to expose him to the American public. He was bracing himself for what he knew would be a hard and dangerous campaign in Alabama, targeting Selma in the heart of the Black Belt. His marriage, even before Coretta opened Sullivan's package, was going through a difficult time. Although she said she never discussed anything so 'trivial' as the possibility that either of them might be 'involved with another person', she must have been aware of absences, looks, rumours. She was shocked when her husband gave the whole of his Nobel Prize, worth over $50,000, to charities linked to the SCLC. The Kings – contrary to the FBI's suspicions of slush funds and Swiss bank accounts – lived frugally. Martin drove a ten-year-old Pontiac, and they lived in a small rented house. Coretta thought some of the money should be put aside for the children's college tuition, but Martin was adamant. In the end it took his friend Harry Belafonte to arrange some provision for the children.

Back in New York, there were moments of glory. At least eight thousand crammed into the 369th Regiment Armory on 142nd Street in Harlem to hear King speak. There were fourteen television cameras at a reception at City Hall. Nelson Rockefeller flew the Kings in his private jet to Washington, where President Johnson received them graciously at the White House. As he remarked to Johnson, he was not used to people saying such nice things about him.

It did not last long. Events were in the saddle,* and would ride him wildly towards new and painful stages of his journey.

---

* 'Things are in the saddle, and ride mankind,' wrote Ralph Waldo Emerson. This is often misquoted as 'Events are in the saddle'.

10

Mississippi Burning

To live habitually as a superior among inferiors, be the
superiority intellectual or economic, is a temptation to
dishonesty and hubris, inevitably deteriorating.

William Alexander Percy, *Lanterns on the Levee* (1941)

When Lyndon Johnson invited Martin Luther King to the White House
on his return from the Nobel Prize acceptance a ceremony, he was only
one of hundreds of pieces in the chess game the old grand master of
politics was playing on half a dozen boards.

Johnson had to establish himself quickly as John Kennedy's legitimate successor, and if possible as his superior, not least when it came
to passing a historic and decisive civil rights act. So by 25 November,
only three days after he flew back from Dallas to Washington with his
predecessor's dead body in Air Force One, Johnson was already
schmoozing with King, calling him Martin. King seized the opportunity to declare that 'one of the greatest tributes that we can pay in
memory of President Kennedy is to try to enact some of the great progressive policies that he sought to initiate.'[1]

'I'm going to support 'em all,' said Johnson, 'and you can count on
that.' Then, slipping in the southern plural to enlist King's sympathy as
a fellow southerner, 'I'll have to have you-all's help. I never needed it
more than I do now.' To pass the civil rights act, Johnson had to put
together a coalition, something the Kennedy brothers sincerely doubted
could be done. He must also think about how he was to be, first, selected
by the Democratic Party as its candidate in the 1964 presidential election, and then re-elected as president in his own right. Normally, it
would not have been too difficult for a sitting president to win his own
party's nomination. But these were not normal times. The country was
stirred, deeply and in unpredictable ways, by the racial crisis which, after
Birmingham, had forced its way to the top of the political agenda.

Already, George Wallace was marching north to challenge President

Johnson by running for the Democratic Party's presidential nomination. He meant to show that the North, too, was angrily divided by the civil rights movement.[2] Subtly changing his tune from the defiant southern leader who had cried, 'Segregation now! Segregation tomorrow! Segregation forever!', Wallace was entering the primary elections in three northern states – Wisconsin, Indiana, Maryland – and in each he was attracting precisely those working-class white voters who were the core of the 'Roosevelt coalition' in the Democratic Party to which Johnson might expect to be heir.

In the North, Wallace did not talk about segregation. He appealed to raw class resentment. In his campaign literature he asked, 'Can a former truck driver who is married to a former dime-store clerk and whose father was a plain dirt farmer be elected President of the United States?' By the end of the 1964 primaries, Wallace had got between 30 and 42 per cent of the vote in those three industrial northern states, enough to show that the answer to his question just might be 'He can.'

So Johnson had to think about the primaries, the first half of the electoral process. He also had to keep himself positioned to beat a Republican in the autumn. Though in the end he destroyed the Republican candidate, Barry Goldwater, by a record margin, he had to keep his eye on the pieces or that board too.

As president, of course, he must concern himself with a myriad other problems: the economy, the Soviet Union, Cuba and other foreign issues. He worried with his intimates about rumours that he might be caught up in scandals, about kick-backs or call girls, generated by the easy-going lifestyle of his former favourite, Bobby Baker.[3] He had to establish himself to the world as a confident, masterful player. He was almost morbidly sensitive to the idea that Americans, and foreigners too, would see him as a crude 'corn-pone' politician from Texas, or, as he put it to one of the Kennedy appointees in his administration, as 'this country-hick, tobacco-chewing Southerner'. He resented, and exaggerated, the contempt he thought sophisticates felt for his southern, his Texan, ways. And that sensitivity took one specific, almost paranoid, form.

Johnson was mortally afraid of 'the Kennedys' – by which he meant both the family and in a wider sense his predecessor's political family – but most especially Robert Kennedy.[4] In his private telephone calls, the obsessional quality of the President's fear of his dead predecessor's brother comes across again and again.[5] Kennedy wanted Johnson to make him Vice-President. Johnson viscerally resisted the idea. 'They're going to try to get us fighting,' Johnson told Kennedy. 'I hope we don't have to.' And a few days later, only half as a joke, Kennedy said he thought J. Edgar Hoover 'sent reports over [to Johnson] about me plotting the overthrow of the government by force and violence'. The President indignantly denied the suggestion. But already the veneer of civility that covered their mutual dislike was beginning to crack.[6]

The analogy with playing chess on several boards at once, however, only goes so far. For the worst of Johnson's difficulty was that each of his problems was linked to the others. To establish his legitimacy, he must commit himself to the civil rights bill. Because he was a southerner, he must do so, visibly, with even more conviction than John Kennedy had shown. To control the primaries, he must show he could pass a civil rights act – but he must also at all costs avoid infuriating the white South and its powerful champions in Congress any more than he absolutely needed to, and at the same time prevent George Wallace eating into his northern working-class support.

In everything, he was at the mercy of events in the struggle that was unfolding in the South. In those events, the role of Martin King would be crucial. Edgar Hoover was telling the President that King was a hypocrite, a monster, the communist agent of foreign conspiracy. Well, thought Johnson, maybe he is, maybe he is not. In any case, he needs me, and I need him. So as 1964 unrolled, the preacher and the president, so different in many ways, found themselves inextricably dependent on one another.

King's situation was scarcely any easier. His Montgomery reputation had been damaged in Albany. Although in the end Birmingham had helped to put civil rights at the top of the national political agenda, the SCLC's strategy in Birmingham had almost failed. Only the 'children's crusade' against Bull Connor's dogs and fire hoses – something Martin had explicitly opposed – had turned defeat into victory. The letter from Birmingham jail and the great speech at the march on Washington would establish Martin's reputation for ever as the most eloquent champion of racial equality. But the SCLC strategy of challenging segregation, state by state and city by city, was not working as reliably or as quickly as King had hoped. More and more people in the movement – in SNCC, in CORE and in The Council of Federated Organizations (COFO, the alliance of both with the local NAACP), which was tackling the toughest resistance of all in Mississippi – were turning to the conviction that voting, not demonstrations, would prove the key to progress.

Another partial success would again call into doubt the credentials of the SCLC and of King as its champion. This happened in a strange place, St Augustine, Florida.[7] The French had settled there first, in 1565, but two years later they were chased away by a Spanish expedition. Founded forty-two years before Jamestown, Virginia, the little town with its narrow streets, Spanish *plaza* and colonial buildings could claim to be the oldest city in the United States, and it earned a modest living attracting tourists on their way to the better-known Florida resorts. Its genteel charm, however, had been shattered by the activity of a very angry black dentist, Robert Hayling, who organized a series of sit-ins to challenge the almost total segregation of the small town that liked to be called the Ancient City. Hayling decided to try to photograph and record a meeting of the very active local Klan. He was spotted and beaten almost to death. When Klansmen drove into the Negro part of town in October, however, they were met by a hail of bullets and one Klansman was killed.

Demonstrations were planned for Easter 1964, and a number of SCLC leaders got involved, especially Hosea Williams, who had organized successful demonstrations in nearby Savannah. What put St Augustine on the front pages nationally was the arrival of a delegation of New England ladies led by the extremely well-connected Mrs Malcolm Peabody, wife of the Episcopal Bishop of Massachusetts, grandmother of seven and flower of upper-class Yankee respectability. With great pluck she waded into a situation well over her head. She was promptly arrested and jailed for attempting to bring the (very pale-skinned) Negro wife of another northern bishop, together with five hastily recruited black cooks, into a white motel.

King and his advisers were attracted by the possibilities of a campaign in St Augustine, not least because they thought the upcoming quatercentenary celebrations would put their campaign on the national map. After a number of reconnaissances, King himself arrived in town in an attempt to persuade Dr Hayling to forswear arms and to mount a series of colourful night marches. These duly took place, provoking a violent response from the Klan led by two very nasty characters, J. B. Stoner from Georgia and the Revd Connie Lynch, a visiting neo-fascist from California. They were reinforced by local allies in the shape of more than a thousand members of the Ancient City Hunting Club, led by a caricature of the beer-bellied redneck racist, one Holstead 'Hoss' Manucy. In the second week in June, King was once again arrested on a public order charge and spent two days in jail before being bailed out to go to preach at Yale.

Events unfolded in a fashion at once serio-comic and potentially very dangerous indeed. A group of rabbis desegregated the swimming-pool at the motel where Mrs Peabody had been arrested. A later 'swim-in' at the beach could have turned extremely nasty, as Hoss Manucy's thugs tried to lure Hosea Williams and his men out into deep water to be drowned. The local police blatantly sympathized with the Klan and its allies, but the Governor of Florida, Farris Bryant, anxious to keep the federal government from intervening, sent in a couple of hundred state lawmen to prevent serious violence. By late June, King and his colleagues were keen to get out of a situation that had failed to have the positive national impact they had anticipated. Once again, non-violent demonstrations alone did not deliver the substantial progress southern blacks now expected. In the meantime other, ultimately more significant, dramas were being played out.

In June 1963 President Kennedy, acknowledging the urgency of the situation, had indicated at long last that he would support a strong civil rights bill. Before it can receive the President's signature and become law, however, a bill must travel along an obstacle course in which its original intent risks being substantially modified, even watered down. In the early 1960s, a civil rights bill would have to run the gauntlet of a whole series of committees, first in the House of Representatives, then in the Senate. Many of these committees were chaired and more or less tightly controlled by veteran southerners, some of them notorious opponents of any use whatsoever of federal power to interfere with the South's 'way of life'.* In late October 1963, the civil rights legislation had cleared the first hurdle when it was 'reported out' of the House Judiciary Committee. The legislation had already been softened by the senior Republican, an elderly and conservative member from Ohio, William McCulloch. To be voted on by the whole House, though, it would need 'a rule', defining exactly how it would be debated and voted on, and that would have to come from the House Rules Committee, chaired by the most stubborn and reactionary segregationist in the entire House, 'Judge' Howard Smith of Virginia.

Then came the Kennedy assassination. Whatever expectations of Lyndon Johnson might have had, he moved very swiftly to make it plain that he was not less, but far more, determined than his predecessor to pass a decisive civil rights act. Shrewdly, he did not take an active part in lobbying himself, but deputed that to Robert Kennedy, Nick Katzenbach and Burke Marshall at the Justice Department, to Clarence Mitchell (the NAACP's veteran lobbyist in Washington) and to the well-known liberal and labour lawyer, Joe Rauh. The President limited himself to saying, publicly and often, that he wanted a strong bill and would not compromise in order to get it.

By mid-January 1964, when President Johnson met Martin King, with the other major civil rights leaders – Roy Wilkins of the NAACP, Whitney Young of the National Urban League and James Farmer of CORE – in the White House to get them, too, involved in lobbying Congressmen, it was clear that Smith would do everything he could to hold up the legislation. He held hearings at which only the most conservative members of his committee were asked to speak, and they did so in the most dilatory way. Smith's lock on the bill could be opened only by a 'discharge petition', which would take a majority of the whole house, or 228 votes, and Johnson had only about 178. So the President, with more than his usual mixture of charm and menace, persuaded the

---

* Because the South, and in particular the 'Deep South', was, at least as far as congressional elections were concerned, virtually a one-party state, and because, until the rebellions and reforms of the 1970s, sub committee chairs of congressional committees were allotted on the basis of seniority alone, the South was massively overrepresented in the power structure of Congress. This was especially true when the Democrats were in control of Congress, as they were for all but four years between 1933 and 1969.

Speaker and the Republican leader, Charlie Halleck of Indiana, to mount a rebellion against Judge Smith in his own committee.* J. Edgar Hoover did not help by going before Judge Smith's committee and testifying that the civil rights movement was riddled with communists. But by 30 January the House Rules Committee voted 11 to 4 to bring the bill to the floor of the whole House for debate on the following day, with a final vote scheduled for 10 February.

On 3 February the House took up 'Title II', the section of the bill that guaranteed equal access to public accommodations. Southerners appealed to the crassest prejudices, suggesting that white barbers could not cut black hair and even that white chiropodists would find that black people's feet smelled. It brought them no honour, and it did them no good. Title II passed by 116 votes to 69. Five days later Judge Smith tried what he no doubt intended as an obstructionist ploy, but which was to have immense and, ironically, beneficent consequences. Title VII banned discrimination on the basis of race, religion and national origin. What, asked the old Judge, of discrimination by sex? He may have imagined that would make the bill harder to pass, though to be fair he had himself supported an equal rights amendment for women since 1945 and his sister had served in the state legislature of West Virginia. At any rate, five of the eleven women members of the House rose to speak in favour of extending Title VII to cover discrimination against women. The amendment passed by 168 to 133, backed by a strange alliance of segregationists and feminists.

Smith's obstruction succeeded in adding not a single racially reactionary amendment to the civil rights bill as envisaged by President Kennedy and as marginally strengthened in the House Judiciary Committee, chaired by an old New York radical, Emmanuel Celler. The bill passed the full House by a vote of 290 to 130.

Now it faced its hardest test, in the Senate. The Founding Fathers had given the Senate the privilege of unlimited debate, precisely so as

---

* He won Halleck over, the Congressman told the press, by asking him to breakfast and serving just the kind of sausage a country boy would appreciate, (author's recollection). Although Senator Goldwater, already likely to be the Republican candidate in the autumn, had come out against the civil rights bill, Halleck was probably influenced more by his sense of the need to keep his party from seeming too reactionary than by gastronomic sympathy.

to protect the states from being tyrannized by a majority. In 1919, faced with the Versailles Treaty and the debate over the League of Nations, the Senate had adopted Rule 22, allowing the Senate to apply 'cloture', ending debate immediately by a vote of two-thirds of its membership. (Later, in 1975, that requirement was reduced from 67 to 60 votes.)

The pro-civil rights forces, liberal Democrats and some moderate Republicans, could easily amass the fifty-one votes needed to pass the bill. But to get the bill to the floor they needed sixteen more. The diehard opposition was led by Johnson's intimate friend, Senator Richard Russell of Georgia. But Johnson said to him in so many words: 'If you get in my way, I'm going to run you down!' A photo records the moment, Johnson jutting his face out at his friend, the picture of aggressive determination.[8] There were sixty-seven Democrats in the Senate, but Russell would be able to count on twenty of those, including his own, plus the vote of one Republican, John Tower of Texas. The liberals would therefore need to harvest at least some Republican votes. Some would have to come from Republican moderates (a species that is now all but extinct) like Jacob Javits of New York and Clifford Case of New Jersey. The bottom line was that the bill could not achieve cloture without the agreement of the Republican leadership.

The crucial figure was that of Everett Dirksen of Illinois, the Republican leader in the Senate, haggard under his tight white curls (he suffered from stomach ulcers) and given to flowery oratory. He was often compared to a Shakespearean actor-manager. Dirksen was instinctively conservative, but he was also proud of his state's and his party's inheritance from Abraham Lincoln, and he aspired to earn the gratitude of the republic. On such a man, pompous, ambitious and ultimately well intentioned, Lyndon Johnson could play like a master musician. It was a sign of Dirksen's willingness to be persuaded that he appointed as his floor manager Thomas Kuchel, a (relative) liberal from California who was the number two in the Republican hierarchy in the Senate.

First came the filibuster. Russell and his men could not go down without demonstrating at least symbolically their commitment to the fight. The truth was that Russell and his fellow diehards (among them James Eastland and John Stennis of Mississippi) were always destined to lose. Younger Republicans might be conservative, but they were not as tied, as men of Russell's generation were, to the absolute primacy of preserving segregation for ever. Attempts at compromise were pushed aside both by Russell and by the liberal leader, Hubert Humphrey of Minnesota, whose national career had begun when he came out for civil rights legislation fifteen years earlier.

Humphrey opened the debate by putting it in a world context. 'If freedom fails here in America,' he asked, 'what hope can we have for it surviving elsewhere?' He quoted travel guidebooks to show that there were more hotels in the South that would accept dogs than would register black guests. The southerners, in reply, 'droned and drawled' for hour after hour. At one point, when there was talk of compromise, Martin Luther King played a crucial part. He told a national television audience that he would rather have 'no bill at all' than negotiate away the banning of discrimination in employment or the desegregation of public accommodations. He was only one of many clergy to fight the good fight. Ministers from all the national Protestant denominations (though not white southern evangelicals or Pentecostals) joined with Roman Catholic priests and nuns and rabbis to lobby the Republicans. Militant black groups began to demonstrate their impatience with the filibuster with disruptive tactics, such as a 'stall-in' of thousands of cars on the Long Island Expressway, one of New York City's busiest commuter routes. Mainstream civil rights organizations quickly reacted, aware of the danger of a white backlash, to douse down the wave of demonstrations.

By late March, after nearly three months of southern rhetoric, Dirksen was ready to compromise. No army is stronger, he misquoted Victor Hugo in his diary, than an idea whose time has come. There were still southerners who could not accept that. Robert Byrd of West Virginia, a former member of the Ku Klux Klan and later an eminent defender of the Senate's privileges, made the final defiant speech, lasting more than fourteen hours. The night before the vote on cloture, Humphrey called Johnson and said he had 68 votes. By morning, he had 71. The roll-call began. It was one of the classic scenes in the history of the Senate Chamber. In alphabetical order, the senators said either 'Aye' or 'No'. There was a moment of drama when Clair Engle, Democrat of California, who was dying of a brain tumour, was carried in. He could not speak, he could hardly move, but he pointed painfully to his eye. Carl Hayden of Arizona, another Democrat, at eighty-six the oldest member, wanted to vote no, but did not want to let his party down. He was told his vote was not needed, and he could vote as he wanted. In the end 44 Democrats and 27 Republicans voted for cloture. Nine days later, after more than a hundred roll-call votes on amendments, the Senate voted by 73 to 27 for final passage. When the bill went back to the House of Representatives as amended, but essentially in the form it had been introduced by President Kennedy exactly a year before Senate passage, the House endorsed it again by 289 to 126.

Martin and Coretta King had hoped to have a quiet August in 1964. Their marriage had been under strain, not just from the FBI's attentions, but also from Coretta's feeling that Martin spent too much time away from the children. There was a trivial but revealing row when the children went into hospital to have their tonsils removed: Martin, in Washington for the signing ceremony of the civil rights bill, forgot to call home to find out how the operations had gone. They were lent an apartment by friends in New York, and planned to take the children to see the sights of the big city. Although they managed to visit the World's Fair, where Marty, aged five, thought it was wrong that the family should be taken to the front of the queue to see the exhibits, his father spent the summer in a maelstrom of political and racial tension. The SCLC was angrily divided. Jim Bevel and his wife Diane were pressing for an all-out voter-registration drive in Alabama, while Hosea Williams, excited by the dramas of Savannah and St Augustine, argued for more demonstrations. Even more difficult for King were the tensions and invidious comparisons caused by the situation in Mississippi.

In 1963 Robert Moses, one of the few figures in the civil rights movement who could challenge Martin King in terms of sheer moral authority, had started a voter-registration drive in the Delta. That vast oval plain, celebrated in the novels and stories of William Faulkner, with cotton plantations interspersed with woodland, is some two hundred miles from north to south. It is not the delta of the Mississippi in the usual sense, though the great river is its western boundary: the geographical delta lies downriver from New Orleans. This is the heart and epitome of the Deep South, where for more than a century black men worked in the broiling sun under the guns of white bosses. It was no accident that this was the home of the blues, the music in which black sharecroppers and landless labourers expressed their sorrow and their dreams. By the 1960s, the cotton economy was being transformed by mechanical picking. The cotton kingdom was moving west to California. Many young black men and women moved north, to the factories of Detroit and the 'black metropolis' – as it was called in a classic 1945 study of urban poverty – on the South Side of Chicago. But the Mississippi social system, the harsh enforcement of white supremacy and rigid segregation, stayed behind.

Fewer than 7 per cent of blacks in Mississippi, who made up almost half the population of the state, were registered to vote. They were prevented by numerous dodges, including cynically unfair literacy tests in which black labourers and maids were given questions to answer that would have baffled PhD students, while white morons were at perfect liberty to vote. It was then that SNCC, CORE and the local NAACP joined forces to start COFO, the Council of Federated Organizations, to challenge this injustice. Since 1961 Moses and a handful of volunteers had been working to change the system by going into rural black communities. For 1964, COFO planned two new initiatives: 'freedom schools' to help poor, semi-literate blacks to challenge the laws and regulations that banned them from voting, and a Mississippi Freedom Democratic Party, to compete with the state's all-white delegation to the 1964 presidential nominating convention to take place in Atlantic City. It was a desperately dangerous business, both for the blacks and for the white volunteers who were trying to help them. The countryside and its little towns were ruled by often brutal sheriffs and their deputies. Many of them joined the 'White Knights' of the Ku Klux Klan, which was winning new recruits as the propaganda against 'race mixing' and federal interference in the South's tradition's intensified.

In April Sam Bowers, the Imperial Wizard of the Mississippi Klan, made a speech in Neshoba County. 'We are here to discuss,' he began, 'what to do about COFO's nigger–communist invasion of Mississippi'. The Klan picked out as its special target one of the white volunteers, Mickey Schwerner, from New York. He was a political radical, he was a Jew, and he wore a beard. The Klansmen called him 'Goatee'. On 30 May, Schwerner and a black volunteer called J. E. Chaney went to Mount Zion, a black Methodist church near Philadelphia, the seat of Neshoba County, to check out its suitability for a freedom school. COFO had been busy recruiting almost a thousand volunteers, four-fifths of them white, from northern universities, many of them from the most prestigious and expensive ones. On 14 June the first batch of these volunteers arrived at a small campus in Ohio for training in non-violence. They were taught to protect themselves as best they could, and they were warned that they must expect some of their number to be killed.[9]

On 16 June the Klan went to Mount Zion Church hoping to find 'Goatee' there. He was not, but they firebombed the church anyway. Five days later Schwerner, Chaney and another volunteer, Andrew Goodman, went to Mount Zion to see what had happened. On the way back they were stopped for speeding by Deputy Sheriff Cecil Price, a Klan member. He detained them for hours, released them, then after nightfall arrested them again. They were driven to a remote place, where Schwerner and Goodman were shot and Chaney, the African-American, was first savagely beaten, possibly tortured, then shot. Schwerner's last words, recorded by the sheriff's men, were 'I know exactly how you feel, sir'.[10]

News that the three civil rights workers had disappeared arrived at Oxford, Ohio, where the volunteers were being trained to go to Mississippi, with devastating effect. Bob Moses was at his best, comforting Schwerner's wife Rita, and doing what he could to raise the morale of the terrified volunteers while urging those who had no stomach for the fight to go home while there was still time. Lyndon Johnson, alerted by James Farmer, told his civil rights aide Lee White that he had asked Hoover to 'fill up Mississippi with FBI men, infiltrate everything and haul 'em in' – meaning the Klansmen – 'by the dozens'.

For Johnson, indeed for the whole nation as the summer of 1964 wore on, events seemed to be breaking at an ever dizzier pace. On 2 July, the civil rights bill passed Congress and Johnson signed it, murmuring to his aides as he did so that he might have lost the South for the Democratic Party for a generation. Before the month was over, rioting had broken out in Harlem after a white cop shot dead a black teenager, fifteen-year-old James Powell. Disorder spread to other cities, first in New York State and then across the country. In addition, newspaper readers were beginning to hear of the doings of Malcolm X and of his murderous feud with Elijah Muhammad and the other leaders of the Nation of Islam.

King was bounced around on the surface of these events like a ping-pong ball on a jet of water. He was desperate to get out of St Augustine, but he could only leave, he said, if he could leave with honour, if he could honestly declare a victory.[11] There was so much else that needed to be done. Black communities in Selma and other Alabama towns were begging him to come to their help. In early July he went out to the West Coast to give evidence about civil rights before the platform committee of the Republican convention. It was about to nominate Barry Goldwater as its candidate for President, after cheering to the rafters his ringing statement that 'extremism in the defence of liberty is no vice'. King did not conceal his dismay. He called the nomination 'unfortunate and disastrous', saying that Goldwater's new brand of conservatism 'gave aid and comfort to the racist'.

Then he headed for Mississippi, where another front in his campaign was opening up. There, for the first time openly, the hostility between King and the SCLC preachers, on the one hand, and the dungaree-clad field secretaries of SNCC broke the surface. When King spoke, they called him under their breath 'de Lawd', the derisive nickname by which they would refer to him for the rest of his life. King had been threatened that the worst might happen if he set foot in Mississippi. He knew his life was in danger, though J. Edgar Hoover, unwillingly and under pressure from the White House, arranged protection for him. King was a reluctant hero, but whenever his courage was tested, in the end he always did what he had to do. He had been angry when SCLC staffers told him he had no alternative but to go to Mississippi, and had stalked off, but he knew they were right.

On 23 July there was a summit meeting with James Forman of SNCC, James Farmer of CORE, Bob Moses of COFO, Bayard Rustin and others at the black Tougaloo College. There were issues to be decided on, not least the planned challenge by the black Mississippi Freedom Democratic Party at the national party's convention in Atlantic City. Lyndon Johnson wanted the convention to be his coronation, and planned to use it to humiliate Robert Kennedy by banning him from the vice-presidency. King and Rustin were insistent that the civil rights volunteers must not spoil Johnson's great day. But the young men, toughened by months of watching their rear-view mirror to see if a carload of Klan killers was after them, did not want to be told to behave themselves.

King had hoped for a brief vacation, but there was no chance of that. After James Powell was shot dead, New York's mayor Robert Wagner called him in to help calm Harlem down. The rioting brought the split in the movement on to the national stage. Roy Wilkins of the NAACP wanted a moratorium on all demonstrations so as to head off a potential white backlash, and Whitney Young supported him. Farmer of CORE and John Lewis of SNCC were bitterly opposed. King told Rustin he was afraid of being called an Uncle Tom. The way out of his political impasse was to emphasize what had been his perception of the key to the African-American dilemma all along – the search for economic justice. But it was all too easy for this to seem like a diversion from the rage in the streets.

Meanwhile white Mississippi was insisting that the disappearance of Schwerner, Chaney and Goodman was a hoax. Jim Eastland, the state's powerful Senator and chairman of the Senate Judiciary Committee, no less, tried to persuade Lyndon Johnson of this. 'I believe it's a publicity stunt,' he said. However little sympathy Hoover might have for civil rights, though, he had made his reputation by getting his man, and not always by orthodox methods of detection. He realized that the Bureau's reputation depended on finding out what had happened in Neshoba County. So a mafioso from New York, Gregory 'the Grim Reaper' Scarpa, was recruited and briefed. He was offered $30,000 if he could find out the truth. Having lured a Klan suspect out of his shop on the pretext of buying a television, he beat him for a while, then stuck a pistol into the man's mouth and said, 'Tell me the fucking truth or I'll blow your fucking brains out.' He was told the bodies were out at the 'old Jolly farm', buried in a new earth dam, and there they proved to be.

The bodies were unearthed with a bulldozer on 4 August. Two days before that, and twelve thousand miles away, the mysterious episode known as the Tonkin Gulf incident took place. South Vietnamese clandestine operations, authorized by President Johnson in April 1964 as

Op Plan 34-A, had been attacking bases from which the North Vietnamese were mounting operations against South Vietnam. At the same time US intelligence vessels, so-called De Soto patrols, were gathering electronic intelligence on North Vietnam and on China. North Vietnamese patrol boats, probably on orders from a local commander, came out and attacked a US destroyer, the *Maddox*. The destroyer, supported by aircraft from the US carrier *Ticonderoga*, sank one patrol boat and damaged two others. The incident enabled President Johnson to obtain from Congress the 'Tonkin Gulf resolution', with only two negative votes in the Senate. The episode, systematically distorted by the Johnson administration at the time, laid the foundations for the expansion of the war – which was ultimately to destroy the Johnson presidency, and to have immense implications for Martin Luther King's career. But in the immediate future, both men were more concerned with the Democratic Party's national convention in Atlantic City.

For President Johnson, the 1964 convention was the culmination of his struggle to establish himself as President in his own right, a struggle which in his own mind, largely took the form of resisting Robert Kennedy's claim to be his vice-presidential running-mate. Johnson achieved this, after teasing his rivals and the media, by appointing Hubert Humphrey, the hero of the civil rights bill, vice-president. And he did indeed turn the convention into a coronation for himself, though not without some anguish as to whether he really wanted to be president at all. (The issue was apparently resolved by an affectionately supportive note from his wife on the eve of the convention.[12]

For King, more important was the attempt of the Mississippi Freedom Democratic Party to gatecrash Lyndon Johnson's party. On 6 August the MFDP held its own convention at the Negro masonic temple in Jackson. It heard an impassioned keynote address from Ella Baker, and a measured assessment of the political situation from Bob Moses. Then Joe Rauh, the white liberal lawyer who represented the United Auto Workers in Washington and who was retained to argue the MFDP's case before the Democratic convention's credentials committee, laid out the odds. If the breakaway party could collect 10 per cent of the 108 votes on the committee, or just eleven votes, then it could bring to the floor of the convention a motion to seat the (mainly black) Mississippians either instead of, or alongside, the all-white party regulars.

Once the issue could be brought to the floor, the MFDP's chances were not negligible, because in November white Democratic politicians in Mississippi and also in Alabama were already beginning to peel off in support of Barry Goldwater and the Republican ticket. Lyndon Johnson was desperate, of course, to avoid a major fracture of the party. He was also keen to play down the MFDP's case, for fear that, even if there were no major Dixie rebellion in the party, too much damage could be done to the Democrats' reputation by what the Mississippi radicals might say. So when Joe Rauh produced Fannie Lou Hamer to give evidence to the credentials committee about how she had been beaten and insulted when she tried to register to vote, the White House's men arranged for her testimony to be heard in a room too small for TV cameras.

The Johnson administration offered the MFDP a parsimonious compromise. Promises were made for future conventions. But for the present, the rebels would be given only two tickets for 'at large' delegates: one for the MFDP's leader Aaron Henry and one for a white radical, the Revd Edwin King. None of the white regulars would lose his seat. The MFDP refused the compromise, and there were unseemly scenes as both delegations tried to grab seats. King had given evidence to the credentials committee in his usual sonorous style, but he was marginalized in the convention's furious politicking. Joe Rauh, Hubert Humphrey, even Bob Moses had more taste and more talent for that.

Perhaps the clearest indication he gave of how lucidly he saw the political changes taking place came after the convention and after his return from his audience with the Pope, in the speech he made to five hundred delegates at a convention of the new Southern Christian Leadership Foundation. King admitted that the situation was delaying, and perhaps cancelling, plans for a systematic attack on the denial of voting rights in Alabama. He analysed the implications of three major events in 1964: the murder of the three civil rights workers in Mississippi, the spread of rioting to the northern cities, and the impact of the presidential election. Once again, he demonstrated that, while he had little talent for political manoeuvring and manipulation, he had a great gift for grasping the strategic impact of events. For the tumult of 1964 would indeed be the prelude to a new phase in American politics, and a turning-point in King's own political career.

11

The Hinge

There goes the South!
> President Lyndon B. Johnson on signing the Voting Rights
> Act, 1965

The five years from the assassination of John Kennedy in November 1963 to the election of Richard Nixon in 1968 were the hinge on which the door closed on one epoch in American history and opened on another. Those years saw the end of Democratic domination in national politics and the rise of a new ideological conservatism, replacing the liberal consensus created by the New Deal. That new right, moreover, was making long strides towards capturing the Republican Party, one of the two parties that had shared political power in America since the Civil War.

They were years of rage. American society was convulsed by the convergence of the civil rights revolution and the war in South-East Asia. An age of conformism gave way to pervasive doubt. In the political system, in the universities, in the churches and the armed forces, at school and at work, in marriage and in the family – everywhere authority was challenged, questioned, insulted and ultimately reasserted on wholly different terms. Public rage was matched by deep, often anguished introspection. Abruptly, a complacent, conventional society began to question everything.

In Martin Luther King's life they were to be years of triumph and frustration, physical and mental exhaustion, changed goals, changed circumstances and methods, defeat, doubt and ultimate martyrdom. Sometimes King seemed close to living out his dream. Often, those were the moments when tragedy struck, and fulfilment was snatched away. He had to fight on half a dozen fronts at once: against vicious racism in the Deep South and against complacent indifference elsewhere, against brutal policemen and tricky politicians, against extremists within his own movement and false friends outside it. There were divisions within every regiment of the army that he was striving to lead, between movement activists, black preachers and liberal politicians alike. There were fierce differences over tactics and strategy, between those whose priority was social equality and those focusing on the right to vote. There was an underlying argument between the apostles of non-violence and those who thought non-violence futile and even unmanly.

Yet, in spite of all the difficulties and setbacks, the fight he fought in those years established him as a heroic figure, of lasting consequence for the character of American life. People recognized that in his lifetime. As his friend and wise counsellor Stanley Levison told him, he was slow to realize that he had become one of the most powerful figures in the country – 'a leader now not merely of Negroes but of millions of whites'.

In those years, the temper and even the name of King's first followers had changed. Negroes now insisted on becoming 'blacks', but were not yet African-Americans. In their thousands, then in their millions, they began to do what King had most wanted them to do: to stand up and claim their rights, without self-doubt or fear. Some of them began to demand, not desegregation or integration, but black power. The battlefield of their struggle for freedom, rights and equality shifted to the whole country. In the South, black people won, first the right to be treated as at least nominal equals in the eyes of the law, then the political power that comes from the right to vote. Abruptly, white people across the nation were made aware by rioting in hundreds of towns and cities that black people were scarcely, if at all, more free or equal, and hardly, if at all, more desegregated, in the North than in the South. The focus of struggle shifted from de jure legal equality in the South to de facto economic equality in the North. New York, Los Angeles, Chicago, Detroit, Washington itself, the cultural, entertainment, commercial, industrial and political capitals of the United States, all heard the sounds of police sirens, strident demonstrators, angry mobs, gunshots.

The consequences of this time of troubles were felt in every street in America, and in every corner of the American psyche. Chains of action and reaction, many of them ultimately anchored in racial conflict and racial fears,[1] transformed the America of the Roosevelt coalition into the America of the conservative ascendancy. The working-out of this process of transformation took time: twelve years elapsed between Nixon's victory in 1968 and the Reagan landslide of 1980. But the core of the process was crammed into a few weeks in the spring of 1965. That was the crucible in which all the conflicts troubling the nation reached incandescence.

Over a mere dozen weeks, the actors at the centre of the stage – not least Lyndon Johnson and Martin Luther King – were left no time for reflection, scarcely even breathing space. The briefest chronology makes the point. Two major plots were unfolding simultaneously, fragmented and confused by other threads and themes. In February and early March, the Johnson White House had to cope with a series of breaking waves, each of which rocked King's frail boat and almost swamped it.

From 1 to 5 February he was in jail in Selma, Alabama. On 6 February, the Viet Cong attacked the American Special Forces camp at Pleiku in the central highlands of Vietnam, killing ten American soldiers, wounding over a hundred, and destroying ten American aircraft. That led directly to the first American bombing of North Vietnam.* A couple of days later King was in Washington, discussing with the Attorney General the drafting of a new and decisive bill to guarantee southern Negroes' right to vote: legislation that would, as the Voting Rights Act of 1965, turn American politics upside down – with the right side up. On 7 March, the world watched in amazement as Alabama police, state troopers and assorted goons charged into a peaceful march of black and white clergy in Selma with clubs, bull whips and electric cattle prods. The next day 3,500 United States Marines, the first to deploy in Vietnam, went ashore at Danang. The civil rights revolution and the war in Vietnam were a double helix. Twisted together in a few weeks during the spring of 1965, they changed America. Given American power and influence at the time, that changed the world.

*

---

* Over the next eight years the United States dropped more ordnance on that middle-sized developing country than was dropped by all sides in the Second World War in Europe and Asia combined.

On 2 January 1965 Martin King drove across country from Atlanta to Selma, in the Alabama Black Belt, with his oldest friend and sharer in his double-dating adventures, Ralph Abernathy. As they went, King told Abernathy that he had decided to make him his successor. He was well aware that his life was in danger, and the Kennedy assassination had made everyone in political life sensitive to the danger of dying without an appropriate heir. King was also aware of Abernathy's jealousy of his friend's reputation and success. There had been that unseemly scene on the day of the Nobel Prize ceremony in Oslo, when the Abernathys had tried to push their way into the same limousine as the Kings and had been relegated by Norwegian protocol to a less prominent vehicle. Ralph Abernathy's resentment signalled only one of a whole network of feuds and quarrels within the SCLC. Hosea Williams and Jim Bevel were at daggers drawn. Everyone had resented the pretension of Wyatt Walker to represent King, while Andy Young was detested by many for his virtues of modesty and charm. On the long drive the two preachers, quick as ever to switch from moral earnestness to an engaging, almost adolescent ribaldry, amused themselves by adlibbing each other's funeral sermons.

They were going to stay in Selma with old friends who typified the network of bonds that linked those comparatively few blacks who had achieved some status in life in spite of Jim Crow. Sullivan Jackson, 'Sully', was a dentist who had led an unsuccessful campaign to win easier registration for educated Negroes in the town. His wife Jean was a childhood friend of Abernathy's wife Juanita, who was also the great-niece of Coretta King's first music teacher in nearby Perry County. Ralph and Martin celebrated their arrival in a friendly home with a pillow fight. It was a comfort to both to have a base with such hospitable old friends. But the fight they were about to find themselves in was anything but playful.

On a bend in the Alabama River,[2] Selma, the county seat of Dallas County, was then a country town of some twenty thousand people, two-thirds of them black. It was a citadel of segregation. The Jim Crow system was kept in place there, as in neighbouring counties on either side of Montgomery, fifty miles to the east, by the denial of the vote to all but a handful of black people. In two nearby counties, Lowndes and Wilcox, no blacks at all were registered to vote.* In Selma, almost total deprival was maintained by a loaded interpretation of literacy tests set by state law. That unfair system was ultimately kept in place by economic boycotting and by the strong right arm of the police who saw maintaining the racial code as their first duty.

But white leadership in Selma, as in much of the South, was passing to a new generation. Where once town and county had been ruled by a 'Bourbon' oligarchy of big plantation owners, the new mayor, Joe Smitherman, was a young refrigerator salesman. A firm segregationist, he nevertheless saw himself as a modernizer who would defend segregation by moderate means, and presented himself as the representative of a new business class that was 'too busy to hate', as the business leadership in Atlanta liked to say. His idea was to offer to pave the streets in the Negro neighbourhoods if the Negroes in gratitude would keep Martin Luther King out.

In Albany, King had been frustrated by Sheriff Laurie Pritchett, who was wily enough to avoid confrontation for the most part. In Birmingham, he had faced defeat from the undisguised violence of Bull Connor. In Selma, the civil rights forces had to cope with both styles of resistance. The maintenance of law and the racially repressive order was in the hands of two sharply contrasting men. The town's police and fire chief was the urbane Wilson Baker, who had once seriously considered studying for the Lutheran ministry. He tried to kill the civil rights movement, if not with kindness, at least with suavity. The sheriff of Dallas County was Jim Clark, a loud-mouthed bully of the old school, armed with pistol, club and electric cattle prod. The two men despised one another, and Baker's dislike of Clark was reinforced by the fact that Clark had beaten him in a close and bad-tempered election for sheriff.

Two separate causes had drawn King to Selma. The less important

* Voting in the United States has traditionally been regarded as a privilege rather than as a right. Historically this is because each of the two national parties had an interest in keeping blocks of people from voting. The Democrats supported their southern wing by denying the vote to black people in the South, while the essentially Protestant Republican Party resisted (albeit with limited success) the spread of the vote to Catholic and Jewish immigrants in the North. On this whole subject see Professor Alexander Keyssar of Harvard, *The Right to Vote: The Contested History of Democracy in the United States*, New York, Basic Books, 2001.

was an invitation from Amelia Boynton. A number of Negro women had quit their jobs at a care home in sympathy for two colleagues who had been disciplined for taking part in a Freedom Day after the murder of the four girls at Sixteenth Street Baptist in Birmingham. Mrs Boynton wanted King to help buy modern sewing-machines so that these women could support themselves as seamstresses. On a much bigger scale were the ambitions of the Alabama project promoted by Jim Bevel and his wife Diane Nash. To commemorate the Birmingham victims the Bevels proposed to stage what amounted to a non-violent revolution in Alabama, focusing on winning the vote for every Negro in the state. Their plan envisaged emasculating the state government by means of strikes and other industrial action and at the same time attempting to persuade the federal government to cut its funding to the state. In order to do this Bevel wanted to send a 'non-violent army' into Alabama, whose leaders and followers alike would be willing to go to jail and stay there for as long as it took. (The Bevels' marriage was a disaster. Bevel is said to have slept with every female member of the movement willing to be seduced, including the wives of colleagues who were in prison for their civil rights activities. Diane Nash contrasted physically as well as in style with her country-bred, volcanically emotional husband. By now, humiliated by his infidelities, she had thrown Jim out of the matrimonial home, but she still worked loyally for the cause.)

By the time King arrived in Selma at the beginning of 1965 the Bevel plan in its full version had been abandoned as impracticable. King was determined, however, to mount a major campaign in the Alabama Black Belt. A local judge, James Hare, had issued a draconian order banning all meetings of more than three Negroes. (Hare was a believer in what he called scientific racism; his hobby was identifying the physical characteristics of Negroes according to their putative descent from various African tribes or nations.) King arrived at Brown Chapel, a large red-and-white brick building with twin towers, and preached to seven hundred local people. They might have been disunited, but they were determined enough to ignore Judge Hare's injunction. King's focus was now squarely on the vote. 'We are not asking,' he ended, 'we are demanding, the ballot.'

For the next two weeks he was in Atlanta and Washington, occupied among many other things with the personal and political fall-out of the FBI's recent blackmailing operation. On 14 January he was back in Selma, staying this time not at the Sullivan Jacksons' but at the Hotel Albert. This is by a wide margin the most notable building in Selma, an elaborately carved replica in wood of the Doge's Palace in Venice, built in the flush times of the cotton boom before the Civil War. ('That's slave work,' an elderly African-American bellhop proudly told me when I registered there myself that spring.)

When King checked in, he was confronted by George Lincoln Rockwell of the American Nazi Party, who challenged him to debate. King invited him to address a mass meeting at Brown Chapel. At the hotel, when he went to speak to another near-fascist white supremacist, one James Robinson of the National States Rights Party, Robinson punched him in the face, knocking him down, and kicked him in the groin. King was rescued by his brother A.D. King and Wilson Baker. Willy-nilly, Selma was integrating. King went on to lead a march to register voters at the courthouse. On that first day, the demonstrations were handled by Baker, who succeeded in restraining Clark. The next day Clark arrested sixty-two people and, in front of national press and TV cameras, dragged Amelia Boynton by the collar halfway down the block. Baker told the reporters Clark was 'out of control'.

Two days after King and his party integrated the Hotel Albert, Lyndon Johnson was inaugurated as president in his own right. Almost immediately he was caught up in the escalating crisis in South Vietnam. On 27 January, the day that, despite all the efforts of the FBI and local segregationists to denigrate him, fourteen hundred Atlantans paid for tickets to a city banquet to celebrate King's Nobel Prize, there was a military coup in Saigon. Soon Johnson was getting confidential reports from General Maxwell Taylor, his ambassador there, as well as from Robert McNamara, the Defense Secretary, and McGeorge Bundy his National Security Advisor, that the United States was losing the war against the Communist VietCong guerrillas.

In Selma, by the end of the month, dozens more had been arrested in spite of a restraining order by a federal judge. A positive sign from the SCLC's point of view was that a hundred teachers, normally a cautious segment of the Negro community, marched defiantly to the courthouse. On 1 February King himself defied Judge Hare's banning order and led a march to the jail. Now Baker arrested him, Abernathy and 265 others, and in the afternoon they were joined in prison by five hundred schoolchildren. Over the next two days a total of 2,600 demonstrators were sent to jail, more than a tenth of the population.

On 5 February the *New York Times* published a 'Letter from Martin Luther King, Jr., from a Selma, Alabama Jail', which pointed out that there were more black people incarcerated in Selma than there were black voters. The next day King sent Andy Young, from jail, a list of twelve points to be borne in mind. They give a revealing insight into King's priorities at that moment. The strategic goal was voter registration, but the tactical focus was on keeping national attention on Selma. Young was to call President Johnson direct, to persuade him to intervene. He was also to 'keep some activity alive every night this week', including a night march to 'let Clark show his true colors'. There is a sense in which King, in Selma, was indeed, as his opponents claimed and as some historians have agreed, engaging in 'non-violent provocation', relying on Jim Clark to behave in such a way that the nation, and the national government, would be moved to intervene. Jim Clark was ever ready to oblige.

On 9 February, released from jail, King was in Washington to discuss the outlines of a voting rights bill with Vice-President Hubert Humphrey and Nicholas Katzenbach. Although Johnson was preoccupied with the crisis in Vietnam, King was spirited across to the White House to meet him, smuggling Ralph Abernathy along too. At long last the federal government was stirring itself to mandate the rights of Negroes to vote, even in the more benighted corners of the Deep South, just as it had finally moved to ban segregation in education and then in public accommodations.

On 18 February the situation in Alabama turned nasty, as had always been on the cards. It happened not in Selma but in Marion, the county seat of Coretta King's native Perry County. King was away in Atlanta preaching, and in his absence C. T. Vivian preached at the wooden Mount Zion Church in the main square. The giant James Orange, Bevel's local lieutenant, was arrested and jailed, and there were serious fears that he would be lynched. Two local clergy bravely led a night march to the Perry County courthouse. State troopers broke up the march and some of them chased an eighty-two-year-old black man into a café and started beating him and other Negroes there. The old man's daughter tried to protect him, and was thrown to the floor. Her son, Jimmy Lee Jackson, tried to save his mother, and a trooper shot him twice in the stomach, then beat him with truncheons into the street, where he collapsed. He died later in hospital.

Jimmie Lee Jackson's funeral took place in Marion on the 28th. The little Mount Zion Church heard a fervent sermon from James Bevel. He took a text from Acts: 'Herod killed James, the brother of John, with a sword, and when he saw that it pleased the Jews, he proceeded to arrest Peter also.' 'I'm not worried about James,' Bevel bellowed. 'James has found release from the indignities of being a Negro in Alabama. I'm concerned about Peter, who is still with us.' And then he moved to a second text, from the Book of Esther. She was charged, his audience would recall, to 'go unto the king, to make supplication unto him, and to make request before him for her people'. Then Bevel, thoroughly excited, shouted over and over again, 'I must go see the king! We must go to Montgomery to see the king!'

King preached at a memorial service for Jimmie Lee Jackson in Marion. 'Who killed him?' King asked, and answered his own question with one of those inimitable rhythmic sequences of repetition that were the key to the power of his oratory.

He was murdered by the brutality of every sheriff who practiced lawlessness in the name of the law. He was murdered by the irresponsibility of every politician from governors on down [a shaft there at George Wallace] who has fed his constituents the stale bread of hatred and the spoiled meat of racism. He was murdered by the timidity of a federal government that is willing to spend millions of dollars a day to defend freedom in Vietnam, but cannot protect the rights of its citizens at home. And he was murdered by the cowardice of every Negro who passively accepts the evils of segregation and stands on the sidelines in the struggle for justice.

On 2 March Dr King was in Washington for the centenary of Howard

University. In cap and gown, he delivered an adapted version of his Nobel Prize speech. But this was the day of the first American bombing raid on North Vietnam. King's comment on this was brief, but pregnant with future developments. He was sympathetic to President Johnson's problem in South-East Asia, he said but then added, 'The war in Vietnam is accomplishing nothing.'

King spent two hours with President Johnson that day, trying to persuade him that a new civil rights bill was needed, this time a voting rights bill that would confirm the right of black people, everywhere in the nation, to vote. Johnson said little, but did not disagree. He referred King to Nick Katzenbach, and unknown to King, the process of making a bill began. This involved not only drafting the text of it but also negotiating with both Senator Everett Dirksen, the Republican leader in the Senate, and Senator Russell Long of Louisiana. Long, son of Huey Long, the near-fascist Governor of Louisiana in the 1930s, known as the 'Kingfish', had signed the pro-segregation 'Southern Manifesto' and attacked the 1964 Civil Rights Act. Yet now he supported Johnson and Humphrey, and was perhaps the most liberal of the great southern barons in the Senate. The fact that he seemed to be taking part in drafting the bill raised hopes that southern opposition would no longer be monolithic.

Back in Selma, King was now committed to leading a march on Montgomery. He had hesitated. Ironically, the radicals of SNCC opposed the march, asking what good it would do. But their leader John Lewis took his place, nonetheless, in the front row with Hosea Williams. On Sunday 7 March, thousands of marchers breasted the steep slope of the Pettus Bridge, its summit towering a hundred feet over the Alabama River. It was called after the confederate general who, with the help of the Ku Klux Klan, had restored order after the Civil War. As they reached the top, the demonstrators could see their way blocked by the big cruisers of the Alabama highway patrol. Behind them about 150 armed men were lined up across the four-lane road. The state troopers wore blue uniforms; Sheriff Clark's deputies and his posse were in khaki, a dozen of them on horseback. As the marchers approached they saw that the state's forces were wearing gas masks – these, plus their goggles, making them look like sinister pachyderms from some surreal horror movie. To the side, in the car park of an establishment called 'Chicken Treat, Home of the Mickey Burger', dozens of white spectators, some standing on cars to see the fun, waited like the crowd at a public execution.

Major Cloud, a bespectacled aide to Colonel Al Lingo, the commander of George Wallace's state troopers, stepped forward, and Hosea Williams asked for a word. 'There is no word to be had,' said Cloud, and gave the marchers two minutes to turn around. After just one minute and five seconds, he gave the troopers their order. They charged into the unarmed Negroes, the horsemen too, crashing into them and screaming with rage, while the marchers howled in fear and pain. A crack sounded as the first tear-gas canister was fired, and the pungent cloud spread fast over the fleeing, coughing men and women. As they fled back over the bridge, the troopers lashed out at them with truncheons, stock whips, electric cattle prods, even rubber hoses and clubs wrapped with barbed wire. The stentorian voice of Sheriff Jim Clark could be heard: 'Get those god-damned niggers! And get those god-damned white niggers!'

Within half an hour the streets were clear. The marchers were choking. More than a hundred, some badly hurt, crowded into Brown Chapel for refuge. Over fifty were given emergency treatment at the Catholic Good Samaritan Hospital, and others at an old folks home in the black neighbourhood. These were the only two institutions that would treat Negroes. Some, like John Lewis, whose skull had been fractured by a trooper's club, were kept in hospital for several days.

In the movement, that Sunday came to be known as 'Bloody Sunday'. (It was only relatively bloody. No one was killed. On another Bloody Sunday, 30 January 1972, in Derry, Northern Ireland, no fewer than thirteen civilians would be shot dead by British soldiers.) Alabama's state troopers and Dallas County's posse men did not fire live rounds. What struck the marchers and the SCLC staff, however, as they listened to minute-by-minute accounts on a WATS line to Atlanta, and what overwhelmed television viewers that night and later when they saw countless reruns of the film, was the sheer vicious racism of armed white men flailing with every weapon they could wield at unarmed, mainly black men, women and children.

The spectacle remained one of the abiding images of the civil rights movement. Its message was hardly new to the South, or to African-

Americans anywhere. But white people, and especially white church people, were severely shocked. The anger of many southern whites – manifested in their determination to treat black people who demanded their rights with contemptuous cruelty, and their feeling that they were perfectly justified in doing so – was not, as most white Americans outside of the South had vaguely assumed, assuaged or moderated, but was as visceral and unapologetic as ever.

Dr King was in Atlanta. He and his lieutenants sent out an urgent message to every religious leader whose address they could find. 'In the vicious maltreatment of defenseless citizens of Selma,' it read, 'we have witnessed an eruption of the disease of racism which seeks to destroy all America . . . I call, therefore, on clergy of all faiths . . . to join me in Selma for a ministers' march to Montgomery on Tuesday morning, March 9.' The immediate response was that thousands of white people poured into Alabama to affirm their own anger and shame at the mores of the white South, and their determination that things must change. White ministers of religion of every denomination, Catholics, Unitarians, Quakers, Anglicans, Methodists, priests and pastors and dozens of rabbis, began to arrive at Montgomery airport on their way to Selma to take part in a great movement for black enfranchisement. 'You could say,' said one distinguished northern Methodist bishop, 'that I heard the Macedonian call.'

Although not present in Selma, King had able and undaunted lieutenants there, beginning with Hosea Williams and Andy Young, not to mention SNCC volunteers like John Lewis who, if not strictly under his leadership, nonetheless shared his goals. King also sent lawyers ahead to try to get permission for the movement, reinforced by highly reputable outsiders, to march the fifty-odd miles from Selma to Montgomery. There, however, King and the SCLC came up against the multi-tiered constitutional texture and legal quiddities of American political life. The local federal judge, Frank Johnson, had been a staunch and understanding ally of the civil rights movement. He did not, however, like to be taken for granted. He was asked to overrule the state and the local officials' refusal to permit the march, and he refused. King first accepted his ruling, then, seeing the immense response to his own plea, he changed his mind and said the march would go on. Judge Johnson issued an order, stressing that no 'irreparable harm' would arise if the march was delayed until after a court hearing on Wednesday.

King now faced a quandary. If he defied the judge's order, he would risk losing the all-important support of the federal government he had worked so hard to earn. If he did not, he risked infuriating the good people, the activist conscience of America, who had responded to his appeal. Later he quipped that there were those who had come to bear a cross, and found they had only to bear a toothpick. All Monday night the debate rolled on at dentist Sullivan Jackson's house in Selma, and over the telephone wires. The Attorney General spoke to King on the phone for an hour and failed to get him to agree to cancel the march. From New York, Bayard Rustin and the NAACP's lawyer, Jack Greenberg, urged him to go ahead. To back down now would damage the non-violent movement, perhaps fatally. King's dilemma was as acute as ever. President Johnson sent a trusted emissary, LeRoy Collins, a moderate former Governor of Florida, now head of the government's community relations service. He flew into Selma on a government plane and worked out a compromise that might have saved King's reputation and his movement.

Collins met Sheriff Clark and George Wallace's man Lingo secretly in the back of a second-hand car dealership in Selma. In true southern political style, a deal was done, though never publicly acknowledged. It is likely, but not certain, that King was in on it. Collins persuaded the men of violence not to attack the non-violent marchers provided that the march stopped when ordered to and went back to Brown Chapel.

King was up until the small hours, wrestling with his dilemma and his advisers, with New York urging him to defy the injunction, Washington beseeching him to obey it. He appeared at Brown Chapel late in the morning, to find three thousand people there, most of them keen to march. King spoke to them as Mr-Valiant-for-Truth. 'Nothing will stop us,' he told the crowd, 'not the threat of death itself . . . We will not be turned around. The world must know that we are determined to be free.' He had made his choice, he ended. 'I have got to march. I do not know what lies ahead of us. There may be beatings, jailing, tear gas. But I would rather die on the highways of Alabama than make a butchery of my conscience.'

If, as is probably true, King did know rather more about what lay ahead than he had told his people, that speech may sound more than a little cynical. It should be remembered, though, that even if a deal had been discussed, no one could be sure that it would be kept. George Wallace, Al Lingo, Jim Clark had all given plenty of proof of violent hostility to black people and their aspirations, and it was far from sure that they could be trusted to keep an agreement. King might have been set up for a humiliation. He might even be taking several hundred people into a death trap.

At any rate, some fifteen hundred people set off at last from Brown Chapel. They marched through black Selma, singing bravely 'Ain't Gonna Let Nobody Turn Me Around', wheeled right at the river bank and then left on to the bridge. At the foot of the steep upward slope a federal court official stepped forward. King stopped the march, and the official read out Judge Johnson's order. King listened courteously, then said politely he was aware of the order and was going to ignore it. The federal official said he would let the march go. The more dangerous test was to be on the other side of the bridge.

As the civil rights leaders and the famous white clergymen in the front ranks reached the top of the bridge, they could see the troopers lined up in their blue plastic helmets, though not now with gas masks. They stood silent, their clubs in their hands under the traffic lights, which went on changing from green to red and back to green again, as if to King's hesitations. Major Cloud allowed him to come within fifty feet before shouting through his bullhorn: 'You are ordered to stop and stand where you are. This march will not continue.'

'We have a right to march,' King answered. 'There is also a right to march to Montgomery.'

Cloud repeated his order, and King asked if they could pray. Cloud said they could, but they must then return to the church.

King asked the marchers to kneel, and the whole line, almost a mile long, sank to their knees. Prayers were given by a Methodist bishop, a Presbyterian pastor and a rabbi. Then a strange thing happened. Major Cloud ordered his troopers to open the road. King, though, gave the word for his marchers to wheel around and back they marched to Brown Chapel, some, in conscious or unconscious irony, singing 'Ain't Gonna Let Nobody Turn Me Around'.

Why did Cloud open the way? Had he forgotten the agreed script? Did he never know of it? Was it a trap? Did George Wallace plan to let the marchers head blindly into the wild country of Lowndes County, helpless victims for ambush? Did Wallace want to discredit King with his more passionate followers? We cannot know. But if the march ended as an embarrassing anticlimax, King's decision was nevertheless the right one.

The country, as he had long hoped, was at last rallying to his cause. The White House was surrounded by demonstrators, and so was the Justice Department, where Katzenbach had sat, chain-smoking, as he waited to hear what had happened when the march met Wallace's troopers. There were huge marches and sit-down strikes in Chicago and New York, in Boston and Cleveland and smaller cities. The biggest of all was in Detroit.

One of the northerners who had come south to march was a Unitarian minister from Boston, the Revd James Reeb, a committed supporter of civil rights who had moved with his family into Boston's black ghetto. He had reached Selma by car from Atlanta, and after the march he accepted a lift to go straight back. He even threw his suitcase into the back of the car. Then he changed his mind and went downtown to eat at a black-owned 'soul food' restaurant. When he and his two friends had finished eating, he called his wife in Boston to tell her he was staying another day in Selma. Then, disastrously, the three white ministers, leaving the restaurant, took the wrong turning and found themselves heading towards the Silver Moon café, a notorious haunt of Ku Kluxers and other white hard men. Four of these hoodlums were lurking in the shadows outside.

'Hey, you niggers!' they shouted as the three harmless and very white clergymen passed. Two of them were hit, but managed to escape. Reeb was caught by a swinging blow to the side of the head with a baseball bat or a steel bar. He fell, and could not stand up. His speech was 'jumbled', he could not see clearly, and he was in unbearable pain from his aching head. His friends got him to the black infirmary and the doctor, one of only two African-American doctors anywhere near Selma, tried in vain to take an X-ray, then decided to get Reeb to the university medical centre in Birmingham. On the way there the ambulance broke down, and the sheriff's deputies refused to escort the doctor's own car. After a nightmare journey over dark country roads through hostile territory, the patient arrived at the Birmingham hospital, four hours after he had been attacked. It was too late. He was diagnosed with a massive skull fracture, a blood clot and pneumonia. Within two days he would be dead.

Reeb's death shocked the country even more than the spectacle of Wallace's troopers gassing and beating the marchers on Bloody Sunday. There were marches, demonstrations, everywhere. A handful of demonstrators even managed to 'sit in' inside the White House. Selma remained in a state of neuralgic tension. But the focus of decision and of attention now shifted to Washington, where the Attorney General was closeted with congressional leaders to hammer out the text of a bill to guarantee the vote to the Negroes of the Deep South. George Wallace came up from Alabama to plead with the President, as a fellow southerner, to understand the South's sensitivities and its pride. Johnson would have none of it. Towering over the bantam-weight governor, Johnson left him in no doubt that he meant to establish the rights Wallace was trying to forestall.

'What do you want left when you die?' Johnson asked. 'Do you want a great big marble monument that read "George Wallace – He Built", or do you want a little piece of scrawny pine board that reads "George Wallace – He Hated"?' Johnson called on the governor to declare that black people could vote.

Wallace insisted he didn't have that power.

'Don't you shit me, George Wallace!' said the President, as one country boy to another. 'You had the power to keep the President of the United States off the ballot [in Alabama]. Surely you have the power to tell a few poor country registrars what to do?'

Finally Wallace appeared to agree that Dr King and his supporters would be allowed to march from Selma to Montgomery. The next day, back in Montgomery, he went back on his word – if he ever quite gave it – saying he would allow a march only if the federal judge ordered it.

Neither the civil rights movement nor Congress quite understood how fully Lyndon Johnson was now committed to passing a decisive voting rights bill. Two days after his meeting with Wallace he removed every last lingering doubt. The Speaker of the House had suggested that the President come to present his bill to Congress in person. Armed with a speech part-written by a speechwriter, Johnson left the script and soared into what is generally regarded as the speech of his life. The issue of equal rights for Negroes, he declared, was an issue that went 'to the values and purpose and meaning of our beloved nation. Even if the country defeated every enemy, doubled its wealth and conquered the stars', if it fails to rise to the issue of equality for Negroes 'we will have failed as a people and as a nation'. For with a country as with a person – here quoting the Gospel according to St Mark – "What is a man profited if he shall gain the whole world and lose his own soul?" There was no Negro problem, he went on, only an American problem. 'It is not just Negroes, but really it's all of us who must overcome the crippling legacy of bigotry and injustice. And we shall overcome!'

Listening southern Congressmen could not believe what they had heard from their former leader. Johnson's best friend in the Senate, Dick Russell of Georgia, called him to friends a 'turncoat'. And in Sullivan Jackson's home in Selma, Martin King's intimates, sitting round the television to watch the speech, could not believe it either. 'Can you believe he said that!' they shouted. As King listened, friends reported, a tear rolled down his cheek. Once again, he was in a cleft stick, caught by the cross-pressures of the unfolding drama. He had been invited by the President to hear him deliver the speech, and had turned down the invitation because he was scheduled to speak at James Reeb's funeral in Selma. And Judge Johnson would still not lift the ban on the march to Montgomery to which King was now committed.

Attorney General Katzenbach called the judge to ask when he would rule on the order. Judge Johnson said he would not rule until he was assured that the federal government would back him, and he needed to hear that from the President himself. Meanwhile in Montgomery the local sheriff, mounted on horseback and wearing a cowboy hat, had led a group of deputies who proceeded to beat up Negro demonstrators, including James Forman, one of the leaders of SNCC.

Not for the first time, King was stymied by the law. He dared not ignore a federal court order; he dared not disappoint the followers, black and white, who had come from all over the country to march from Selma to Montgomery, and who had twice been frustrated. As in Albany and in Birmingham, his whole movement risked losing momentum. The President had committed himself in the most public way to a voting rights bill. But would the march go forward? Once again, King was in the process of trying to put the best face on his disappointment when his aide Andrew Young pushed through the crowd and whispered to him. King's face changed. Then 'Let me give you this statement, which I think will come as a source of deep joy to all of us,' he announced to all those assembled. 'Judge Johnson has just ruled that we have a legal and constitutional right to march from Selma to Montgomery.'

And march they did. On 21 March, just two weeks after Bloody Sunday, three thousand people set out, unimpeded, over the Pettus Bridge. After only seven miles, they settled down to camp for the first night. The next morning, on they went, through the marshland and forest trees of Lowndes County. The Spanish moss and kudzu vine drooping from the trees lent a romantic and at the same time sinister air to the highway. After three days King left his marchers to keep a speaking appointment in Cleveland, his feet sore from the sixteen miles covered the previous day. By then they had made their point. On the fourth day King, with Coretta and Ralph and Juanita Abernathy, plus twenty-five thousand marchers, returned home in triumph to Montgomery, and Dexter Avenue Baptist, where his political journey had begun. This was not perhaps the high point of his political career. It did not touch the peak of the march on Washington, nor the Nobel Prize. But it came close to it: the most intimate, the most satisfying moment, the point at which he could feel that he had indeed overcome.

The response to the violence in Selma, King told the huge crowd, had been 'a shining moment in the conscience of man'. There would still be a 'season of suffering', he predicted, but it would lead to 'a society at peace with itself, a society that can live with its conscience'. How long will it take? he asked. 'However difficult the moment, however frustrating the hour, it will not be long.' And he repeated the question, and the answer. 'How long? – Not long!'

Martin and Coretta, together for once, went back to Atlanta in a mood of elevation. But as so often in their life, a peak of triumph was followed by tragedy, a sign that the season of suffering was not over.

Violet Liuzzo was the white wife of a union official in Detroit, the daughter of a Tennessee coalminer. She had come south to join in the march, and to drive marchers where they needed to go in her Oldsmobile. After the march, she set off from Selma to Montgomery to take people home – with her a young black SNCC volunteer. In the dangerous country of Lowndes County she was shot and killed in cold blood by Klansmen. One of the four men in the murder car happened to be an FBI informer. Prurient suggestions were soon being whispered about why this forty-year-old mother of five was travelling at night with a young black man in her car.

The Selma campaign led directly to the early passage of the voting rights bill of 1965. That in turn led to the defection of many conservative southern whites from the Democratic Party. 'There goes the South!' It was in itself a turning-point in the transformation of American politics from the age of liberalism to the conservative ascendancy. For Martin King, it marked the end of his campaign against legal segregation in the South, and the opening of a far harder struggle for equality across the nation. Less predictably, perhaps, it was the moment when the hidden rifts within the black civil rights movement itself now broke into the open.

12

Walks on the Wild Side

This is a great city. It can be an even greater city.
Martin Luther King Jr to Mayor Richard J. Daley of Chicago

By the autumn of 1965 Martin King had been on active service for a decade. There had been few breaks of more than days. The first substantial one came in early 1967 when he flew to Jamaica to get on with writing his book, *Community or Chaos*. It was, one historian has written, the first time in his life that he was free from the demands of meetings, the telephone and an insistent schedule.

He had been arrested and imprisoned half a dozen times. He had become accustomed to fear and often acknowledged to his friends and colleagues that he well knew that his life was at risk. He travelled constantly, and spent time much hurrying to catch planes and criss-crossing the continent. He was constantly in demand as a speaker, frequently several times in a day, and had learned to recycle favourite sermons and to improvise around familiar ideas and tropes, such as his favourite verse from the Book of Amos about 'justice [rolling] down as waters, and righteousness as a mighty stream'. The movement he had created was heavily dependent on his ability to raise startling sums of money by accepting an endless stream of invitations to speak.

The burden had been heavy, and its effects were showing. Martin, who in his Crozer days had been able to take his good health and abounding energy for granted, now frequently checked into hospital for bed rest and routinely went down with what his friends called his 'regular' virus, so often did it appear at critical moments of a campaign; he also suffered from occasional bronchitis and persistent laryngitis, the direct consequence of overusing his exceptional speaking voice. He remained an inspiration to his supporters and a delight to his friends, for his warmth and kindness and not least for his irrepressible humour.

Martin's home life had taken much of the strain. Coretta stayed with him, loyally, while trying to keep up the pretence that she was untroubled by the FBI's tape and other hints of his numerous infidelities. 'Coretta was most certainly a widow long before Dr King died,' said a friend' He continued to slip away to be with women, to seek some relaxation from the threats of his enemies and the quarrels amongst his friends.

His children were a joy to him, but they were undoubtedly aware of, and affected by, the tensions between their parents. Coretta worried constantly about their future, and about money. He earned vast sums, but kept little for himself. She could not help resenting his indifference to such material concerns. She chivvied him about what she felt was the inadequacy of the house, shabby and rented, where they lived on Johnson Avenue in Atlanta. She wrote later that he was 'reluctant in the first place to own a house because this would set him apart' from his followers and might be 'inconsistent with his philosophy'. Early in 1965 she succeeded in persuading him to buy, for the very modest sum of $10,000, an unpretentious brick house on Sunset Avenue in a 'better' neighbourhood. He agreed that Coretta should carry out some renovations, but then grumbled to friends that they were too ambitious.

After the victory in Selma and the triumphal return to Montgomery, Martin was so depressed that his friends worried about his health. Part of his low mood was occasioned by the sheer intransigence he encountered at every turn, from Ku Klux Klan killers, southern sheriffs and national Democratic politicians alike. But part, too, was caused by the internal problems of the movement. Selma had replenished the organization's coffers. Large sums came in from speaking engagements and from wealthy northern donors, including Nelson Rockefeller, the Republican Governor of New York. But within months the SCLC was broke again.

Hosea Williams, his reputation made by his successful organizing in Savannah and his brave leadership in St Augustine, had persuaded King to allow him to go ahead with a project called SCOPE (Summer Community Organization and Political Education). The idea was to pour a thousand volunteers into 120 Deep South counties to educate and register black voters. There was much to be said for the concept. But it fell victim to Williams's arrogance and lofty indifference to administrative discipline. SCOPE haemorrhaged money. Randy Blackwell, who had taken over from Wyatt Walker the thankless task of administering the SCLC, was driven to distraction by it, and ultimately to resignation. Before he left he sent an overwrought confidential memo to King, urging that SCOPE be shut down as soon as possible 'without inviting public inquiry'. Rental cars used by the project were returned in an indescribably filthy condition. 'It has cost . . . ten times what it should have,' Blackwell wrote, '. . . the project has degenerated in the main to an experiment in liquor and sex, compounded by criminal conduct, no less than a series of reported rapes.'

Martin King had surrounded himself with a group of men possessing towering egos, confident, aggressive and tough. They had to be, to put up with the hardship and danger they brought on themselves by challenging the deepest prejudices of a violent southern society. Their mutual relations were at best suspicious, at worst poisonous. Hosea Williams and Jim Bevel were bitter rivals. Williams wanted the SCLC to focus on voter registration, Bevel still cherished ambitious dreams of boycotting the government of Alabama. Their differences over strategy were exacerbated by open personal rivalry, and Bevel's private life was if anything even more out of control than Williams's. All of the leaders resented Ralph Abernathy because he was King's closest friend and designated successor. Most of them disliked Andrew Young, for his virtues. Some suspected he was an FBI informer and even called him an Uncle Tom to his face.

As for SNCC, resentment and even contempt for King were spreading in its ranks. Many in the organization had never fully shared King's total commitment to non-violence. They had survived for weeks and months in the most dangerous corners of the rural South, where the poor blacks on whom their own survival depended saw nothing wrong in using guns to defend themselves. They had not only lived in terrible danger, they had lived in apostolic poverty while, as they saw it, King and his acolytes were flying from one expensive hotel to another. King made little attempt to control these rivalries and jealousies among his lieutenants or to impose any kind of discipline. Indeed, it is possible that, like Franklin Roosevelt, he tried to use them as a form of 'creative tension'. Certainly, his response to the competing strategies of Hosea Williams and Jim

Bevel was to accept both of them. As for SNCC, his way of dealing with the growing estrangement from him largely consisted in a teasing humour.

Administrative chaos, financial worries and rampant personality conflicts were not the worst of the problems King faced in late 1965 and early 1966, however. The civil rights movement as a whole was now at a crossroads. All but a committed handful of King's supporters in the North, the likes of Stanley Levison and Harry Belafonte, had decided that, after the apparent conversion of the Johnson administration and the passage of not one but two major civil rights bills, the war in the South was won. All attention now shifted to the 'cities', as the journalistic shorthand put it: to the residential segregation, police brutality, injustice, poverty and rage of the ghettos where African-Americans lived in every city in the land, from South Central Los Angeles to Roxbury in South Boston, by way of Chicago, Detroit, Cleveland and New York, and in hundreds of smaller places too.

At this time, Martin King was developing his own thinking, in farsighted and personal ways. We shall come back to his growing conviction that non-violence was an international value, which drove him to risk everything he was working for with the intensity of his opposition to the Vietnam War. His thinking about America's domestic politics was also evolving swiftly. Long-held social democratic ideas were driving him to see that he ought to be campaigning on behalf of all poor people, not only for blacks. Therefore his focus should not be limited to the South, but should be national and even international.

His immediate response to the crisis, though, took the form of a decision to bring non-violent direct action from the South – where it had succeeded in overthrowing the most blatant legally enforced racism – to bear against the subtler but still intolerable oppression of black people in the North. King and the SCLC undertook a reconnaissance of the North's great cities. They looked at Boston, Philadelphia, Cleveland, New York, Chicago. There were problems with each of them. Adam Clayton Powell, the rascally African-American Congressman who controlled Harlem, had as good as warned King off. In the end, they chose to focus on Chicago, America's second city, home to the vibrant 'black metropolis' of more than a million people, and also to some of the worst slums in the nation. It had its own acute problems, especially in residential segregation, and housing, and it had a vigorous native protest movement. As one writer has put it, the SCLC didn't so much choose Chicago as Chicago chose them.

As part of the process of deciding where to launch the first big northern campaign, King went to Chicago in July 1965 and made about twenty speeches in two days, including a major speech to a crowd of thirty-five thousand. (The experience was so exhausting that he had once again to see a doctor for a check-up.) There was already in existence an umbrella organization, the Coordinating Council of Community Organizations (CCCO), which brought together some forty protest groups focused on changing Chicago's segregated school system and the rigid pattern of racial segregation.

In the last three months of 1965 a dozen SCLC workers, led by Jim Bevel, moved into Chicago's West Side ghetto and started making contacts and reconnoitring the situation there. A rising star in the SCLC, Jesse Jackson, a theology student not yet ordained as a minister, had started Operation Breadbasket, the extension to Chicago of a scheme that had proved successful in Atlanta. The idea was to use the consumer power of black customers to put pressure on corporations dependent on retail shoppers to hire more black employees, and it worked.

Some of Martin's closest friends warned him, nonetheless, that Chicago would be too tough a nut to crack. Bayard Rustin said bluntly that he would be 'wiped out' if he went there. The nation's second city was run by a tacit alliance between tough, pragmatic businessmen and one of the last old-fashioned Democratic political 'machines' in the country, ably and ruthlessly controlled by the mayor Richard Daley, known to his friends as 'Hizonner', to many as 'the boss' and to many African-Americans, raised on Old Testament tales of oppression, as 'the Pharaoh'. Daley's Democratic legions were supported, albeit warily, by the unions, as well as by a network of ethnic organizations – Daley, remember, thought that 'affirmative action was nine Irishmen and a Swede'. The Daley regime was passionately committed to the expansion of the city and to the highway, construction and real estate industries. Under his reign its business district, the Loop, acquired skyscrapers as tall as or taller than those of New York. Chicago boasted – and it did boast, incessantly, with the inferiority complex of a second city – of a great, if in Dr King's day very conservative, newspaper, the *Tribune*; a great symphony orchestra; the Art Institute, one of the greatest art galleries in the world; opulent hotels, magnificent department stores; and in the University of Chicago one of the most successful research institutions in the world.

Daley himself, a pious Catholic from a working-class background, had been a devoted supporter of the New Deal, keen to encourage its social and economic help for the city. The Daley machine also maintained a subterranean but effective cooperation with the Mob. It included a whole ancillary machine to represent and control African-Americans in the sprawling ghettos of the South and West Sides and the outlying areas into which black citizens had spread. The black alderman and Congressman William Dawson was Daley's chief lieutenant with power over the black metropolis, or 'Bronzeville'.

By the time Martin Luther King arrived in town, African-Americans made up more than a third of the population, which peaked at around 3.7 million in the late 1950s.* In spite of the Daley machine's inclusion of Dawson and his men, Chicago exhibited some of the worst ghetto conditions in America. In public housing 'projects' like the fearsome Robert Taylor homes, high-rise jungles stalked by drug dealers, muggers and armed gangsters, a minimum of order was kept by trigger-happy police. Segregation was as absolute both in Chicago schools and in housing as in Memphis or Birmingham, and the Chicago police department kept order in the black neighbourhoods as brutally as any Deep South sheriff.

Ever since the Great Migration of the 1910s and 1920s first brought thousands of southern blacks north to work in Chicago's mills, stockyards and factories, race relations in the city had been frankly terrible. In the summer of 1919 a black youth swam into water reserved for whites at a Lake Michigan beach and drowned after being hit on the head with a rock. In five days of wild rioting, twenty-three blacks and

---

* The population of Chicago, like that of London and other great cities, peaked not because of any real decline but because so many of its inhabitants moved to suburban homes outside the city's boundaries.

fifteen whites were killed. Two historians who in general avoided partisan attacks on Daley concluded of this episode that the seventeen-year-old Richard 'was an integral member of a youth gang that played an active role in one of the bloodiest anti-black riots in the nation's history'.[1] They also pointed out that Daley's mentor at the time actively encouraged attacks on Negroes, and that within a few years Daley was chosen as leader of the gang in question. This was the city, and this the leader, that Martin Luther King chose to persuade to share his dream of the 'beloved community'. Here was a clear clash between two visions of the city's future. Daley dreamed of a city of orderly, stable white communities, clustered round their large Catholic churches, and growing affluent thanks to the wealth generated by the commercial giants in their skyscrapers and to the massive investments he would conjure out of the Democratic administrations in Washington. King dreamed of an Open City, where two racially divided communities would become one in peace and brotherhood.

King was clear that he should not stay in one of the 'bourgeois' hotels, as he called them, in the Loop. On 26 January 1966 he, Coretta and the children moved into a tenement flat at 1550 South Hamlin Avenue in Lawndale on the West Side, a grim slum belying its bucolic name. The apartment had four rooms, on the third floor. The rent was $90 a month. Next door a neighbourhood restaurant, Belinda's Pit, served beef stew with black-eyed peas, turnip greens and peach cobbler for 96 cents.

Although Martin had tried to keep his arrival in the apartment secret, by the time the Kings arrived they found plasterers, painters and electricians hard at work fixing the place up. Even so, the family found it cheerless, and a sophisticated visitor from New York was surprised to find that King had not made himself more comfortable. The Kings noticed that in the apartment's confined space the children were more fractious than at home. Martin had his church to look after in Atlanta, speaking trips to make to raise money, and necessary visits to New York and Washington. So he decided to make it his practice to spend from Wednesday to Friday every week in Lawndale. Already there were tensions to be soothed over between his battle-hardened southern troops and the local CCCO activists, who felt brushed aside by Bevel and his men.

In early February a local priest brought parishioners to see him who were freezing in an unheated building in Chicago's bitter winter weather. Then King took reporters to a rat-infested building at 1321 South Homan, and a few days later his aides seized it – which of course was illegal. It was also unwise, and it backfired in publicity terms: it turned out that the landlord was desperately poor himself, very old and mortally ill.

In March, for the first time, King met Mayor Daley, who was pleased when he explained that 'I'm not leading a campaign against Mayor Daley, I'm leading a campaign against slums.' Daley was a very wily operator, who was not about to reveal his deep reservations and resentment at King's invasion of his city. Instead, he stressed to everyone, from local reporters to President Johnson himself, how much his administration in Chicago was already doing to improve slum housing and invest in the city's housing stock. By late May, nonetheless, King and his Chicago Freedom Movement, as they now called themselves, had decided on a strategy and tactics that could not fail to anger Daley, famous for his almost daily rages.

The strategy would be to focus on housing, slums and residential segregation. The most controversial tactic would be a series of marches through the lily-white neighbourhoods of what was known as the Bungalow Belt, inhabited by white working-class people, many of them of Irish or Polish descent. King also announced that there would be a massive rally at Soldier Field, now the home of the Chicago Bears American football team, then a venue, cherished by Chicagoans, that had seen such varied exertions of the human spirit as a Marian service attended by more than a quarter of a million Catholics in 1954 and the Jack Dempsey–Gene Tunney heavyweight world title match in 1927. Then, King said, he would march to Daley's City Hall, and – like his namesake on the church door at Wittenberg – nail, or rather tape, there a manifesto of his righteous demands.

On 6 June, events disrupted their plans. On the first two days of the month Lyndon Johnson had held a White House conference entitled 'To Fulfil These Rights'. Already, King was out of favour, chiefly because of his persistent criticism of the war in Vietnam. He was relegated to a secondary role, and allowed to speak only once, at a minor meeting. Press reports hardly mentioned his presence, let alone his opinions. While the conference was sidelined by ill-tempered bickering about Daniel Patrick Moynihan's celebrated (and badly misunderstood*) report on 'The Negro Family', James Meredith, the awkward hero of the desegregation of the University of Mississippi mentioned earlier, suddenly announced that he proposed to march from Memphis the length of the Delta to the state capital, Jackson. He was marching to appeal for voting rights for Mississippi's blacks, he said, but also to free them from fear.

Within hours of crossing the state line, Meredith was shot from ambush by an unemployed hardware salesman called Aubrey James Norvell. (He was arrested, and would convicted and sentenced to only five years in prison.) The weapon was a shotgun, and the wounds, because of the range they had been fired at, were less serious than was at first feared.

Even so, this was a crisis for the whole civil rights movement. Martin King announced without hesitation that he would continue Meredith's march, and many of the leaders of what was already a divided and somewhat dispirited movement said they would join him. News that Meredith had been shot arrived in Atlanta on Monday afternoon, 6 June. By Tuesday morning, King and a handful of aides had reached Memphis and met Meredith at his hospital bedside, where they were joined by Stokely Carmichael, who had replaced John Lewis as chairman of SNCC, and other SNCC members. The feisty radical black comedian Dick Gregory had already visited Meredith. That same afternoon twenty-one marchers, led by King, set out from the spot where he had been shot and started to march, harassed by Mississippi highway patrolmen who insisted that they keep off the carriageway.

The march lasted from 7 to 26 June. The SCLC, SNCC and CORE were all represented. It was an act of great courage – King and the others

---

* Moynihan, an assistant secretary at the Department of Labor, argued in the report that black Americans were caught up in a 'tangle of pathology' due to damage done since slavery to the Negro family. Many Negroes and some white liberals attacked him for racism, saying that he was 'blaming the victim'. Some journalists accused him of outlining a reactionary strategy for the Johnson administration. Moynihan was so upset that for a time he joined the nascent neo-conservative movement. After his election to the Senate in 1976 he moved back towards his original position as a liberal Democrat.

were putting their heads into the lion's mouth. White Mississippians buzzed the marchers in their cars, deliberately missing them by inches. They shouted insults and threatened them with pistols. The highway patrol, the state's police force, who were supposed to be protecting them, tear-gassed them instead. Byron de la Beckwith, the murderer of Medgar Evers, showed up and drove up and down the marching column. King made a detour to Philadelphia, in Neshoba County, where the three civil rights workers had been murdered. He was met by Sheriff Rainey and his deputy, Cecil Price. Price was later convicted and Rainey acquitted of the killings.

'You're the one who had Schwerner and those fellows in jail?' King asked quietly.

'Yes, sir!' Price answered.

King held a brief memorial service for the murdered men, while a growing crowd, up to three hundred whites, booed and tried to drown his prayers.

He said he believed the murderers were somewhere around.

'You're damn right,' Price growled, 'they're right behind you right now.'

King said afterwards that Philadelphia was 'a terrible town, the worst city I have ever seen'. To go there was one of the bravest things he ever did.

Two days earlier, while he was away on a quick trip to speak in Detroit, his movement encountered for the first time a political threat from its own supporters potentially as dangerous as anything the Klan could do to it.

Tall, handsome and debonair, Stokely Carmichael had worked in the Mississippi Delta. He knew it, he despised its white supremacist law men, and he knew what he thought it, and they, needed. He was just as brave as King, but he did not have much time for non-violence and he was impatient with what he saw as King's political timidity. On 16 June in Greenwood, in the heart of plantation country, Carmichael's patience snapped. When he spoke at a meeting that night, the march was threatened by a man with a gun. Police protection had been reduced. Carmichael and two colleagues were arrested for trespassing. When he spoke at a meeting in a park that night, he was angry, and he did not hide it.

'Every courthouse in Mississippi ought to be burned down,' he shouted, 'to get rid of the dirt.' The Delta needed black sheriffs, and its black people ought to demand 'black power'. 'We want black power!' Carmichael shouted, and the crowd yelled back, 'We want black power!' This was the first time that slogan, inspiring, provocative, yet misleading, had been uttered. It was, after all, less inappropriate in a hot Delta town where only that afternoon the marchers had been threatened with drawn pistols, and where whites, far outnumbered by blacks, were protected in their privileges by armed white men, than in America as a whole.

The next day, King heard the cry for the first time. Carmichael used it in his presence, and his friend Willie Ricks picked it up and led the crowd in rhythmically chanting it. Hosea Williams tried to start a competing chant of 'Freedom now!' But the rift in the movement was now out in the open.

There had always been an ambivalence in SNCC towards non-violence.[2] There were those in the movement who did not buy it. Once, at a SNCC meeting, Carmichael asked everyone who had a 'piece' to put it on the table. A dozen guns appeared. In Mississippi, south-west Georgia or the Alabama Black Belt civil rights workers, the resident rebels as well as the incomers, had long assumed that their survival might depend on a well-aimed shot. This non-ideological realism was reinforced by a rather pervasive suspicion of King, and even more perhaps of others in the SCLC, who seemed to live high on the hog while SNCC volunteers were living in fear and on starvation wages.

Now, in Greenwood, Mississippi, these tensions broke the surface. And it was not long before the reporters had fastened on the story. King himself was well aware of the issue. On the first day of the 'Meredith march', he and Stokely Carmichael were marching arm in arm when a Mississippi state trooper was so rude to Stokely that he made a move as if to hit the man. King held his arm, and recalled later, mocking his own pulpit voice, that 'I restrained Stokely *non-violently!*' The march staggered on to Canton, then Tougaloo, and finally the few miles further into Jackson. In Canton the state troopers who, the federal government had promised, were to protect the participants tear-gassed them, then clubbed them. At Tougaloo, the splits in the ranks could no longer be concealed. When the march reached Jackson, though the

SCLC, SNCC and CORE were all still theoretically allied, the movement seemed on the brink of dissolution.

Reporters from the national news media were obsessed with the Black Power slogan and queued up to interrogate King about what it meant. Did it announce the abandoning of non-violence, a wave of revolutionary violence, even race war? Stokely Carmichael and others such as Willie Ricks and Hubert 'Rap' Brown did not help by pouring out inflammatory rhetoric which hinted at violent action by blacks, which they well knew would be counterproductive and could only lead to violent repression. To some extent, this was a natural outburst of anger at the violence of some white southerners and the impunity of notorious racist murderers. Byron de la Beckwith openly threatened the marchers. Cecil Price taunted them. Klan leaders were in court to gloat at the acquittal by a white jury in Lowndes County of the murderer of the white Episcopalian seminarian Jonathan Daniels, killed at point-blank range with a shotgun for what was still seen there as the crime of working for civil rights.

There was another reason for the neuralgic effect of the Black Power slogan on white Americans. The Black Muslims, or Nation of Islam, founded in the 1930s by W. D. Fard, had developed under Elijah Muhammad what seemed to whites a doctrine of black separation. At the same time the charismatic Malcolm X was attracting attention by scathing denunciations of white racism. Many confused the Black Power slogan with the doctrines of the Nation of Islam.

The moral weather was darkening. The Watts riot, in central south Los Angeles, had erupted on 11 August 1965. Since then, there had been demonstrations, confrontations and riots in hundreds of other northern cities. This was the background to growing resentment, on the part of many working-class whites and their political leaders, of the Johnson administration's 'Great Society' programmes to help blacks. Mayors complained that government money was going not to their elected administrations, but to civil rights activists and even street gangs. Sometimes, in truth, it was not easy to tell the difference between the two. At the same time there was resentment among blacks that the President, torn between the demands of the war in Vietnam and the anger of his

Democratic colleagues, no longer seemed care to about their problems. To some extent, the black power slogan was put forward to 'raise consciousness' among blacks, to persuade them to stop thinking of themselves as powerless. It was also of course, in part a political device with which young rivals hoped to win support away from Martin Luther King as the leader of the movement.

King had insisted on the day Carmichael and Ricks first floated the banner of Black Power, as he explained to me in a lengthy interview shortly afterwards,[3] that it would be sheer folly for Negroes, who were little more than one-tenth of the population, to think they could win full freedom by force. He was absolutely right. Yet to many in the media his message of non-violence was dull and stale. Black power and white fear made a better story. To some blacks, King's non-violent philosophy seemed naive, ineffective, even cowardly. To many whites those who hinted at violence must be revealing more honestly than King what black people really felt, and why it was absurd to think they could be embraced in a 'beloved community'.

It was with these metaphorical clouds over his head that King turned northwards to Chicago, sweltering under a heat wave. On 10 July, he spoke in 98-degree heat at a rally at Soldier Field. He and his fellow organizers had hoped for a crowd of 100,000, but the most they could claim was 60,000; the city government said it was 23,000. Undeterred by that disappointment, King, with his children, duly marched to Daley's City Hall and taped fourteen demands on its locked door.

The next day, 11 July, he met Daley for the first time. To blunt the rally's sting, Daley had announced with pedantic pride that his administration had repaired 102,847 apartments. He was civil, but sought to contrast his achievement record with King's Open City approach. There was no meeting of minds, but Daley was playing it long, playing it clever. As ever, his concern was for his vision of the prosperity of his beloved city. As ever, he was watching the political situation. Already there had been signs that the Republicans were beginning to make inroads in the massive vote the Democratic Party traditionally received from the white working class in their suburbs in the Bungalow Belt. The marches and the prospect of an end to the all-white character of those suburbs were tearing great lumps out of Daley's traditional support.

The day after his meeting with King, one of those trivial incidents occurred that so often trigger a riot if the situation is tense enough. An ice-cream delivery truck got stuck in a pot-hole on the West Side.[4] In retrospect, the incident can be seen as an ironic rebuttal of the mayor's claim to have brought progress in a racially even-handed way to the whole city. At the time, it was just an opportunity for local kids, who helped themselves to the ice-cream. The marooned driver called for police assistance. When the cops arrived, the driver told them the culprits were turning on the fire hydrants and cooling off in the spray, so the cops turned them off. By ancient unwritten custom, city kids in America on hot summer afternoons have used the fire hydrants as improvised whirlpool baths. So the kids were furious. They complained that the hydrants in a nearby Italian neighbourhood were still on, and that the local swimming-pools did not admit black kids. Police arrested a boy. He shouted to the crowd, 'Why don't you do something about it?'

They did. Martin and Coretta King were on their way to dinner with the immortal gospel singer Mahalia Jackson when they became aware of the riot. Martin dashed instead to the 12th District police precinct and bailed out six bedraggled teenagers. But he could not stop the mayhem. The first wave of violence lasted five days, and reached within half a block of the Kings' apartment on Hamlin Avenue. The children, fascinated and fearful, looked out of the window at the noise and fury down the street. 'Get away from that window,' Coretta shouted, her words recorded by two reporters who happened to be present, 'or you'll have your heads blown off!'

By the time the riot had ended, the South had come north, to Chicago. Five hundred people were arrested, and two, both black, were killed. Mayor Daley was reduced to asking for the National Guard to come into the city. He lost his cool and accused King's staff of 'instructing people in how to conduct violence', a charge he had to retract when Archbishop Cody took King's side. But Daley told his friend Lyndon Johnson on the telephone that 'King is not your friend. He's against you on Vietnam. He's a god-damned faker!'

Two top aides from the Johnson White House arrived at the apartment to find Martin leading a bizarre seminar on non-violence with dozens of tough kids from Chicago's street gangs – the Vice Lords and the Roman Saints, the Blackstone Rangers and the Cobras. King attached great importance to the idea that the members of Chicago's youth gangs could be converted to the gospel of non-violence. Although some gang members were impressed by the guts of some of King's team, like the colossal Jim Orange, who got his nose broken in an attempt to break up a gang fight, the effort was doomed to failure. King hoped for great things from these tough young people, but Coretta later admitted in her memoirs that while he was preaching non-violence to them, many were still saying, 'We believe in violence.' One of the Vice Lords threatened to shoot Jim Bevel, who had praised him for being non-violent.

The first skirmish of a second wave of rioting came on 29 July, when some African-Americans picketed a real estate agency in Gage Park and were driven away by a white mob. The next day a racially mixed group marched through the park in protest, and local whites showered them with stones and bottles. The day after that, the whites wrecked two dozen of the cars that had brought in the demonstrators, and injured sixty people. Jesse Jackson and the Revd Al Raby were both hurt. So it went, day after day. On 2 August, 140 policemen fought a thousand protesters in Belmont-Cragin, a white neighbourhood near Lawndale. On the 5th, the confrontation had grown: one thousand policemen were protecting 800 civil rights marchers against a white crowd of 4–5,000. As King got out of his car, a stone the size of a base-ball hit him on the head. He was shaken for a moment, but recovered his self-control enough to make a wry joke: 'It hurts,' he said, 'but it's not an injury.'

The marches continued: Jesse Jackson and Raby took 1,500 through the Belmont-Cragin neighbourhood on 7 August, and on the 10th Jim Bevel led five hundred through the Loop, the downtown heart of Chicago. Bevel and his marchers stopped outside the Chicago Real Estate Board, who were blamed for the city's rigid residential segregation.

The most frightening news, however, was announced by Jesse Jackson, on 8 August. There would be a march, he said, in Cicero, an all-white suburb inhabited by working-class Italian, Polish and other Central European families; and controlled, since Al Capone made it his headquarters in the 1920s, by the Mob. Cicero was technically an enclave, not part of the city; known as the Walled City of the Syndicate, it was run by fearsome characters with names like Frank 'the Enforcer' Nitti and Tony 'Big Tuna' Accardo. In 1951 a black bus driver, Harvey E. Clark, rented an apartment there. Five thousand whites turned out, broke into the apartment and burned the furniture. The idea of non-violent marchers running the gauntlet in Cicero put the fear of God into civil rights workers, the city's administration, the police and most other Chicagoans alike. It acted as an effective pressure to bring the establishment to the table to confront the civil rights organizations.

King was not in Chicago when Jackson made his announcement about Cicero. After being hit on the head he had flown to Atlanta for a couple of days' rest before the SCLC annual meeting, to be held in Jackson. King introduced Senator Edward Kennedy as the keynote speaker, then retired to bed with a virus. It was certainly a time of crisis, for him and for the movement he led. He admitted that he was thinking of changing the SCLC's name to make it less southern, more national. His speech was read to the meeting by Andrew Young. King attempted to tackle the issue of black power by stating that since 'the majority of our people are now powerless ... self-determination for an oppressed people requires power'. The meeting passed a resolution criticizing the federal government's failure to enforce the 1964 and 1965 civil rights laws, and another sharply attacking the Vietnam War.

The marches might have shown how far thousands of white people would go to keep Chicago from becoming the Open City of King's vision, but they did have their effect. Daley and the city government were more than ever anxious to bring mass demonstrations to an end. Faced with the more or less genuine fear of a massacre in Cicero, the city and the surrounding Cook County were threatening the civil rights movement with an injunction that would limit the size of marches and the circumstances in which they would be permitted.

An opportunity to negotiate now appeared. The Chicago power structure – the political and business leaders – decided it was time for a high-level summit between the city government, the real estate interests and the civil rights movement. The movement kept up the pressure, holding three neighbourhood marches on the same day, and there were plans to picket City Hall and the Real Estate Board. A body called the Chicago Conference on Religion and Race – backed by big businessmen from the steel and telephone companies and other business organizations, but also by the Roman Catholic archbishop John Cody, the Episcopalian bishop James Montgomery, as well as by Rabbi Robert Marx of the Union of American Hebrew Congregations – announced that the summit would take place on 17 August.

Mayor Daley suggested that the meeting should be chaired by Ben W. Heineman, a railroad executive who had been in the chair at the recent White House conference on race in Washington. It met at the St James Episcopal church house. King was backed by no fewer than fourteen representatives of the civil rights movements, including Bevel, Raby, Jackson and Young as well as local leaders. Daley attended in person, and so did representatives of the real estate industry, the mortgage banks and other bankers.[5]

The discussions were frustrating. The Real Estate Board offered little beyond theoretical support for the principle of open housing. Mayor Daley was prepared to go beyond that, and put some pressure on the real estate men to pass an ordinance obliging their members to post notices in their offices promising equal access to housing for black people – but only if King would end the marches. 'It always seemed to me,' said an observer, 'that Daley was not trying to figure out how to deal with the broader race and housing problems in Chicago. It was about stopping the marches, which were tearing at the heart of the Democratic party.'

The atmosphere became tense and angry, and it looked as if the summit would collapse. Then King intervened, with what was called by another observer 'a grand and quiet and careful and calming eloquence'. The city was tired of demonstrations, he said, and so was he. 'I am tired of demonstrating. I am tired of the threat of death. I want to live. I don't want to be a martyr . . . But the important thing is not how tired I am: the important thing is to get rid of the conditions that lead us to march.' The marches – he called them 'our humble marches' – had revealed a cancer. He did not see enough reason to end them but he wanted to continue the dialogue, with love and non-violence. 'We have not used rocks. We have not used bottles ... This is a great city,' he ended, 'and it can be a greater city.'

King had saved the summit. Andy Young quickly suggested a sub committee to work out specific proposals, and Heineman accepted. After the meeting King went to a church where he made a moving speech again admitting how tired he was, how afraid of martyrdom. 'I don't march because I like it,' he said. 'I march because I must.'

Only two days later, the city sought and was given an injunction banning marches by more than five hundred people. It made little difference to the movement, which simply switched its attention to the suburbs. But it did dissipate much of the goodwill caused by King's intervention. Attention switched back to the threatened Cicero march. The sheriff of Cook County said it would be 'almost suicidal'. King still refused to promise that it would not happen.

The second session opened at the famous Palmer House Hotel, with the Freedom Movement representatives along one side of a huge U-shaped table, the city officials and the real estate industry opposite them, and the men of religion in the middle. The men on King's side of the table were wary, suspicious. They found it hard to believe that either Daley or the real estate men meant what they said. But an agreement was reached, and eventually accepted. It amounted to little more than the expression of an intention to end segregation in Chicago's housing. Once again, King spoke calmly, taking the discussion to a higher plane. He had seen hatred in the faces at Gage Park, he said, a hatred born of fear, and that fear was born of separation; he was not threatening more marches, but if the agreement did not work, marches would be a reality. He praised Daley, and he looked forward to making Chicago a city of brotherhood.

It was not, however, in that spirit that the agreement was received – by his own people least of all. Chicago's black leaders, for the most part, saw the deal as a sell-out. The size of the problem that remained is best measured by the fact that the agreement envisaged black people becoming a minimum of only 1 per cent in each of Chicago's seventy-five neighbourhoods. That was modest enough. Yet nothing of the kind was achieved. More than four decades later, the rigid segregation of Chicago's schools and neighbourhoods is essentially unchanged. Indeed, it is measurably worse than in big cities in the South. What has moderated it to some extent has been demographic change and in particular Hispanic immigration. Cicero, for example, is now 77 per cent Hispanic. Nationally, at the time, King's venture into Chicago was widely seen as a defeat, and not unfairly.

There was one remaining irony. King never did launch a march into Cicero. But on 24 September that year some two hundred and fifty marchers, led by Robert Lucas of CORE and SNCC's Monroe Sharp, did breach the Walled City. Two thousand National Guardsmen and hundreds of Cook County police succeeded in protecting them from several thousand white folk, screaming invective and hurling rocks. Some of the marchers wore baseball mitts to catch the stones and throw them back. Yet no one was killed or even seriously hurt. Martin Luther King could not allow the march, or take part in it. But Lucas was touched that King called him the night before to wish him luck.

In Montgomery, in Albany, and in Birmingham, King was able to snatch victory out of the jaws of defeat for one reason above all. In each case, he was ultimately supported by the authority and the power of the federal government. That, in turn, had been because southern sheriffs and police chiefs, both the rough and the smooth, could be relied on to go too far. Images of police horses and dogs, tear gas and cattle prods, the deaths of civil rights workers – especially of white civil rights workers Mickey Schwerner, Andrew Goodman, James Reeb, Jonathan Daniels and Violet Liuzzo – unsparingly reported in the national media, always brought irresistible pressure on the federal government to do something to bring the segregationist South into line with northern dislike of legally sanctioned segregation. That did not mean that there was a universal determination in the North to be rid of segregation. Far from it, as George Wallace had understood.

But Chicago proved that in the North the political dynamic was different. Mayor Daley, and the civic, religious and business elite of the great northern metropolis, did not make stupid mistakes. They did not reject – they shared, or at least said, and no doubt thought, they shared – King's vision of racial harmony. They were just not prepared to do what would have been necessary to bring it about. Although they shared

King's conviction that Birmingham, or Philadelphia, Mississippi, were bad places, communities vitiated by racial separation and hatred, they could not bring themselves to share his growing belief that racial separation and injustice were not peculiar to the South, and that for black people Chicago, too, was not a good place. So Chicago was a defeat for him. It also strengthened his understanding that there was an even higher and more dangerous mountain to climb.

13

Vietnam and Beyond

The war in Vietnam is but a symptom of a far deeper malady within the American spirit.

Martin Luther King, at a sermon at Riverside Church,
New York, 4 April 1967

On 14 January 1967 Dr King flew to Ocho Rios, on the north coast of Jamaica, for a working vacation. He needed time to draft the book that would be called *Where Do We Go from Here: Chaos or Community?* He did a good deal of writing there in spite of a lightning visit from Jim Bevel, who had chivvied Andy Young into revealing where Martin was hiding.

At the Atlanta airport on his way to Jamaica he bought an issue of *Ramparts* magazine. The main feature was a twenty-four-page article called 'The Children of Vietnam'. Introduced by America's favourite paediatrician Dr Benjamin Spock, who was now emerging as one of the principal critics of the war, it was written by a young American lawyer, William Pepper, who had spent much of the previous year in Vietnam. It was illustrated by terrifying pictures of children killed by American weapons – mutilated, burned, napalmed. King was travelling with his aide Bernard Lee. As he looked at the magazine, he pushed his food away. Lee asked what was the matter. King said bleakly, 'Nothing will ever taste good for me until I do everything I can to end the war.' That was by no means the first time that King had thought hard about Vietnam. Almost two years earlier, as soon as President Johnson had ordered the first bombing of North Vietnam, King was speaking at Howard University. It was then that he first expressed his sympathy for Johnson's dilemma, but he also stated firmly that the war in Vietnam was achieving nothing.

A few days later he called the President and in the course of an edgy, difficult conversation went out of his way to express his appreciation of the President's problem, emphasizing that he had criticized the war as a minister of the Gospel, not as a politician. Johnson, for his part, was almost apologetic, saying he didn't want to be a warmonger, but he could not come home from Vietnam with his tail between his legs.

That did not stop the President, shortly afterwards, in July, passing to J. Edgar Hoover a request for the FBI to investigate King's position on the war, to which his attention had been drawn by his colleagues, Roy Wilkins of the NAACP and James Farmer of CORE. (A little later, when King had an uncharacteristically angry exchange with Whitney Young, accusing him of not speaking out on Vietnam because he might lose a foundation grant, Young pointed to King's waistline and said, 'You seem to be eating well!') The civil rights movement was increasingly divided and confused about the war. In August, in the course of an anti-war demonstration, Bob Moses argued: 'Negroes better than anyone else are in a position to question the war. Not because they understand the war better, but because they better understand the United States.' A few days later, during the SCLC convention in Birmingham, King admitted that 'few events in my lifetime have stirred my conscience and pained my heart as the present conflict which is raging in Vietnam'.

In September, apparently at the President's instigation, King met Arthur Goldberg, the veteran labour union lawyer and later member of the Supreme Court, who was Johnson's ambassador to the United Nations. King put his researchers, including Bayard Rustin, Levison and Harry Wachtel,* to work to brief him fully on the background. King took a strongly anticolonial line. He argued to Goldberg that the United States had missed an opportunity to be an ally of Ho Chi Minh. He admitted that Ho was a communist, but saw him as primarily a Vietnamese nationalist and fighter against colonialism. He tried to persuade the ambassador that the United States, by financing France's war to retain colonial power in Vietnam, had backed the wrong side. Goldberg took time out to deal with a crisis that had arisen between India and Pakistan, then came back and denounced King in a press conference. At the same time Senator Thomas Dodd of Connecticut came out with a statement calling King arrogant for 'undermining' the President's foreign

---

* Harry M. Wachtel, who died in 1997, aged 78, was a Manhattan lawyer who met Dr King in 1962 and helped him with advice, fund-raising and introductions.

policy. King was sure Johnson was behind these attacks, and felt he had been mouse-trapped by the President. But he also told his advisers, including Levison, to their chagrin, that he felt he could not fight on two fronts at once.

At this stage Johnson himself was ambivalent, or at least ambiguous, about Vietnam. In his State of the Union speech at the beginning of 1966, for example, he said the war was 'a crime against mankind'. 'There are poor to be lifted up,' he went on, in his best preacher's manner, 'and there are cities to be built and there's a world to be helped.' Yet, he added, 'we do what we must'. Johnson's policy was conditioned by a fear of being thought ignorant in foreign policy matters. He was anxious to be accepted by the great figures of the Cold War, men like Dean Acheson and the imagined chairman of the 'foreign policy establishment', John J. McCloy. Later Johnson summoned them among a group of 'wise men' whom he hoped to persuade to support his commitment to the war, and in 1968 their dissent was to be an important part of his motive in deciding not to run for re-election. But in 1966 the President was becoming surer than ever that he must do everything he could to bring back victory from Vietnam. As the year went on, and even more in the course of 1967, he was angered by those who opposed the war and especially by Martin King, whom he saw as having betrayed his trust.

Throughout 1966, King held to his resolution not to risk the goals of the civil rights movement by diverting his energies into the campaign against the war. It was hard. All his instincts, his commitment to nonviolence, his Christian pacifist beliefs, urged him to denounce the war, but his political judgement told him not to get involved. His wife was even more certain that the war was immoral, and for a time he thought he could leave it to her to campaign against it. He was particularly annoyed by those who said he wanted to merge the civil rights movement and the peace movement, though in truth he was attracted by the opportunity the war offered of creating a broad, interracial coalition on the left of politics.

Before leaving Jamaica, he wrote to the Nobel Prize committee, nominating a Vietnamese monk for the peace prize. Still he hesitated to come out publicly against the war. It does seem to have been his emotional reaction to the pictures accompanying Bill Pepper's *Ramparts* piece that made something snap. He came back from Jamaica, and after a few more days working on his book at a hotel in Miami Beach, he made up his mind to speak out.

That spring, opposition to the war was mounting. Allard Lowenstein, the Yale University chaplain William Sloane Coffin and Rabbi Abraham Heschel were busy organizing Clergy and Laity Concerned About Vietnam (CALCAV). In early March Robert Kennedy spoke publicly against the war. King himself attended a conference in a Los Angeles hotel with four Democratic Senators who had broken with the administration on the issue, and expressed his concern in uncompromising language. At a Chicago theological seminary he called the war 'a blasphemy against all America stands for'. Yet by the end of March he had still not spoken out unambiguously and in public. His most respected advisers all begged him not to do so. Even Stanley Levison, to whom he paid more attention than to anyone, warned against the dangers of joining a 'squabbling, pacifist, socialist, hippie collection'. Martin stood firm. His mind was made up.

The opportunity came with an invitation to move a lecture scheduled for CALCAV to Riverside Church on 4 April 1967. This is a huge neo-Gothic basilica, Baptist but interdenominational, modelled on Chartres Cathedral and seating thousands. It was built by John D. Rockefeller I next to Columbia University on the Upper West Side of New York City. The Riverside pulpit had long been occupied by the thunderous Harry Emerson Fosdick, one of Dr King's models as a preacher, and was also associated with another of his mentors, Reinhold Niebuhr. A sermon at Riverside could be assured of coverage in the national media, and national attention is exactly what it got.

The Riverside speech was among King's most carefully wrought and emotionally powerful. It was also one of the worst-received. He began by saying that his conscience left him no choice. Over the past two years, he said, he had moved 'to break the betrayal of my own silences'. There was an obvious connection between the struggle for civil rights and the war. 'We were taking the young black men who had been crippled by our society, and sending them eight thousand miles away to guarantee liberties in Southeast Asia which they had not found in southwest Georgia and East Harlem.' He repeated the argument he had made to

Arthur Goldberg, that America had chosen the wrong side in Indochina. The Vietnamese 'must see Americans as strange liberators'. The United States had vigorously supported the French for nine years as they sought to recolonize Vietnam. After the Geneva Conference of 1954 the Vietnamese had watched as the United States conspired with Ngo Dinh Diem, whom he called 'one of the most vicious modern dictators', to prevent elections that would surely have brought Ho Chi Minh to power.

He now stepped boldly into the political domain he had so far avoided, proposing five things the American government should do. It must end all bombing in Vietnam, South and North, and declare a unilateral ceasefire. It should stop the war spreading by ending the build-up of US forces in Thailand and interference in Laos. It must realistically accept that the National Liberation Front, America's enemy in the war, must play a part in negotiations and in any future Vietnamese government. It must set a date for pulling out all foreign troops from the country.

That was bad enough, from the point of view of the Johnson administration and therefore of those in King's own movement who were afraid of the consequences of a diversion into the peace movement. But King went further. The war in Vietnam was 'but a symptom of a far deeper malady within the American spirit'. If Americans ignored that fact, they would find themselves organizing committees for the next generation to campaign against US policing and marching to protest against American actions in a dozen countries in Asia, Africa and South America. He quoted a 'sensitive American official overseas' who had judged that the United States was 'on the wrong side of a world revolution'; the 'shirtless and the barefoot people of the land were rising'. Communism was a judgement against American failure to make democracy real. Americans must recapture the revolutionary spirit and declare 'eternal hostility to poverty, racism and militarism'. History was 'cluttered with the wreckage of nations and individuals that pursued this self-defeating path of hate'. And he ended by quoting James Russell Lowell, nineteenth-century abolitionist:

Once to every man and nation comes the moment to decide,
In the strife of Truth with Falsehood, for the good or evil side.

He had expected his views to be unpopular, but he seems to have been surprised by the breadth of the annoyance he had caused, and by its vehemence. The *Washington Post* said his speech contained 'sheer inventions of unsupported fantasy'. The *New York Times* charged him with 'recklessly comparing American military methods to those of the Nazis'. President Johnson's new adviser, John Roche, called King 'ambitious and quite stupid', commenting that he had 'thrown in with the commies'. *Life* magazine said the speech 'sounded like a script for Radio Hanoi'. Another Johnson aide, George Christian, put up the African-American columnist Carl Rowan to attack the speech. Even many of King's allies were uncomfortable, or plain hostile. The NAACP's board passed a resolution against any attempt to merge the civil rights movement with the peace movement. This is what King explicitly denied he was doing. 'Everyone has a duty to be in both the civil rights and peace movements,' he explained but he was not urging 'mechanical fusion' of the two.

As a leader and as a man, Martin Luther King had nailed his colours to the mast, his theses to the cathedral door. A few days after the Riverside speech, he took a prominent part in the mobilization against the war – the 'spring Mobe'. He marched among the leaders of the peace movement at the head of 125,000 demonstrators in New York. Just over three weeks later, in the church he had inherited from his father in Atlanta, he made his case again. And again, he held nothing back. Much of the sermon reused material from the Riverside speech, as anyone who was asked to speak as often as he was might well have to do. But to his own congregation in Atlanta he restated in the Baptist idiom they loved his reasons for believing 'why we should not be in Vietnam'. The Ebenezer sermon was less political, but just as intransigent as the lecture at Riverside.

He agreed with Dante, he began, that 'the hottest places in hell' are reserved for those who in a moral crisis remain neutral. 'We are called to play the Good Samaritan on life's roadside,' he said, 'but that will only be an initial act. One day we must come to see that the whole Jericho road must be changed.' Again, he broadened the scope of the cause. He spoke, in his richest baritone, with an intensity rare even for him:

Don't let anybody make you think that God chose America as his divine, messianic force to be a sort of policeman of the whole world. God has a way of standing before the nations with judgment, and it seems I can hear God saying to America, 'You're too arrogant! And if you don't change your ways, I will rise up and break the backbone of your power, and I'll place it in the hands of a nation that doesn't even know my name. Be still and know that I am God.

And with that he swung into his inimitable rhetoric, stirring the voices of the ancient and modern prophets into a prayer of faith, to 'hew out of the mountain of despair a stone of hope'. And he ended with a plain line from one of his favourite Negro spirituals: 'I ain't gonna study war no more.'

Some journalists had accused him of embracing the anti-war movement only because the air was going out of the civil rights movement. That was not his motive. No one could deny the real moral anguish, the moral commitment, that had driven him to take such risks with everything he had worked for. Yet it is true that at this time he was bogged down in the petty and the mundane. The SCLC was broke, as usual. The rows between the staff were more furious than ever. Hosea Williams was more impossible, and King suspected that Jim Bevel had actually gone mad. The first major sortie in the North, into Chicago, had been a rebuff, if not a defeat. King himself was depressed and frustrated. He found comfort in a secretive affair he had begun in 1964 with an older married woman, the Kentucky state senator Georgia Davis. It was not apparently a particularly intense relationship. King called, and Davis came to him. But she fulfilled his need for relief from almost intolerable pressures.

Once he was a declared champion of the peace movement, King found himself in demand politically. He was courted by the movement's leaders, including such diverse figures as Dr Spock, John Kenneth Galbraith, Allard Lowenstein and even Robert Kennedy, who came out against the war his brother had expounded, at first cautiously but eventually in the most unambiguous fashion, by running against Johnson for the presidency. Apparently there was some discussion of King running in 1968, either for President as a peace candidate or as a vice-presidential running-mate for Kennedy. His children have said so, and although many have been sceptical, it is not impossible.

Since 1966, a peace movement of a kind had been growing across America.[1] It was a loose agglomeration of groups that intersected only through the furious efforts of a handful of leftish political activists, among them Al Lowenstein and Curtis Gans, a staff employee of the liberal organization Americans for Democratic Action. There were also members of a liberal intellectual establishment that had adored Jack Kennedy and never quite accepted his successor: people like Galbraith, the historian Arthur Schlesinger Jr, and Richard Goodwin, all of whom had worked for President Kennedy and had become disenchanted first with President Johnson and then with the war.

Then there were the students, especially from the great graduate schools like Columbia, Harvard, Yale, Berkeley, Wisconsin and Michigan. Hundreds of them had already signed up for the dangerous campaign for civil rights in Mississippi. Their fury at the war was fanned for some by the possibility that they might be drafted to serve in it; movements to resist the draft and oppose the war were spreading among them like wildfire. Demos, mobilizations, teach-ins, alternative journalism and every variety of grass-roots political activism were finding new recruits every month for a great political that only needed leaders. Such leaders might be found among the small but growing group of successful Democratic politicians, especially in the Senate, people who were aware of the damage the war was doing to their party, to the economy, to domestic tranquillity and to America's reputation in the world. The acknowledged leaders of the party, many of them southerners, like Richard Russell of Georgia, John Stennis of Mississippi, Robert Kerr of Oklahoma, were Lyndon Johnson's friends and loyal supporters of the Cold War wherever it must be fought. But the 'doves', as they were coming to be known, included some respected names too, among them Bill Fulbright of Arkansas, Wayne Morse of Oregon, George McGovern of South Dakota, and a man who would be available as a presidential candidate to challenge President Johnson in 1968 because he was not up for re-election to the Senate – Eugene McCarthy of Minnesota.

At the centre of these intersecting groups, inscrutable as a Buddha but by no means as silent, was Robert Kennedy. He hated Lyndon Johnson; it is not too strong a word.[2] He dreamed of succeeding his elder brother in the White House. From a distinctly conservative position on many issues he was gradually moving leftward. He had been especially moved, and changed, by a brief visit to South Africa. But he also regarded himself as a cautious political pragmatist. Throughout 1966 and 1967 he was watching, taking soundings, and keeping his counsel about whether he would risk everything by running against Johnson himself.

For twelve months of excited politicking, among the most dramatic in twentieth-century American history, King was a player. Even those who could not visualize him as a presidential or even vice-presidential candidate, in an age when his race alone would have been an all but insuperable barrier in the Democratic Party, recognized that he had imposed his presence as a national figure. Many thought that he had been beached by what they saw as the collapse of the civil rights movement. Many highly politicized young black people thought he had been leapfrogged by the advocates of Black Power, by SNCC, the Black Panthers, the Black Muslims or the insurgent followers of Malcolm X. They saw him as too cautious, too bourgeois, too Christian, too southern. For others he was too radical, too earnest, unrealistic in his non-violent faith, and unlikely to survive in the shark-infested waters of presidential politics.

King himself was not tempted by electoral politics, but the campaign of conscience he had undertaken against the Vietnam war was only one aspect of a new conception of American politics that had been maturing in his mind for a long time, indeed since his student days. He was broadening his concern from the injustice meted out to black people in the South, to injustice to the poor and powerless everywhere in America, and indeed from the national to the international scene. In the year he had left to live after his speech at Riverside, his efforts to develop a new revolutionary politics in America were doomed to failure, even to something close to farce. But this new political vision was to survive him.

14

The Last Campaign

Precious Lord, take my hand!
Old Baptist hymn

On 4 December 1967 Dr King summoned the media to a press conference at which he announced his most ambitious and – many thought – his most ill-judged and desperate venture. It came to be called the Poor People's Campaign. The concept was that the Southern Christian Leadership Conference would lead 'waves of the nation's poor and disinherited' to Washington, where they would mount the biggest, the most radical, the most aggressive lobby of both Congress and the President.

The Poor People's Campaign was different in both strategy and tactics from the campaigns King had conducted from Montgomery to Selma. For one thing, it was targeted not only against racism, but against economic inequality and injustice in general. It would not be a one-day march on Washington like the happy and unthreatening triumph of 1963. It would be 'a trek to the nation's capital by suffering and outraged citizens who will go to stay until some definite and positive action is taken to provide jobs and income for the poor'.

The strategy of the campaign reflected King's adjustment to the changed realities of the late 1960s. At least in theory, the target of his southern campaigns had been met. The Civil Rights Act of 1964 and the Voting Rights Act of 1965 committed the government and the law to guarantee to African-Americans desegregation and the right to vote, though in practice the walls of Jericho would by no means come instantly tumbling down. The rioting in northern cities had drawn national attention to the economic injustices there, and the seething anger of their black inhabitants. King's own actual and potential followers were perplexed and divided over the issue of Black Power and more generally of what tactics might work in the northern context. His own experiences in Chicago and elsewhere had shown him, if he ever doubted it, just how tough it would be to deal with the subtle, half-veiled, unadmitted, stubborn racism of the North.

The event, planned for April 1968, was not aimed, like King's earlier campaigns, at improving life for southern blacks. His aides fanned out and tried to recruit as participants Native Americans, Puerto Ricans, Hispanics and poor Appalachian whites. The project reflected a strand in King's thought that was not new, but which had been occupying an ever bigger place in his analysis of the situation. This was the conviction that the difficulties of African-Americans were not solely due to racism, but that the American capitalist system as a whole, in the way it had developed, made inequality and injustice inevitable.

The seed of the idea for the Poor People's Campaign came from a young African-American lawyer, Marian Wright, who later married one of Robert Kennedy's closest associates, Peter Edelman. (There are suggestions that she had been put up to suggesting the campaign by Kennedy himself as he wrestled with the decision of whether or not to oppose Lyndon Johnson openly for that year's Democratic presidential nomination.) She proposed a sit-in at the offices of Johnson's Secretary of Labor, the well-intentioned Willard Wirtz.

There were precedents. In 1894, a year of economic depression, one Jacob Coxey, a quarry owner from Massillon, Ohio, led an army of protesters to Washington. Preceded by a Virgin on a donkey, they marched under a banner that read 'Peace on earth, goodwill to men, but death to interest-bearing bonds!' In 1932, in the depths of another depression, discontented First World War veterans, who had not been paid the bonus promised to them when they volunteered for service, marched on Washington. They camped on the Anacostia Flats, across the river from the Capitol, before being dispersed by troops with fixed bayonets led by Major George Patton under the command of General Douglas MacArthur, and their shanties were burned down. (Eisenhower, it was said, who was a major on MacArthur's staff at the time, disapproved of the violent way in which the marchers were dispersed. George Patton had no such qualms.)

The Poor People's Campaign attracted a good deal of ridicule, not least because sharecroppers' shacks were to be shipped from Mississippi on flatbed trucks and mule carts to be parked on the Mall between the

Lincoln Memorial and the Capitol. More seriously, it marked the total breakdown of relations between King and President Johnson, who now began to credit the poisonous information dripped into his ear by Hoover, in particular about the supposedly 'communist' influence of Stanley Levison. One historian drew a perceptive parallel between the two men, as 1967 turned into 1968. 'Lyndon Johnson and Martin Luther King, now avowed political enemies, faced identical dilemmas: how to end an escalating war, with mounting casualties, which was siphoning funds from the dream they still shared of a more just society – and how to deal with increasing hostility from each other as well as from their own hard-won constituencies.'[1]

King's own constituency seemed to be crumbling. Increasingly, he was being attacked as too cautious – even by some as an Uncle Tom – by SNCC extremists like Stokely Carmichael and Hubert 'Rap' Brown. King was rightly infuriated by their reckless advocacy of violent struggle, which he constantly pointed out was suicidal on the part of a group numbering little more than 10 per cent of the population, especially given that the majority had a near-monopoly of organized force, not to mention resources of every kind. Yet many young African-Americans were attracted by the Black Power slogan and its champions. Many more were outraged by the brutal repression of the rioting in Detroit, Newark, New Jersey and other cities, where black casualties far outnumbered white.

King's immediate allies were divided and disorganized. Many were unhappy both with his stance on Vietnam and with the Poor People's Campaign. James Bevel and Hosea Williams were still at daggers drawn. Bayard Rustin, now at last ensconced in a salaried job in the trade union movement, strongly opposed King on both issues, and he was far from alone. In October 1967 King had hired a very able African-American businessman, William Rutherford, who had made a success of a public relations consultancy in Geneva, to sort out the SCLC headquarters. Part of Rutherford's brief was to examine how SCLC staffers on modest salaries could live so plenteously. At his first meeting with the leadership, Rutherford described how shocked he had been at an SCLC party where prostitutes had been brought in and a young female assistant had almost been raped. The assembled Baptist ministers and civil rights workers laughed aloud at Rutherford's naivety.

The truth is that, in this last winter of his life, 1967–8, King was suffering from many of the symptoms of severe depression. He was drinking heavily. He had difficulty in sleeping. He frequently expressed pessimism about his movement and about the country as a whole. He was consumed with guilt, about his personal failures generally and specifically about his persistent sexual infidelities. In the past, he had built up an elaborate justification, pointing out to anyone who showed an interest that many great moral and religious leaders, including Martin Luther and St Augustine, had been sexual libertines or sexually obsessed. Now, in his thirties, he was confronting the moral ambiguity of his behaviour. He did not stop seeing other women. But at Ebenezer he preached more and more unambiguously about his own sinful nature. In the end he was guilty of appalling, though apparently unthinking, cruelty towards Coretta. On 24 January 1968 she was taken into hospital for an emergency hysterectomy. When she came home, he chose that moment to confess to her the most emotionally significant of his numerous relationships with women, that with an African-American graduate who lived in California.

During this frustrating and miserable period, he spoke even more frequently than before about his own death. It was about this time that he said, on hearing of President Kennedy's assassination, 'This is what is going to happen to me. This is such a sick society.' He used almost the same expression when a plane he was about to fly in had to be evacuated because of a bomb threat.

By now, many people thought King had lost his grip. He seemed to be making increasingly wild and radical analyses of American society. He was, of course, far from alone in talking in such terms. The Tet Offensive in early 1968 made many question whether the United States could win the Vietnam War. These doubts, afflicting even those who had no objection to the war in principle, and the fierce moral anger it provoked in many other Americans, coinciding with shock and concern over the causes of the urban rioting, which reached something of a climax in Detroit in 1967, provoked a neurasthenic, despairing mood. This was a time when many young Americans emigrated to Canada and others spelled their country's name with a K: 'Amerika' had a sinister, Central European ring to it.

Yet it is important to understand that, however stressed and pessimistic King was – and he was now contemplating the frustration of his whole life's work – his radical analysis was neither new nor shallow. Ever since theological college, as mentioned earlier, he had suspected that the inequalities and injustices of American society might be too great to be healed except by a shift to the left. After the passage of the great civil rights statutes of 1964 and 1965, as he turned from desegregation and Negro emancipation to the more elusive problems of the northern ghetto, he became more and more convinced that, if black and white Americans were to live together in the beloved community he dreamed of, it would have to be in the context of some kind of democratic socialism.[2]

Of course, he was well aware that it would be fatal to his other political aims to speak openly about this belief. Late in 1967 he spoke at a meeting at the Ford Foundation, which was thinking of putting substantial funding into training SCLC workers: 'Something is wrong with capitalism as it now stands in the United States,' he said. 'We are not interested in being integrated into this value structure. Power must be relocated, a radical redistribution of power must take place.' Then he asked for the tape recorder to be turned off while he talked about his conviction that American capitalism would have to be replaced by democratic socialism.

King masked his personal beliefs. He sometimes spoke like a Cold War liberal. But since his early visits to Ghana and India his sympathies had lain with the ex-colonial societies that were trying to emerge from powerlessness. He always saw powerlessness as essentially an economic rather than a psychological condition. His confrontation with Mayor Daley in 1966, and his experience of the economic system as it worked for black people in Chicago, drove him to a more radical view of American society which by 1967 was explicit, if not exactly trumpeted abroad. By 1968 he was talking openly about class struggle. So the Poor People's Campaign and the attempt to create a broad alliance between poor blacks and poor whites were not the desperate expedient of a leader who was losing control of his followers. It was the logical, if ill-fated, conclusion drawn from more than a decade's reflection on American society. Like many an American radical before him, he could see that poor whites and poor blacks must work together, but he did not know how to persuade them to do it.

King now set out on a series of journeys across the Deep South, trying to recruit poor people to come to Washington in April. The results were disappointing. Then preparations for the campaign were interrupted by a phone call from Jim Lawson, one of Martin's oldest and most respected friends.

On 12 February black sanitation workers in Memphis had gone on strike. They were angry about a whole culture of discrimination. The immediate cause of their walking out was a typical incident: black employees were sent home without pay when the weather was bad, while white workers continued to be paid. Demonstrating strikers were beaten by the police. The strike became bitter. The city authorities denounced it as illegal, and while national union officials and African-American leaders including Rustin and Roy Wilkins tried to mediate, the tension, and its openly racial dimension, got worse. Lawson, the former Nashville students' leader, now pastor of a major African-American Methodist church in Memphis, had tried several times to get King involved but he had pleaded his heavy speaking schedule. Finally, on 17 March, he agreed to stop off, between a fund-raising tour of Los Angeles and further efforts to drum up sharecroppers from Mississippi and Alabama to bring their mule carts to Washington.

King finally reached Memphis on 28 March for what was intended to be a non-violent march through the city in support of the sewage workers. The mood, however, was anything but non-violent. Sullen youths gathered at the back of the procession, many with bottles of booze hidden in paper bags. Lawson's authority was openly challenged by a group of students who called themselves 'the Invaders'. In a half-baked way they had adopted Stokely Carmichael's militant ideas. It is questionable how much responsibility the Invaders bore for what happened. Certainly their motives were mixed. They may have been critical of what they saw as King's moderation, but they were happy to be paid by the SCLC. When the march swung into Beale Street, famous as the home of the blues in an earlier generation, hundreds tore the placards they had been issued with off the sticks and used the sticks for smashing shop windows. Criminals appeared in their dozens, and the supposedly peaceful demonstration turned into an orgy of looting and disorder.

The Memphis police reacted as they had been trained to do. They beat the marchers and the looters with their night-sticks indiscriminately. They fired tear gas, and then live rounds. Sixty-two people were injured, by no means all by the police. But a sixteen-year-old African-American boy was shot dead by a police bullet. The situation was ugly by any standards. One of King's aides commandeered a car and he and a few others escaped with a police motorcycle escort. The police would not allow him to go to the hotel where he was already checked in, the elegant Peabody, but he ended up in another white hotel.

The next morning he learned for the first time of the divisions within the Memphis African-American community and in particular of the bad blood between Jim Lawson and the Invaders. Any way he looked at it, King faced a public relations disaster. Within hours the FBI was circulating whispers that if the Poor People's Campaign reached Washington, worse violence could be expected. At a hastily called press conference, King sought, with limited success, to give reassurance that his legions of the poor would be strictly non-violent.

Even those liberal papers that had supported him, if not uncritically, now took it for granted that the poor people's descent on Washington would end with looting and rioting. Both the *New York Times* and the *Washington Post* came out against the march, and the *St Louis Post-Dispatch*, usually a reliably liberal voice, called Martin 'one of the most menacing men in America today'. As for southern papers and southern legislators, they were delighted by his misfortunes in Memphis. 'Chicken à la King,' headlined the local paper, the *Memphis Commercial Appeal*, mocking King's flight from the demonstration. Southern Senators, led by John Stennis of Mississippi, called upon the federal government to turn back the marchers at the city limits of the District of Columbia.

On his way back to Atlanta, King sat up late in New York arguing with two of his closest friends and drinking far too much whisky. On 30 March, he was back in Atlanta, licking his wounds. There was a strategy meeting at Ebenezer, which turned out to be one of the most important and the tensest in the organization's history. Ostensibly, the issue was whether to persevere in Memphis, or to carry on with plans for the poor people's march on Washington. It was plain to many that King's leadership was in jeopardy.

The meeting began badly. The leaders were divided about strategy. Martin began by telling his friends and veterans of the struggle, 'We are in trouble.' He was not personally committed to either Memphis or Washington, he said. He could not make up his mind. That was for the staff to decide. One by one they gave their opinions. Andy Young was for delaying the march on Washington for a year, to give time to assemble an impressive army. Bevel said that was so much bullshit: 'We need to stop this war'. Jesse Jackson thought they would be better focusing on his Operation Breadbasket, a hitherto rather successful effort to get corporate help and jobs to the black poor. Then, uncharacteristically, Martin stormed out. But before he did so, he did something else he had never done before: he turned the withering power of his speech on to his friends, individually. Young had given in to doubt, he charged, Bevel to 'brains' – meaning to intellectual conceit – and Jackson to ambition. Jackson shouted down the stairs to him, 'Doc, doc don't worry! It's going to be all right.'

King stopped and shouted back up the stairs, 'Jesse, everything's not going to be all right. If things keep going the way they're going now, it's not the SCLC but the whole country that's in trouble.' If Jackson wanted to carve out his own niche in society, he went on angrily, he should go ahead, 'but for God's sake don't bother me!' And off he tore. It seems that, as in other moments of frustration and stress, he went to see a lover, this time his long-established Atlanta mistress. Wherever he was, the paladins were left dumbfounded.

The day was saved by one of the least known of the ministers. It was Joseph Lowery,* as Stanley Levison remembered, who said quietly, 'The Lord has been in this room this afternoon. I know he's been here because we couldn't have deliberated the way we did without the Holy Spirit being here. And the Holy Spirit is going to be with us in Memphis and Washington, and I know we're going to win.' At this the whole group, traumatized and profoundly moved, stood up and shook hands. Ralph

---

* Joseph Lowery, from Huntsville, Alabama, was one of the founder members of the SCLC in 1957. He became president of the organization in 1977. He was very active in opposing apartheid in South Africa.

Abernathy, who alone knew where King had gone, fetched him. It was decided they should do both Memphis and Washington. In effect, the meeting had led the whole group, whatever the personal or doctrinal interests of individual members, to see that Memphis and Washington were not alternatives, but two ways of making the same points. They would dramatize racism and poverty as two facets of the same injustice in American society.

The third-floor conference room at Ebenezer Church was not the only place where emotions were running high that weekend. This was a moment of crisis not just for King, but for his former ally, now enemy, Lyndon Johnson. Once again, the two narratives, Vietnam and race, were plaited together. In the previous week, LBJ had consulted the veteran foreign policy experts he called his 'Wise Men'. For the first time, they were reluctant to go along with sending yet more troops to Vietnam. On the Sunday, 31 March, King preached at the episcopal cathedral, in Washington, St Alban's, which generated misleading headlines about alleged threats that he had in fact not uttered.

That same evening, President Johnson addressed the nation on television. Only his wife and a handful of aides and technicians had any inkling of what he had in store for them. After thirty-five minutes speaking, he said abruptly, 'Finally, my fellow Americans, let me say this. Of those to whom much is given, much is asked.' He had done his best, he said, borrowing Lincoln's hallowed phrase, to 'bind up the nation's wounds' since the Kennedy assassination. Now he felt he could no longer 'devote an hour or a day of my time to any personal partisan causes . . . Accordingly I shall not seek and I will not accept, the nomination of my party for another term as your President.'

The SCLC decided to schedule the second march in Memphis for 5 April. James Orange, he who had known how to intimidate Chicago's Blackstone Rangers, was sent on to deal with the Invaders. Others, led by Andy Young, went to work out a plan with James Lawson and his community organization and with the unions.

On 3 April King himself arrived in Memphis. This time he and his immediate entourage were staying at an African-American motel, the Lorraine, on the south side of downtown. His journey was not without incident. Eastern Airlines flight 381 was delayed on the ground at Atlanta Airport for an hour because of a bomb scare. When he got to Memphis, he found that the city had successfully asked for an injunction from the federal court banning the march planned by the sanitation workers for the following Monday. There were also whispers of death threats.

It was a stormy day. Tornadoes killed a dozen people across the Middle West. High winds and heavy rain reached Memphis around the time King was due to speak at the cavernous Mason Temple. Reports came in that, either because of the storms or perhaps because of fears of violence, only two thousand had turned up to hear the speech, in a venue that easily held fifteen thousand people. King was loath to speak to so few. He was afraid it would generate newspaper stories about no one wanting to hear what he had to say. He asked Ralph Abernathy to speak in his place. Instead, Abernathy acted as a warm-up man. He kept what audience there was in a state of feverish excitement, and then, as the storm reached its height, he went to the telephone and begged Martin to come and speak.

Giving in to his friend's appeal, he delivered one of the two or three most memorable speeches of his life. It did not start in a particularly promising way. He seemed to some of the listening ministers, experienced preachers all, to have reached his peroration prematurely, before he had given the audience something they could take home and dwell on. He trotted through many of his standard tropes, than offering a lighting tour of world history to show why he would have chosen, of all ages, the late twentieth century to live – namely, because of the opportunities it afforded for freedom, not just in the United States but in the former colonial world as well. He was in a mood to share with his audience, more than he usually did, some very personal thoughts. He touched, as he had rarely done before, on the assassination attempt by Izola Ware Curry in 1958. He told them about having been informed that if he had sneezed it would have killed him, then quoted a letter from a white teenager, saying how glad she was that he had not sneezed. That set him to counting his blessings.

With mounting rhetorical emphasis he recited the speeches, the demonstrations, the victories he would have missed if he had sneezed.

This train of thought brought to mind the morning's bomb scare and the threats he had heard when he arrived in Memphis. That, in turn, triggered a burst of authentic emotion, a rhetorical power of a calibre few, if any, other speakers of his time could reach, as he accepted and dismissed the probability of his own martyrdom, savouring every word.

He went on, his magnificent voice reaching a new intensity:

Well, I don't know what will happen now. We've got some difficult days ahead. But it really doesn't matter with me now, because I've been to the mountaintop. And I don't mind. Like anybody, I would like to live a long life. Longevity has its place. But I'm not concerned about that now. I just want to do God's will. And He's allowed me to go up to the mountain. And I've looked over. And I've seen the Promised Land. I may not get there with you. But I want you to know tonight, that we, as a people, will get to the Promised Land! And so I'm happy, tonight. I'm not worried about anything. I'm not fearing any man! Mine eyes have seen the glory of the coming of the Lord!

After the speech, Martin disappeared with Ralph Abernathy, out on the town. They got back to the Lorraine motel at four in the morning, just in time to see a car with Kentucky plates pulling into the parking lot.[3] 'There's the Senator!' King cried out in pleasure. The car held King's friend, Kentucky Senator Georgia Davis, who had just been elected to the Kentucky legislature as both the first African-American and the first woman in that body. Davis was the best friend of a girlfriend of Martin's brother, the Revd A.D. King, who had introduced her to Martin. He now disappeared into Davis's room, 201, for the rest of the night.

The next morning, he was up at around 9 a.m. to brief lawyers for the hearing on the injunction against the sanitation workers' march. Then he primed Bernard Lafayette, the aide who was to take his place at a press conference, describing the planning for the poor people's march. For lunch, he and Abernathy shared a plate of catfish, and after more business calls, the King brothers together called their mother and talked to her happily for almost an hour.

The plan was for the whole group to have dinner at the home of Billy

Kyles, a local minister. Spirits were high. When Andrew Young returned from a grilling by the city of Memphis's lawyers about the march and the theory of non-violence, a doctrine about which they were both ignorant and sceptical, he was set upon – first tickled, then pelted in an old-fashioned pillow fight. Meanwhile Hosea Williams had discovered that the Invaders, who had been allowed two rooms in the motel, had managed to bill the SCLC for fifteen meals on room service. They were promptly ejected. Now it was time to dress and get ready for dinner at the Kyleses'. Martin was in jovial mood, joshing his friends. The motel's parking lot was filling up with the dinner guests, not to mention a sprinkling of undercover police spies.

Jesse Jackson arrived and introduced a colleague, Ben Branch, who was the singer and saxophonist with the Chicago band run by Jackson's outfit, Operation Breadbasket. Martin remembered him, and his signature tune.

'Ben,' he said, leaning over the motel's balcony, 'make sure you play "Precious Lord, Take My Hand" in the meeting tonight. Play it real pretty!'

Those were the last of his words, words that had changed America and the world. At that moment, the bullet shattered his throat.

15

Detective Story

Judge Battle: 'Are you pleading guilty to murder in the first
degree in this case because you killed Martin Luther
King. . .?'
James Earl Ray: 'Yes.'

Evidence from Ray's trial for murdering Dr King.

For some two months, what was billed as 'the greatest manhunt in history' pursued the wrong man. It was not until June that federal law
enforcement agencies were sure of the identity of the man they were
hunting. He turned out, on fingerprint and other evidence, to be an
obscure professional criminal who had served time across the Middle
West and in California for a number of robberies before being sentenced
to twenty years for an armed robbery in Missouri.

At first they were confused by the various aliases he had used, of
which the chief was Eric S. Galt, the real name of a Canadian employee
of the American corporation, Union Carbide.* To rent a room in Bessie
Brewer's flophouse, with windows overlooking the balcony of the Lorraine motel, he called himself John Willard. To buy a rifle, he called
himself Harvey Lowmyer, the name (misspelled) of a fellow convict from
Missouri. To get a Canadian passport, he used two other names, apparently culled from Toronto newspaper files, Bridgeman and Sneyd. The
favourite alias was sometimes mistakenly written as Eric Starvo Galt,
because of the original Galt's habit of writing the initials of his middle
name (St Vincent) between two rounded dots. In the end, the law
enforcement agencies came to agree that all these names were aliases
for the same man.

He was born in 1928, one of a large dysfunctional family in the Middle
West. He weighed 170 pounds, and stood a couple of inches under six

---

* Since Union Carbide had done a certain amount of secret weapons research for the federal
government, that was enough to excite at least one of the many researchers who set out to
disprove official accounts of the case.

foot tall. He had spent much of his adult life in various American prisons, and had at different times been called also Raines, Rains or Ryan. But the name under which he came to be notorious was James Earl Ray.

On 23 April 1967, just under a year before King's death, Ray, a constant escaper, left the Missouri State Penitentiary hidden in a box of bread being trucked out from the prison bakery. For almost eleven months after that he was on the run. At different times he was to be found in a Chicago suburb, in St Louis, in Canada, Mexico, and California. His life during those months seemed aimless. He worked only briefly, earning a total of less than $700. He haunted seedy bars and occasionally picked up women there casually. He took lessons as a bartender and learned to dance, and he bought some fairly expensive photographic equipment. Then, somewhat abruptly, his life seemed to become more purposeful.

On 17 March 1968 he drove east from Los Angeles. He appears to have started stalking Dr King first in Atlanta, then at Selma, where King was speaking, and finally in Memphis. In Birmingham, he looked at a less lethal gun, then bought a high-powered deer-hunting rifle with a telescopic sight. The circumstances suggested that someone told him to reject the first rifle on offer and choose a more powerful weapon. In Memphis, Ray first checked into a place called the New Rebel motel, then rented a room under the name of John Willard in a rooming house behind the Lorraine motel at 422 1/2 South Main Street – Bessie Brewer's. A bathroom along the hall offered an even better shot at the balcony, if you clambered into the bath first.

After the murder, Ray tried to throw investigators off the track with a story that he had met a mysterious 'Raoul' to discuss selling guns to Mexican criminals, that Raoul had fired the shot and he had been no more than the getaway driver. It was never obvious why Mexican criminals would have to go to Memphis, or indeed would require the services of Ray and Raoul, to buy guns that were on sale openly and cheaply almost as soon as they crossed the Rio Grande. Still less was there any explanation of why Raoul would want to give up his gun-running exploit in order to kill Martin Luther King. Investigators quickly agreed that there never was such a person as Raoul, and that Ray alone stalked and murdered Dr King.

After firing the fatal shot, Ray threw down a bundle containing the rifle which, like other objects in the bundle, carried his fingerprints, before he fled south in a white Mustang sports car. Critics, not unreasonably, pointed out that this was a strange thing to do. Some took it as evidence that Ray was being set up by some mysterious conspiracy. He was, in any case, quick enough to get clear of Memphis before the police could establish a dragnet. This too has struck conspiracy theorists as suspicious. In any event, Ray drove overnight to Atlanta, where he had left some possessions in a rented room. He then travelled north by bus and train into Canada. There is some dispute about how long he took to do so. Using false names, he bought an air ticket to London and acquired a Canadian passport. After staying about a month in Toronto, he duly flew to London on 6 May. He seems to have had it in mind to travel to a country in Africa from which he could not be extradited, and perhaps to sign on as a mercenary. He consulted a journalist in London who had written about mercenaries for information on how to join up. On 7 May he flew to Lisbon, whose troops were still at war with African rebels in Angola and Mozambique. He also showed an interest in emigrating to Rhodesia, now Zimbabwe.

Unable to sign on as a mercenary, he flew back to London and checked into a cheap hotel in Earl's Court, a district then on the route to and from the airport, much favoured by transients. He may have carried out a bank robbery in London; perhaps his money was running out. It was when he returned to Heathrow on 8 June for a flight to Brussels, still pursuing mercenary leads, that the British police arrested him for passport offences and for carrying a concealed weapon, a Japanese-made .38 revolver. He appeared briefly in court in London, then was extradited back to the United States to stand trial for the murder of Dr King.

Ray was represented at first by Arthur Hanes, a former Mayor of Birmingham, Alabama. He also signed a three-way contract with Hanes and William Bradford Huie, a well-known Alabama journalist and writer, who had shown a lifelong interest in the Ku Klux Klan. Huie would pay Hanes $40,000 in trust for Ray, in return for which Ray was to tell Huie what had happened every day since he left prison in April 1967. Huie had no illusions about Ray's truthfulness. But he hoped in this way to ferret out the truth of the question on everyone's mind: not who pulled the trigger, but why and on whose behalf.

Ray, however, perhaps excited by reports of the sums of money he might earn elsewhere, became unhappy with this agreement. He was contacted by J. B. Stoner, from Georgia, the veteran political lawyer and organizer who was something of a national figure on the far right. Stoner, whom we last met stirring up trouble in St Augustine, was associated with both the Ku Klux Klan and the racist National States Rights Party, of which he was at one time chairman. He offered to defend Ray, predicting that 'hundreds of thousands of dollars' would flood in for his defence to pay for batteries of lawyers, and that 'millions of Americans' would thank him for what he had done. He painted a picture of Ray, in short, as the hero of a national conservative movement. In early November, however, at the prompting of one of his brothers, Ray dismissed Hanes as his lawyer and instead briefed a celebrity defence lawyer from Texas, famous for his flamboyant style and huge fees, Percy Foreman of Houston. Foreman proceeded to plea-bargain. If Ray would plead guilty, he would not go to the electric chair, but would receive a long prison sentence instead. (Tennessee law still allowed the death penalty, though it had not been carried out in the state since 1960.)

On 10 March 1969, on Foreman's advice, Ray appeared in the criminal court of Shelby County, where Memphis lies, before Judge W. Preston Battle. Judge Battle may have been a crabby old southern judge with unsympathetic views on African-Americans. But he was very scrupulous in explaining to James Earl Ray the implications of what he was saying. He first asked whether any pressure had been used on him to plead guilty.

'No,' said Ray.

'Are you pleading guilty to murder in the first degree in this case because you killed Dr Martin Luther King under such circumstances that would make you legally guilty of murder in the first degree under the law as explained to you by your lawyers?'

'Yes.'

The judge then asked him at some length whether he understood that by pleading guilty he was waiving a good many rights, including the right of appeal. Again, Ray said simply, 'Yes.' In spite of these warnings, he proceeded to plead guilty to first-degree murder – that is, to the deliberate premeditated killing of Dr Martin Luther King Jr.

It was not long, however, before Ray laid the groundwork for withdrawing that explicit confession, made after those warnings in open court. As an experienced jailhouse lawyer, Ray knew that in certain circumstances a case could be reopened if the defendant repudiated his lawyer. So he quickly fired Foreman, and maintained that he had been duped by the celebrity advocate, whom he referred to, even in official letters, as 'Percy Fourflusher'. It is true that where Hanes stood to make no more than some $20,000 out of defending Ray, Foreman was asking for $165,000. The affair soon disintegrated into a morass of rows and litigation between Ray, Huie and the various lawyers.

In the process Ray withdrew his guilty plea. Indeed, he continued vociferously to protest his innocence until he died in prison in 1998. The fact is, however, that he remains on record as having pleaded guilty to the murder. There is, too, a mass of evidence, accepted by several official reports – even if challenged by various amateur investigators – to link him to the murder, including fingerprints on what is generally taken as the murder weapon.

There is, in other words (in my opinion, though many disagree), little serious doubt that James Earl Ray pulled the trigger of the model 760 Remington rifle and killed Dr King.* The two important questions, and they have been asked and agitated and argued over ever since, are, first, why he pulled the trigger, and, second, did he act alone?

Was Ray, in other words, the agent of a conspiracy? If so, what kind of conspiracy? Was he, perhaps unknowing, the cat's-paw of powerful national political forces: of the FBI, for example, the CIA, or some clique within the federal government, perhaps one in which powerful men had been maddened by King's attacks on the Vietnam War, or panicked by his threat to march on Washington? Was he the victim of some avatar of the Klan, or just of some obscure local racist or reactionary clique? Did he, alternatively, unlikely as it might seem, given the elaborate nature of what he had to do to hunt down his prey, act alone simply because,

---

* The Remington bought by Ray in Birmingham was compatible with the bullet that killed King, though it cannot be proved ballistically beyond any doubt that it was the murder weapon.

for some personal reason or combination of reasons, he wanted to see King dead?

It has to be remembered that King had long been one of the most hated men in the United States. Across the South, but also in many northern subcultures, he was detested as the arch-disturber of the racial status quo. In Georgia, in Alabama and in Chicago, there had been no shortage of voices denouncing him, depicting him as a communist insur-rectionary, a hypocrite, and a revolutionary. People in Iowa were sure that he was sending gangs of black criminals from Chicago into their largely rustic state on motorcycles to kill white people.[1] Similar fantasies were current elsewhere in the inflamed racial climate. There were those in the government, in the FBI and in the Johnson administration who shared such views, which had been vigorously circulated by Hoover and his intimates.

At first, the Justice Department took the FBI's campaign against King with a pinch of salt. When Lyndon Johnson became President, he too at first, as we have seen, was sympathetic to him. But after King denounced the Vietnam War, lending his support to a movement that had come to threaten the stability of the Johnson administration itself, the President had turned against him and began to give more credence to Hoover's increasingly venomous defamation. After all, there was more or less serious discussion of King's running for president or vice-president against him, perhaps on an anti-war ticket with Dr Benjamin Spock, the politicized paediatrician, or – what would have been even more maddening from Lyndon Johnson's point of view – for vice-pres-ident on a ticket headed by Robert Kennedy. As recently as the Sunday before his death, King had denounced the war in bitter language. The war, he told the congregation at the National Cathedral in Washington, 'has strengthened the forces of reaction in our nation. It has put us against the self-determination of a vast majority of the Vietnamese people.' It was enough, in wartime, to anger a great many people all over the country.

In the South, King was almost universally feared and despised. In the proliferating ranks of the old and new right, among Ku Kluxers and White Citizens' Councils and Minutemen, the National States Rights Party, the American Nazis and dozens of other organizations, violent rhetoric against King was habitual. Furthermore, King's belief that he would be assassinated had never been more acute than it was now. He had been to the mountaintop, but he had also looked down from it and beheld the valley of the shadow of death.

At first, there was widespread suspicion, at least in northern and liberal circles, that King's murder would not be thoroughly or carefully investigated, especially given the known hostility of the FBI's leadership to him and all his works. In fact, whatever Hoover's predilections, the technical investigations, both by the Memphis authorities and by the FBI, if not perfect, were at least professionally done. This is perhaps all the more surprising, given the fury of the national reaction to King's death and the intense political sensitivity of the case. In the summer of 1968, there were not a few Americans in pre-insurrectionary mood.

Within hours of the assassination, rioting had broken out and ultimately spread to more than a hundred American cities. Within minutes Stokely Carmichael was out in the streets of Washington's African-American neighbourhoods in incendiary mood, demanding that shops close as a gesture of respect to King, whom he had disrespected for years. The rioting came as close to the White House as Seventh Street, North-west, only a few hundred yards from the Oval Office. For the first time in American history, high officials gathered in the White House situation room to discuss not an international crisis in Berlin, Cuba, the Middle East or Vietnam, but a domestic threat. The Marines mounted machine-guns on the steps of the Capitol, and the Third Infantry deployed round the White House.

In this excited atmosphere, it is not surprising that the investigators in Memphis and elsewhere missed some evidence and misreported or misunderstood enough to allow later conspiracy theorists to come forward with a mass of questions, criticisms and insinuations. Indeed, the furore grew until it was exceeded only by the doubts raised by the Warren Commission's hasty and politicized report into the death of John F. Kennedy. Once again, government and people yearned to be reassured that there was nothing systemically wrong with American society, and that Dr King had been killed by a lone assassin, not coldly targeted by a political cabal. A second and opposite reaction, on the part of a sizeable minority a few years later, was deep paranoid suspicion, especially about the role of the government in King's death. As a reporter covering the events in Memphis at the time, I found it very hard to believe that James Earl Ray had indeed acted alone. Forty years later, my doubts remain. They are not, however, accompanied by any certainty about what did actually happen.

It was not until well on into the 1970s, when Congress turned to investigating King's death in the context of questions about the assassinations of the Kennedy brothers, that official and semi-official attempts to fit the evidence together began to be published. The wider context, of course, was the mood of doubt and confusion that afflicted the United States as a result of the racially motivated urban rioting between 1965 and 1968, the popular disenchantment with the Vietnam War, and the scepticism about government in general and the CIA in particular, generated by the Watergate affair in 1972-3.

In 1975, after a torrent of leaks and rumours about illegal activity on the part of the Central Intelligence Agency, Congress set up two committees, one in the Senate and one in the House, to look into the agency's conduct and in particular into reports that it had been involved in political assassinations, both in the United States and abroad. The background was the Ervin Committee's hearings on Watergate in the Senate and the revelation that Nixon, and also his predecessors, had used the CIA and the FBI in various illegal ways – for example, in attempting to assassinate foreign leaders and in wiretapping and otherwise infringing the rights of American citizens. The first House Select Committee, under Congressman Otis G. Pike of New York, was ineffectual; it expired in early 1976. The Senate Committee, chaired by Senator Frank Church of Idaho, was more tenacious. It published no fewer than fourteen reports and received immense media coverage. Its reports uncovered a mass of material, for the most part suggestive rather than conclusive, about assassination attempts against Fidel Castro in Cuba, Patrice Lumumba in the Congo and General René Schneider in Chile, among others. It also looked into the assassinations of President Kennedy and Dr King. Understandably, the Kennedy assassination received the lion's share of media and public attention. No clear picture emerged from this welter of vigorous, officially sanctioned muck-raking. But certain assumptions about the probity of American government in general, and of the FBI and the CIA in particular, were destroyed, perhaps for ever.

Meanwhile the House of Representatives established a new committee, the House Select Committee on Assassinations (HSCA), which did turn up some interesting new material that might or might not have a bearing on Ray's motivation. The only detailed account of a conspiracy backed by credible, though again by no means conclusive, evidence was produced by the HSCA. Its report suggested that Ray had been supported by his two brothers, Jerry and John. Two of the three of them may have carried out a bank robbery in Alton, Illinois, just across the Mississippi River from St Louis. Without positing any larger conspiracy, that alone could have raised the money to pay for Ray's car, rifle and travelling expenses. The Rays' sister, Carol Pepper, owned, and John Ray operated, a St Louis bar, the Grapevine Tavern, frequented by Wallace supporters, racists and sundry extreme right-wingers.

The report uncovered evidence that two St Louis businessmen with right-wing connections, John Kauffmann, a lawyer, and John Sutherland, a wealthy former stockbroker, drug manufacturer and motel owner, put it about in circles that would have been known to the Rays that they would offer $50,000 for a contract on King's life. These men and their associates had some more or less tenuous connections with Ray through his imprisonment in the Missouri State Penitentiary, and also with Ray's brother John through his tavern. The theory that Ray acted in order to earn this reward is far from proven, but it does have a certain muddled plausibility.

At the end of 1975, the Ford administration's Justice Department ordered a review of the FBI's files to determine whether the investigation of King's death should be reopened. A task force reported in January 1977, both on King's assassination and on the FBI's surveillance of him and his associates in his lifetime. Most recently, in August 1998, the Clinton administration's Department of Justice ordered two separate investigations into King's death. These were the result of publicity about allegations by two members of the public. In December 1993 a man called Loyd Jowers, the owner of Jim's Grill, the bar below the rooming house from which Ray is assumed to have fired the fatal shot, announced on ABC Television that he had been paid by a man with

Mafia associations to hire a hitman to kill King. He proceeded to revive the mythical Raoul, though now with the Spanish spelling, Raúl. Jowers's story was confused, and he never told it on oath.

The other new story came from a former FBI agent, Donald Wilson, who came forward with a most improbable account of how, as a young agent in the FBI's Atlanta bureau, he had found an envelope in Ray's abandoned Mustang containing papers which, Wilson claimed, cast light on both the Kennedy and the King assassinations. The Justice Department's report gave short shrift to both of these tales. Neither allegation was credible, it found; Jowers and Wilson both contradicted themselves. There was no evidence to corroborate either of their claims, and significant evidence to refute them.

Numerous accounts have alleged that the CIA or the FBI, or both, were involved in King's death. The most elaborate of these theses is that of Dr William Pepper, a lawyer who has represented the King family. (It was Pepper's photographs of children in Vietnam that put Martin King off his breakfast on his way to Jamaica in January 1967.) After the assassination, Pepper devoted himself for many years to trying to uncover what had really happened. In this he had the support of some of the King family and of the King Center in Atlanta. Pepper, who also practised as a barrister in England for some years, was involved in the Kings' civil lawsuit against Loyd Jowers. He has published more than one account of his theories, the last, *An Act of State: The Execution of Martin Luther King*, in 2003.[2]

The first investigations of why Ray killed King took it for granted that he was motivated essentially by raw racism. Anecdotes were collected about incidents when he had said nasty things about black people, picked quarrels with black people, and generally displayed racial prejudice. The trouble with this approach is that there is no reason to suppose, on the basis of these data, that Ray was significantly more racist than many working-class Middle Westerners of his generation, let alone than most inhabitants of state or federal penitentiaries.

William Bradford Huie came up with a different hypothesis: it was because Ray was a banal petty criminal that he hankered after notoriety. Specifically, Huie theorized, Ray was a fan of a popular television show of the day, ABC's *The FBI*. Near the end of the show, the FBI would list its 'Top Ten Most Wanted Criminals'. The show was one of Ray's favourites, in prison and outside. Huie 'subsequently came to believe, and [was] ... convinced that Ray, in Los Angeles, finally set a goal for his life. He decided to "make the Top Ten" by killing Dr King.'[3] That would explain, apart from anything else, why he jettisoned personal belongings, including the murder weapon and scope, to identify himself as the murderer.

This explanation, however psychologically plausible, has not convinced everyone as it convinced Bill Huie. While official or semi-official investigations continued to insist that Ray for whatever reason had acted alone, in the post-Watergate era the fashion was for narratives of elaborate conspiracies, involving the FBI, the CIA or even (in the case of William Pepper) the US army. Some of these also found a role for the Memphis police department. Some brought in the Mafia, especially that part of it run out of New Orleans by Carlos Marcello, 'Big Daddy in the Big Easy', a Mafia capo introduced into the public consciousness by theories about his implication in the Kennedy assassination. 'The assassination of Martin King,' Pepper has said, 'was a part of what amounted to an ongoing covert program in which they tried to suppress dissent and disruption in America.'

William Pepper was only one of those who interpreted the King assassination in political terms. Another researcher, Philip H. Melanson, a professor at Southeastern Massachusetts University, in a book called *The Murkin Conspiracy*,[4] uncovered many weaknesses in the House Select Committee's work in order to imply, but by no means prove, that King was murdered as a result of a sophisticated conspiracy, probably by the CIA. Harold Weisberg, famous for his demolition of the Warren Commission's official account of President Kennedy's assassination, also wrote a book about King's death.[5] He concluded that Ray did not fire the shot, but declined to say who did, or to identify the conspiracy behind the murder. Hard as Pepper, Melanson and Weisberg (not to mention Mark Lane and several other investigators, or 'assassinologists', as they sometimes call themselves) worked to track down witnesses and prove the truth of their theories, it is hardly surprising that none of them has come even close to establishing clear proof of government involvement.

Two other types of motivation have been suggested. For many, King was murdered as a result of a conspiracy of the far right. Others, far fewer, have hypothesized that he was the victim of rival African-American organizations, frustrated by King's refusal to join the revolutionary struggle. Such theories can only be speculation, and speculation with a minimum of evidentiary basis.

It certainly does seem possible that James Earl Ray was somehow put up to his crime, and perhaps helped at least with financial support, by *some* kind of conspiracy. Yet for all the irregular goings-on within the FBI and the CIA, which were well documented by the Church Committee and other investigations, it is still hard to believe that the United States government itself so far forgot its own laws as to arrange for King to be murdered, however inconvenient and even threatening he had come to seem to some. If King's death was the result of a conspiracy, a private one seems far more credible. In the feverish mood of the late 1960s there were enough extremists who saw him as a serious threat to domestic tranquillity, and especially to the racial status quo in America. Yet, with the solitary exception of the inconclusive case hesitantly deployed by the HSCA against Kauffman and Sutherland, nothing approaching a trail of evidence has been unearthed to compel belief that any such conspiracy existed, let alone to identify any specific conspirators.

Failing the sudden uncovering of some new cache of evidence, it is safest to conclude that James Earl Ray did kill King, motivated by either racial prejudice or financial greed or some combination of the two. Far more important, ultimately, than the motivation for his death, is the tally of Martin King's achievement, and to that we turn in the next and final chapter.

16

A Voice Crying in the Wilderness

Prepare ye the way of the Lord, make straight
in the desert a highway for our God.

Isaiah 40: 1

On 2 November 1983, in the White House rose garden, President Ronald Reagan signed a bill that designated Martin Luther King Day as a federal holiday. The holiday commemorates his birthday on 15 January, but is held on the third Thursday in the month. The preacher's son from Atlanta, great-grandson of slaves on both sides of his family, had joined the American immortals. Only four public holidays in the United States commemorate the birthdays of individuals: those of George Washington, Christopher Columbus, Jesus Christ – and Martin Luther King Jr.

This is only one of the honours that have been showered on King since his death. One geographer claims that there are no fewer than 730 roads, boulevards, avenues, streets and other thoroughfares named after him in thirty-nine states, almost three-quarters of them in the Deep South, where in most of his lifetime he was not allowed to eat in a restaurant, sleep in a motel or cross an infinity of mean-spirited, if imaginary, lines that segregated his people from their former white masters. There are high schools named for him from Riverside, California, and Seattle to Amsterdam Avenue in New York, and from suburban Atlanta to Detroit.

It should not be supposed that the public holiday was easily won or granted without opposition. Reagan himself initially opposed the idea, as – several years later – did Senator John McCain when it was first proposed to him, though later he was instrumental in overcoming resistance to the holiday in his home state, Arizona. That tower of southern conservatism, Senator Jesse Helms of North Carolina, led the opposition to Martin Luther King Day on the grounds that King was not important enough to deserve the honour and was in any case an 'action-oriented Marxist'. Several states tried to avoid linking the holiday to the name. For a time Virginia pointedly combined King's name with that of two Confederate generals, Robert E. Lee and Thomas 'Stonewall' Jackson, in an incongruous Lee–Jackson–King Day. The idea for the holiday had first been put forward, shortly after King's assassination, by the highly respected African-American Congressman, John Conyers of Michigan. The bill did not come before the House of Representatives until 1979 and at first failed to pass by five votes. It was given a powerful impulse by the success of a 1981 Stevie Wonder record, *Happy Birthday*:

> There ought to be a law against
> Anyone who takes offense
> At a day in your celebration . . .

After that, a petition to pass the bill received six million signatures, said to be the largest number ever gathered for any petition in American history. President Reagan had no choice but to sign the bill when it passed both houses of Congress by massive majorities.

The history of the holiday echoes the history of the man. In his lifetime King won notable victories, some – Montgomery, Birmingham, Selma among them – snatched, as the cliché goes, from the jaws of defeat. He knew great triumphs and received signal honours, from the universal admiration of his speech at the march on Washington to his Nobel Prize. Yet when he died the jury on his political struggle was still out. Some of his darkest hours came in the last year of his short life. It was far from clear whether his second, more militant march on Washington, the Poor People's Campaign, would be a success or the disastrous failure that – many, both friends and enemies, believed – might have ended his political career. The omens, it has to be said, were not good. His opposition to the Vietnam War was prescient as well as courageous, and although there are still those who insist that the United States would have won the war if it had not been for the way the troops in the field were betrayed by the media and public opinion on the home front, King's harsh judgement on the conflict has been endorsed by the majority verdict of history.

At the time it infuriated President Johnson, who had helped to turn King's mass protests into legislative victories. King could expect no help from a wounded and, where he was concerned, bitter President. Moreover, in the first years after his death there was a certain reaction against his style. He was seen as a cautious, middle-class leader in comparison with Hubert 'Rap' Brown or Stokely Carmichael (who later changed his name to Kwame Ture). It was fashionable among liberal journalists for a time to compare King unfavourably with Malcolm X, and even with the Black Panthers, or with Eldridge Cleaver or Angela Davis. Many chortled over the nickname 'De Lawd' given him by angry young radicals who had no patience with Martin's Christian beliefs. But his reputation has rightly outlasted all of these (with the possible exception of that enigmatic, gifted but tragic figure Malcolm X). None of them can claim an achievement to be mentioned in the same breath as King's legacy. Yet that legacy is hard to define with precision, and it is not altogether easy to answer the question: How different would the United States be if King had never lived?

King was endowed with many gifts. He was of course highly intelligent, both in the conventional academic sense and in the more important sense that he grasped intuitively the essentials of the political context he found himself in, whether in the local realities of confrontation in small towns like Albany, St Augustine or Selma, or on the macropolitical scale of national and international politics. When he died, neither American society nor the American electorate had wholeheartedly accepted the central message of his life and ministry: that Americans would never be fully free until they accepted that black and white Americans must be equal. Many complicated emotions and interests have been plaited into the conservative ascendancy that has dominated American politics since the 1960s. But one master thread of that narrative has been the negative response of a large, strategically placed minority to the great emancipatory legislation of the mid-1960s, and especially to the Civil Rights Act of 1964 and the Voting Rights Act of 1965.

Each of those great legislative achievements was made possible, indeed made necessary, by the non-violent civil rights movement in the South which Martin King led. The part played by non-violence in his work is itself controversial, as I have argued. There were those among his supporters who saw it as purely tactical. King himself always insisted that it was futile and frivolous for a minority amounting to little more than one-tenth of a society even to think of appealing to violence in order to vindicate its just claims, when the majority had a near-monopoly of the means of organized violence.

King was well aware that some of his followers, both in traditional Negro organizations and in SNCC, had no difficulty carrying arms for self-defence. For him, non-violence was much more than a prudential expedient. Gandhi's influence on him was indirect and almost theoretical; he was in touch with, and much influenced by, radical American pacifists including A. J. Muste, James Lawson and especially Bayard Rustin. Non-violence was an indispensable element in his conception of the 'beloved community'. This was an idea that had fascinated him all his life. In 1957 in one of his first newsletters for SCLC he wrote that its 'ultimate aim is to foster and create the beloved community in America when brotherhood is a reality'.

King was indeed a significant figure in twentieth-century American history, if only in the negative sense that one important strand of that history was created by opposition to the movement he led. He did not create that movement. 'There go my people,' he liked to say. 'I must follow them, for I am their leader.'* He had the political insight to see how invincible that movement must be in the long run, and the fortitude to stay at the head of it. That took physical courage. He was the target of rocks, shots, bombs and threats of violence of every kind. It also took moral courage. He was constantly placed in situations where his physical courage was challenged by his opponents and doubted by his allies and rivals. It took a particular kind of nerve to be able to say, 'Not this time', to pick the times and situations when he would put his life at risk. As he said, he wanted to choose the 'when and the where of his own Golgotha'.

For twelve years he lived with stresses such as few encounter, even for a brief time in their lives. As well as courage, that demanded inexhaustible physical vitality. The movement depended not only on the heroic virtues:

---

* The quotation has been attributed to Gandhi, but also to Alexandre Ledru-Rollin, the mid-nineteenth-century French radical politician.

leadership, bravery, judgement, and his incomparable eloquence. It also depended on his ability to raise the money to keep it going. Again and again, when his mind and body cried out for rest, he had to take another plane, to New York or to California, to speak to crowds who expressed their faith in his cause by their financial generosity. Again, the leading personalities of the Southern Christian Leadership Conference could not be described as tractable. King frequently found himself facing the rage or scorn of a Jim Bevel, a Hosea Williams or even of his oldest and closest buddy, Ralph Abernathy. It was necessary, for the movement's mere survival, that he possessed in rich measure those essential components of leadership that were so quintessentially his.

His greatest gift, however, the talent that distanced him from other highly gifted men in his movement, such as Andrew Young and John Lewis, was the magic of his mastery of the spoken language. Oratorical ability has always been prized in American politics, and great leaders – Abraham Lincoln, Woodrow Wilson, Franklin Roosevelt, John Kennedy – have been wonderful speakers, as is Barack Obama. None of them, since Lincoln, came as close to the sheer emotive power, the astonishing gift for reaching, touching and arousing an audience, as King at his best.

Some of that magic came from sheer professionalism. Not for nothing had young Martin sat at the feet of Professor Robert E. Keighton and learned the tricks of the preacher's trade, the Ladder Sermon, the Jewel Sermon, the Surprise Package Sermon. His best sermons broke free of such conventions and soared into elevated regions of theology and ethics. He spoke so often. He preached almost every Sunday at Dexter during the bus boycott and later at Ebenezer, even when criss-crossing the country on campaign. He kept up his contact with his own congregation as often as he could, even when he was locked into deadly confrontation with his political enemies. It was in his great political speeches, from the march on Washington in 1963 to his speech at Mason Temple in Memphis on the eve of his death, that his art reached its sublime height.

He was born with an instrument of rare power. His rich baritone could sweep to climax after climax without seeming to tire, though there were times when even *his* larynx needed to be rested. He was capable of intensity, humour, bathos, patient exegesis and sheer irresistible rant. He was a master of rhythm, knowing how to accelerate or slow down for effect. He was also working, much of the time, with audiences who were not only connoisseurs of preaching and speaking, but also given to encouraging the speaker with clapping, interjections, exhortations, even stamping. King's sober congregations at Dexter and Ebenezer did not allow themselves the wilder emotionalism of country preachers in the 'bawl and jump' tradition. But they loved to hear great speaking, and they were well qualified judges of what they heard. The South, white and black alike, has a culture of the word. It values storytellers, wits, poets, novelists, preachers, advocates and political orators. Martin Luther King Jr came out of that tradition. Like all supreme artists, though, he took a rich tradition and enriched it further.

His particular contribution was to bind several distinct traditions. One mined the rhetorical resources of the black Protestant and specifically Baptist churches, and especially the shared culture of Old Testament language. King knew, by instinct, when to draw on the sheer sonority and the emotional resonance of a phrase like his favourite verse from the prophet Amos, fifth chapter, twenty-fourth verse: 'let justice roll down as waters, and righteousness as a mighty stream'.[1] A second source of his language was the rhetoric of American patriotism; he borrowed from the Founding Fathers and especially the Augustan, eighteenth-century prose of Thomas Jefferson and the fastidious oratory of Abraham Lincoln. To the stylistic wealth of these two traditions he added the sometimes pedantic erudition of his early theological education. For some, for example, he was a little too prone to expound on the difference between the four Greek words for love, *philia*, *charis*, *agape* and *eros*. But he could also draw on the astringent thought of modern Protestant theologians like William Temple and Reinhold Niebuhr, and he was never afraid to address the great questions of human life.

In 2008, forty years after King's death, the people of the United States elected Barack Obama, an African-American, as their President. Obama disproved the pessimism of those who predicted that secret racism would falsify the polls predicting he would win. Moreover, although a significant proportion of Americans, as measured in polls and less formal surveys, perhaps a third, continue to have reservations about an African-American as head of their state and government, Obama's election triumphantly demonstrated that the doubters and the prejudiced were a minority. By 2008, African-Americans had already climbed all the other peaks of American life. They had been Congressmen and Senators, judges and justices of the Supreme Court, chief executives of the greatest corporations and of mighty banks. Two in succession have served as Secretaries of State. Many others have earned great respect and great fortunes in sports, entertainment, Hollywood, television and every other field of endeavour. The African-American cause has come a long way in the past forty years. This transformation would not have taken place without the words and the witness of Martin Luther King Jr. Without King's dream, it is plain, and without the efforts of those who shared it, Barack Obama could not have become President.

Yet so far King's dream has not wholly come true. The African-American experience since King's death has been a divided one. Perhaps as many as a half of black Americans, those who were able to take advantage of educational opportunities, to finish high school and graduate from college, or simply to acquire professional or vocational skills, have found that they could aspire to the basic elements of the 'American dream'. They could and did, buy homes, move to the suburbs, and bring their children up to take advantage of the same opportunities – not without resistance and conflict, but with infinitely less struggle than it would have taken in King's lifetime. For a handful of these, there was no limit to their ambition. They could succeed, and if three out of ten white Americans still confessed to prejudice against all African-Americans,[2] a majority of whites were proud that their African-American fellow citizens were now able to succeed.

For the other half or so of the African-American population, and perhaps it is more than half, the dream has not so far been fulfilled. Those who dropped off the educational ladder for whatever reason, or who never advanced more than a few steps up it, could look forward to a life no better, and in some ways grimmer, than their grandparents' in King's lifetime.

By the early twenty-first century, there were more black men in prison than in college. Trapped in inner-city slums or rural dead-ends, they found it almost impossible to get steady work. Black women could expect the burdens of the single mother's life, one which – in spite of heroic exceptions – virtually guaranteed that their children would fail at school and in work. For men, a life of crime, alcohol and drug abuse was all but inescapable. Black unemployment was far higher than for whites with equivalent qualifications. More than a quarter of all black males could expect to spend time in prison during their lifetime, while only 4 per cent of white males ever go to prison. African-Americans make up about 12 per cent of the US population, but about half of all prison inmates, and 40 per cent of those sentenced to death. Even more startling, a third of all African-American males aged twenty to thirty-four are right now either locked up, on probation, or on parole. An argument rages whether this represents discrimination on the part of police officers, judges and other people in authority. Such prejudice no doubt exists. But the discrimination takes place, so to speak, further back. For many young black males, in particular, their whole lifestyle makes it more likely from early adolescence on that they will be arrested and convicted of crimes, whether those who arrest and judge them are prejudiced or not.

Martin Luther King Jr was a living example of the possibilities America society offered to some African-Americans, even as it denied them to others. Son of a man who had himself been strong enough to succeed, Martin Luther King Jr had seized every slim opportunity presented to him. The mother of his children also came from a family with the same discipline and will to succeed. Martin junior was the product of a very peculiar background, the southern black Baptist ministry. He grew up in a world where the men of God, at that time among the few leaders the African-American community was allowed had also to be men of the world. He was bred to take responsibility, to be a leader. He could be personally indifferent to money, in part because his father had counted the pennies. The rewards of the black ministry were psychic and incidentally often sexual. Martin and Ralph Abernathy, Hosea Williams and Jim Bevel, were by no means the only Baptist ministers who took it for granted that women, in their congregation and out of it, would sleep with them. Martin Luther King junior was a 'prince of the captivity'.* He was born to respect, affection, opportunity and self-confidence, and he grew up with more than a touch of personal vanity.

It was, however, in a real sense a captivity. He achieved, through his words and his death, the leadership of a movement to bring legal equality to southern blacks. That success prepared the way for progress for all African-Americans, progress that now, with one of their number in the White House, they may be poised to realize. But King's vision was not limited to the destruction of southern segregation or even to the improvement of the conditions of all African-Americans, North and South. The beloved community he sought was not defined or limited by race. He had arrived at a critique of American society as a whole: he concluded that capitalism, minimally regulated, produced great and growing inequality. In this he saw further than most of his contemporaries. The experience of the four decades since his death has given substance to his vision.

So long as he was dealing with the black middle and working class of Georgia, Alabama and the Deep South generally, he knew exactly what to expect from his flock, and how to find the pressure points in the segregation system. It was hard for him to shift his focus from the struggle for political and civil rights in the South to the struggle for economic and social justice elsewhere in America. This is not to portray him as some kind of primitive, unable to understand the complexities of the wider society. On the contrary, he was highly sophisticated. Early in his life, before his involvement in the civil rights movement, he made a radical analysis of American society. For political reasons, it was not until late in his career, when he had acquired a national reputation and people turned to him for wisdom, that he ceased to conceal, or at least play down, his social democratic instincts and his radicalism. But as we have seen, from theological college onwards, even perhaps from childhood, he understood that the repression and ill-treatment of black people was not – as it suited many whites to maintain – an aberration in an otherwise near-perfect society. It was merely an example of the

* The phrase is the title of a novel by John Buchan, *A Prince of the Captivity*, London, Hodder & Stoughton, 1933. Benjamin Disraeli wrote a novel called *The Prince of the Captivity*. The phrase refers to a Jewish prisoner who became an adviser to Umar, the second Muslim caliph; the story is told in Henry Milman's nineteenth-century *History of the Jews*.

price paid for the wealth-creating power of American capitalism. In this deeper sense, Martin Luther King did not merely make it possible for an African-American to become President. He offered a vision of what the agenda for that President might have to be: nothing less than the rejection of the inequality and selfishness of the conservative ascendancy in favour of a broader, more generous interpretation of the promise of American life.

'Comfort ye,' go the opening words of what is known to scholars as the Second Isaiah, 'comfort ye my people, saith your God. Speak ye comfortably to Jerusalem, and cry unto her, that her warfare is accomplished.' Martin Luther King did not always speak comfortably to Jerusalem, or to his people. He knew that his people's warfare was not yet accomplished, and that they had not, as true penitents, 'received of the Lord's hand double for all their sins'. His message was starker than that – it was 'the voice of him that crieth in the wilderness'. The second author of the Book of Isaiah, writing in the sixth century before Christ, was prophesying the return of the Jewish people from their captivity in Babylon. In the Christian tradition, the text has long been taken to refer to John the Baptist, prophesying the advent of the Messiah. In more recent times, the voice crying in the wilderness has come to designate the prophet who is not honoured in his own time.

King was both honoured and disrespected in his life. He was insulted, imprisoned, brutalized, killed. Yet his voice did not go unheard. He was not a prophet in the popular sense of the word, merely one who predicts events. He was not, so to speak, a John the Baptist making possible the advent of a Barack Obama. He was a prophet in the older and truer sense: one who speaks out fearlessly, demanding that his generation pay heed to great and uncomfortable truths. He was – and this is often not so much forgotten as undervalued – a specifically Christian prophet. 'In the quiet recesses of my heart,' he said, 'I am fundamentally a clergyman, a Baptist preacher.' Steeped as he was from childhood in Christian belief and language, since the 'kitchen conversion' of 1956, he had an evangelical faith in the personal and literal presence of his Redeemer.

For society as a whole it was his political witness and teaching that were his most significant achievement. More forcefully than any other speaker in America, and perhaps as forcefully as anyone anywhere in the twentieth century, he insisted on the injustice of inequality, between races and in other relationships. His reward has been to be honoured by his own people as their greatest leader, and to be counted by sympathetic white Americans as a luminous figure in their history.

He was a man of his time. Although he possessed a compelling vision of a better future, he addressed the problems he saw in front of him. Focusing first on racial injustice and segregation, only slowly did he come fully to understand that African-Americans outside the Deep South, though not segregated by law, were still the victims of institutionalized discrimination and injustice. Even more gradually, he began to speak out about the belief he had long held that American society as a whole, for white people as well as black, was deeply flawed by economic inequality and injustice. Deploying one of those distinctions he was so fond of, called from the philosophical studies of his youth, he preached αγάπη (*agapē*), which he defined as disinterested love. He was killed before he could convey to his countrymen that particular message. As we have seen, he was a man of his time in other ways, too. His attitude to women was unreconstructed. He liked them, and they liked him. But even if some of the evidence collected and perhaps manipulated by the FBI can be dismissed as inconclusive, his sexual behaviour would today be thought inexcusably exploitative.

How much credit can King be given for the change – for there has been a great, if not yet decisive, change – in American attitudes to race? I have already pointed out that some of the consequences of his work were negative. The reaction against his campaigns and against what he stood for strengthened the conservative backlash against the liberal ideology of the Kennedy–Johnson era. There could have been no George Wallace the national figure, and perhaps no President Nixon and no Ronald Reagan, without Martin Luther King.

Yet his influence was far more positive than negative. King's campaigns, his great speeches, his letter from Birmingham jail and his personal example, not to mention his death, had the cumulative effect of making any serious defence of the racial status quo untenable. In that sense, he was not just the most brilliant orator of his age, he was also one of its most influential teachers. 'O thou that tellest good tidings to Zion,' says the Second Isaiah, 'get thee up to the high mountain.' Martin Luther King reached the mountaintop, and the tidings he brought were hard, but good.

Notes

CHAPTER 2 – SWEET AUBURN

1 See www.georgiaencyclopedia.org; Carole Merritt, *The Herndons: An Atlanta Family*, Athens; University of Georgia Press, 2002.

2 For Dobbs, see Gary M. Pomerantz, *Where Peachtree Meets Sweet Auburn: A Saga of Two Families and the Making of Atlanta*, New York, Scribner, 1996.

3 Pomerantz, *Sweet Auburn*, p. 124.

4 W. E. Burghardt Du Bois, *The Souls of Black Folk*, Greenwich, CT, Fawcett Publications, 1961, pp. 53–4.

5 This account of Martin Luther King Jr's ancestry relies on Clayborne Carson (ed.), *Papers, of Martin Luther King, Jr*, vol. I, Introduction.

6 Taylor Branch, *Pillar of Fire, America in the King Years 1963–65*, New York, Simon & Schuster, p. 542.

7 See Carson, vol. I, Introduction, p. 27; Taylor Branch, *Parting the Waters: America in the King Years, 1954–63*, New York, Simon & Schuster, 1988, pp. 44-47.

CHAPTER 3 – A HIGHER EDUCATION

1 The document is published as 'Autobiography of Religious Development' in Carson, *Papers of Martin Luther King, Jr*, vol. I, p. 363.

2 Martin Luther King Jr, *Stride Toward Freedom*, New York, Harper & Row, 1958, pp. 4–5. The account in the book differs slightly from the version in the seminary essay, but is the same in its essential description of a child's response to the realities of segregation.

3 Jimmy Carter, *An Hour before Daylight, Memories of a Rural Boyhood*, New York, Simon & Schuster, 2001, pp. 229–30.

4 Carson, *Papers*, vol. II, pp. 359–63.

5 I was fortunate enough to interview Benjamin Mays in 1966.

6 This statement was made in a written response to a request by Joan Thatcher,

of the Division of Christian Education of the American Baptist Convention, cited by Carson, *Papers*, vol. I, Introduction, p. 44.

7 Taylor Branch, *Parting the Waters: America in the King Years, 1954–63*, New York, Simon & Schuster, 1988, pp. 76–7.

8 Branch, *Parting the Waters*, pp. 88–90.

9 Carson, *Papers*, vol. II, Introduction, p. 25.

10 Martin Luther King Jr, *Stride Toward Freedom: The Montgomery Story*, New York, Harper & Row, 1958, pp. 75–6.

11 King, *Stride Toward Freedom*, p. 77.

12 This account of the Kings' courtship is taken from Branch, *Parting the Waters*, pp. 94–8, citing Coretta Scott King, *My Life with Martin Luther King, Jr*, New York, Holt, Rinehart & Winston, 1969, pp. 67–82; Martin Luther King Sr, with Clayton Riley, *Daddy King: An Autobiography*, New York, William Morrow, 1980, pp. 148–51.

CHAPTER 4 – SICK AND TIRED

1 Juan Williams, *Eyes on the Prize, America's Civil Rights Years 1954–1965*, New York, Penguin, 1987; Putnam, 2007, pp. 106–7.

2 Martin Luther King Jr, *Stride Toward Freedom: The Montgomery Story*, New York, Harper & Row, 1958, p. 39.

3 Speech of 5 December 1955. Clayborne Carson (ed.), *Papers of Martin Luther King, Jr*, vol. III, p. 73.

4 King, *Stride Toward Freedom*, pp. 114–115.

5 *State of Alabama v Martin Luther King and Others*, cited in Carson, *Papers*, vol. III, Introduction.

6 Taylor Branch, *Parting the Waters*, New York, Simon & Schuster, 1988, p. 195.

CHAPTER 5 – THE LITTLE BROWN GHOST

1 David J. Garrow, *Bearing the Cross: Martin Luther King and the Southern Student Leadership Conference*, New York, HarperCollins, Perennial Classics, 2004, p. 68.

2 This thesis is argued by Nick Sharman of the University of Melbourne in a paper entitled 'The Narrative Construction of Leadership in Martin Luther King's Appeal to White America'.

3 Mary E. King, *Freedom Song, A Personal History of the 1960s Civil Rights Movement*, New York, William Morrow, 1987, p. 43.

4 On Levison, see Adam Fairclough, *To Redeem the Soul of America: The Southern Christian Leadership Conference and Martin Luther King*, Athens, GA, University of Georgia Press, 2001, pp. 30–31; David J. Garrow, *The FBI and Martin Luther King Jr*, London, Penguin, 1983, passim, esp. pp. 26–9.

5 On Rustin, see Jervis Anderson, *Bayard Rustin: Troubles I've Seen*, Berkeley, CA, University of California Press, and HarperCollins, 1997; John D'Emilio, *Lost Prophet: The Life and Times of Bayard Rustin*, New York, Free Press, 2003; Fairclough, *To Redeem the Soul*; David Levine, *Bayard Rustin and the Civil Rights Movement*, New Brunswick, NJ, Rutgers University Press, 2000; Bayard Rustin, *Down the Line*, Chicago, Quadrangle Books, 1971.

6 Fairclough, *To Redeem the Soul*, p. 60, citing Southern Regional Council estimates. For Lawson, the Bevels and the Nashville group, see also David Halberstam, *The Children*, New York, Random House, 1998.

7 King, *Freedom Song*, p. 45.

8 Fairclough, *To Redeem the Soul*, pp. 11–34.

9 Acts of the Apostles, 17: 22ff.

10 Branch, *Parting the Waters*, pp. 237–41.

11 Branch, *Parting the Waters*, pp. 308–9.

12 Branch, *Parting the Waters*, pp. 356–66. The conversations between Wofford, Shriver and John Kennedy are from interviews with Shriver and Wofford.

CHAPTER 6 – BETWEEN TWO FIRES

1 There are accounts of the Freedom Rides in Taylor Branch, *Parting the Waters*, New York, Simon & Schuster, 1988, pp. 412–91; James Farmer, *Lay Bare the Heart: An Autobiography of the Civil Rights Movement*, New York, Arbor House, 1985; August Meier and Elliott Rudwick, *CORE: A Study in the Civil Rights Movement 1942–1968*, Urbana, IL, University of Illinois Press, 1975; Juan Williams, *Eyes on the Prize*, New York, Penguin, 1987, pp. 144–61.

2 Ralph Ellison (1913–94) was best known for *Invisible Man* (1953); Richard Wright (1908–60) was the author of *Native Son* (1940); James Baldwin (1924–87) wrote many novels, including *Go Tell It on the Mountain* (1953).

3 Thomas F. Jackson, *From Civil Rights to Human Rights, Martin Luther King and the Struggle for Racial Justice*, Philadelphia, University of Pennsylvania Press, 2006, pp. 123, 124.

4 Nicholas Lemann, *The Promised Land: The Great Black Migration and How It Changed America*, New York, Knopf, 1991, p. 112.

5 See Lemann, *Promised Land*, pp. 6–7.

6 US Census Bureau, 1961.

7 Selz C. Mayo and C. Horace Hamilton, 'The Rural Negro Population of the South in Transition', *Phylon*, vol. 23, 1963.

8 David J. Garrow, *The FBI and Martin Luther King, Jr*, London, Penguin, 1983 (first published New York, Norton, 1981), pp. 46–50.

9 Branch, *Parting the Waters*, p. 483.

CHAPTER 7 – FROM ALBANY TO OXFORD

1 See Selz C. Mayo and C. Horace Hamilton, 'The Rural Negro Population of the South in Transition', *Phylon*, vol. 23, 1963.
2 The following account of the Albany story is based on Clayborne Carson, 'SNCC and the Albany Movement', *Journal of Southwest Georgia History*, 1984, 2, pp. 15–25; Adam Fairclough, *To Redeem the Soul of America: The Southern Christian Leadership Conference and Martin Luther King, Jr*, Athens, GA, University of Georgia Press, 2001; David J. Garrow, *Bearing the Cross, Martin Luther King and the Southern Student Leadership Conference*, New York, HarperCollins, Perennial Classics, 2004, pp. 172–230; Mary E. King, *Freedom Song, A Personal History of the 1960s Civil Rights Movement*, New York, William Morrow, 1987; David L. Lewis, *King: A Critical Biography*, New York, Praeger, 1970, pp. 140–70; Taylor Branch, *Parting the Waters: America in the King Years, 1954–63*, New York, Simon & Schuster, 1988; Juan Williams, *Eyes on the Prize, America's Civil Rights Years 1954–1965*, New York, Viking, 1987, pp. 165–179.
3 King, *Freedom Song*, p. 160.
4 Lewis, *King*, p. 144.
5 Lewis, *King*, p. 144.
6 Branch, *Parting the Waters*, p. 526.
7 Later a successful corporate lawyer in Washington and President Clinton's favourite golf partner.
8 Fairclough, *To Redeem the Soul*, p. 88.
9 Garrow, *Bearing the Cross*, p. 185.
10 Branch, *Parting the Waters*, p. 557.
11 Garrow, *Bearing the Cross*, p. 203.
12 Garrow, *Bearing the Cross* , pp. 160, 219–20.
13 Author's interview with O'Donnell, spring 1962.
14 The author, who had been present at the football match described below, drove with them, and was also present on the Ole Miss campus during the riot.

CHAPTER 8 – IN THE CITY OF VULCAN

1 This chapter is based on the works cited in the notes earlier, especially Branch, *Parting the Waters*; Fairclough, *To Redeem the Soul*; Garrow, *Bearing the Cross*; Clayborne Carson (ed.), *Autobiography of Martin Luther King*; Diane McWhorter, *Carry Me Home*, New York, Simon & Schuster, 2002. The author covered the Birmingham events for the London *Observer* and interviewed Martin King in the Gaston motel. He has many graphic memories of those events, not least being shot at during the

riot of 8 May. He also remembers with gratitude the help of Charles Morgan Jr.

2 See www.peace.ca/kimstory.htm and *The Road from Vietnam*, a film by Shelley Saywell, Canada.

3 McWhorter, *Carry Me Home*, pp. 31–55.

4 McWhorter, *Carry Me Home*, p. 75.

5 Acts 16:9: 'And a vision appeared unto Paul in the night. There was a man of Macedonia standing, beseeching him, and saying, Come over into Macedonia and help us.'

6 Garrow, *Bearing the Cross*, p. 247.

7 McWhorter, *Carry Me Home*, pp. 359, 367.

8 Garrow, *Bearing the Cross*, p. 257.

CHAPTER 9 – THE TIDE TURNS

1 The author was present at the Wallace–Katzenbach confrontation. He can be seen in a photograph taken there reproduced in Wikipedia, though some members of his family are not convinced that the picture is of him!

2 Charles Morgan Jr, later head of the American Civil Liberties Union.

3 Including the author.

4 McWhorter, *Carry Me Home*, pp. 534–5.

5 On King's lifelong commitment to economic and social equality for white as well as black people see especially Thomas F. Jackson, *From Civil Rights to Human Rights: Martin Luther King and the Struggle for Economic Justice*, Philadelphia, University of Pennsylvania Press, 2007.

6 David L. Lewis, *King, a Critical Biography*, New York, 1970, pp. 82–3.

7 Garrow, *Bearing the Cross*, pp. 84, 307, 621, 622.

8 Garrow, *Bearing the Cross*, p. 375.

9 The following account of King's dealings with J. Edgar Hoover and the FBI is based on David J. Garrow, *The FBI and Martin Luther King, Jr: From 'Solo' to Memphis*, New York, W.W. Norton, 1981; Victor Navasky, *Kennedy Justice*, New York, Atheneum, 1971; Richard Gid Powers, *Secrecy and Power: The Life of J. Edgar Hoover*, New York, 1987; Anthony Summers, *Official and Confidential*, London, Gollancz, 1993.

10 *New York Times*, 31 Oct. 1971.

11 Navasky, *Kennedy Justice*, p. 155.

12 Taylor Branch, *Pillar of Fire, America in the King Years 1963–64*, New York, Simon & Schuster. p. 207.

13 I once stumbled on King by accident in a situation with a young woman, at the Gaston motel in Birmingham, that convinced me at the time that they were sexually involved.

14 Quoted in Garrow, *Bearing the Cross*, p. 376.

15 Gospel according to St Matthew, 13:57.

16 For the Nobel Prize trip, see Branch, *Pillar of Fire*, pp. 539–43; Garrow, *Bearing the Cross*, pp. 363–8.

17 Robert Porter.

18 Garrow, *Bearing the Cross*, p. 366, citing an interview Coretta Scott King gave to Charlotte Mayerson after Dr King's death.

CHAPTER 10 – MISSISSIPPI BURNING

1 Michael Beschloss (ed.), *Taking Charge: The Johnson White House Tapes 1963–64*, New York, Simon & Schuster, 1997, p. 37.

2 Dan T. Carter, *The Politics of Rage: George Wallace, the Origins of the New Conservatism, and the Transformation of American Politics*, Baton Rouge, Louisiana State University Press, 1995.

3 Beschloss, *Taking Charge*, p. 158.

4 See Jeffrey Shesol, *Mutual Contempt: Lyndon Johnson, Robert Kennedy and the Feud that Defined a Decade*, New York, Norton, 1997, p. 182: 'President Johnson was obsessed with what aides dubbed, simply, "the Bobby problem".'

5 Beschloss, *Taking Charge*, passim.

6 Beschloss, *Taking Charge*, pp. 447, 460.

7 The following account of events in St Augustine is based on David R. Colburn, *Racial Change and Community Crisis: St Augustine, Florida, 1877–1980*, New York, Columbia University Press, 1985, as well as on the standard histories of the civil rights movement.

8 Published in Branch, *Pillar of Fire*, opposite p. 208.

9 The author attended this training session in Oxford, Ohio, as a reporter.

10 A careful account of the whole incident is in Howard Ball, *Murder in Mississippi: United States v. Price and the Struggle for Civil Rights*, Lawrence, Kansas, University of Kansas Press, 2004.

11 Garrow, *Bearing the Cross*, p. 336.

12 Shesol, *Mutual Contempt*, p. 218.

CHAPTER 11 – THE HINGE

1 On this point see Dan T. Carter, *The Politics of Rage: George Wallace, the Origins of the New Conservatism, and the Transformation of American Politics*, Baton Rouge, Louisiana State University Press, 1995.

2 In this chapter I have used my own notes and recollections of events which I covered as a reporter in 1965, supplemented by a visit in 2005, as well as the standard secondary sources. I am especially grateful for a vividly written memoir by an eyewitness and historian, Charles E. Fager, *Selma 1965: The March that Changed the South*, Boston, Beacon Press, 1974.

CHAPTER 12 – WALKS ON THE WILD SIDE

1 Adam Cohen and Elizabeth Taylor, *American Pharaoh: Richard J. Daley: His Battle for Chicago and the Nation*, New York, Little, Brown, 2000. See also Mike Royko, *Boss: Richard J. Daley of Chicago*, New York, Dutton, 1971. Chicago is also the subject of a classic of sociology, Horace R. Cayton and St Clair Drake, *Black Metropolis*, London, Jonathan Cape, 1946. The original edition was published in the United States the previous year.

2 Mary E. King, *Freedom Song, A Personal History of the 1960s Civil Rights Movement*, New York, William Morrow, 1987, pp. 103–4.

3 For a documentary, shown on ITV in Britain on 13 July 1966, called *The Fire This Time'*. Stokely Carmichael was also interviewed at length for the same programme.

4 The following account draws gratefully on the spirited account in Taylor Branch, *At Canaan's Edge*, New York, Simon & Schuster, 2006, pp. 502–06.

5 This account of the summit is based on Branch, *At Canaan's Edge*; Cohen and Taylor, *American Pharaoh*; Fairclough, *To Redeem the Soul of America: The Southern Christian Leadership Conference and Martin Luther King*, Athens, GA, University of Georgia Press, 2001; Garrow, *Bearing the Cross*; and Nicholas Lemann, *The Promised Land: The Great Black Migration and How It changed America*, New York, Knopf, 1991; as well as on the author's reporting at the time.

CHAPTER 13 – VIETNAM AND BEYOND

1 The following paragraphs are a summary of the reporting in Lewis Chester, Godfrey Hodgson and Bruce Page, *An American Melodrama*, New York, Viking, 1969.

2 See Jeffrey Shesol, *Mutual Contempt: Lyndon Johnson, Robert Kennedy, and the Feud that Defined a Decade*, New York, Norton, 1997.

CHAPTER 14 – THE LAST CAMPAIGN

1 Nick Kotz, *Judgment Day: Lyndon Baines Johnson and Martin Luther King Jr. and the Laws that Changed America*, Boston and New York, Houghton Miffin, 2005, p. 378.

2 Thomas F. Jackson, *From Civil Rights to Human Rights: Martin Luther King Jr and the Struggle for Economic Justice*, Philadelphia, University of Pennsylvania Press, 2007, carefully traces the evolution of King's concern with economic justice.

3 The following account of King's last hours is primarily based on the *Report of*

the *Department of Justice Task Force to Review the FBI Martin Luther King Jr Security and Assassination Investigations*, 1977.
http://www.usdoj.gov/crt/crim/mlk/part2.php

CHAPTER 15 – DETECTIVE STORY

1 Rick Perlstein, *Nixonland*, New York, Scribner's, 2008, p. 142.
2 William E. Pepper, *An Act of State: The Execution of Martin Luther King*, London, Verso, 2003.
3 William Bradford Huie, *He Slew the Dreamer*, London, W.H. Allen, 1970, pp. 111, 159.
4 Philip H. Melanson, *The Murkin Conspiracy*, New York, Praeger, 1989. 'Murkin' was apparently a police code for the murder of King.
5 Harold Weisberg, *Frame-Up*, New York, Outerbridge & Dienstfrey, 1971.

CHAPTER 16 – A VOICE CRYING IN THE WILDERNESS

1 American King James version.
2 PewCenter, 2008, http://people-presswork/reports/, 26 June 2008. The Pew Center is a non-partisan research centre studying press, politics, religion and other matters. It is funded by the charitable trusts established by the Pew family of Philadelphia, founders of Sun Oil.

Index